POSTCARD HISTORY SERIES

Along Pennsylvania's Lincoln Highway

On the front cover: Please see page 100. (Author's collection.)

On the back cover: Please see page 63. (Author's collection.)

POSTCARD HISTORY SERIES

Along Pennsylvania's Lincoln Highway

Richard W. Funk

ARCADIA PUBLISHING

ISBN 978-0-7385-4511-0

Published by Arcadia Publishing
Charleston, South Carolina

Printed in the United States of America

Library of Congress Catalog Card Number: 2006921432

For all general information contact Arcadia Publishing at:
Telephone 843-853-2070
Fax 843-853-0044
E-mail sales@arcadiapublishing.com
For customer service and orders:
Toll-Free 1-888-313-2665

Visit us on the Internet at www.arcadiapublishing.com

Dedicated to that special breed of people known as "road fans," who gladly spend weekends and days off traveling the routes of yesteryear.

Contents

ACKNOWLEDGMENTS

The Lincoln Highway, among other early routes, has fascinated me since childhood, an early indication that I would grow to be a road fan. To some people, a road is just a road, a way of getting from point A to point B. But to the lover of old highways, each mile is an adventure and an old landmark rotting in the weeds can be a thrill. Seeing a landmark still being used is that much better.

Not everyone understands this, and I owe a debt of gratitude to one person who does: Brian Butko. During the compiling of this book, I found myself constantly turning to his two outstanding works, *The Lincoln Highway Pennsylvania Travelers Guide* volumes I and II. Several years ago, I had the pleasure of writing a newspaper review for the second edition and found it to be excellent, concise, and entertaining. At the time, I had no idea the books would become my most valuable reference tools. Thank you, Brian.

Another person who immediately comes to mind is Olga Herbert of the Lincoln Highway Heritage Corridor, based in Ligonier. Olga opened the corridor's collection to me, and while my work as a newspaper reporter did not permit a planned trip there, the fact that it was made available is priceless to me.

I also need to extend thanks to Linda, my significant other. When I would start to lose steam on the project, she encouraged me to move forward. During the time it took to complete this work, my daughter Susan showed all the understanding a 13 year old is capable of—and then some. She realized that between my regular work and this book time was not always available but never complained.

Last, but far from least, I want to thank my Arcadia editor, Erin Vosgien. Throughout the process of assembling both this book and my first, Erin was a patient person who was always there to answer whatever questions I had, and she worked with me through some very trying times.

Introduction

Although the Lincoln Highway was not the only route to cross the country, it is probably the best remembered and most loved. The New York–San Francisco highway, established in 1913, holds the distinction of being the first transcontinental route to be marked by road signs. Carl Fisher of the Prest-O-Lite Company developed the idea in an era when the automobile was the new kid on the transportation block. The road was named in honor of Abraham Lincoln, and the Lincoln Highway Association was quickly established. The overall goal was to make the entire route toll-free, a large order at that time.

While the Lincoln Highway is a historic entity in its own right, the route more or less follows two other transportation paths through Pennsylvania: the Lancaster Pike in the eastern part of the state and Forbes Road to the west.

For those accustomed to horse-drawn or train travel, the novelty of the automobile and the newness of the highway were strong lures. Road trips became a common thing, especially with those who had the means to purchase a car. Others, especially farmers in rural areas, were not thrilled by the prospect of cars whizzing around at speeds of up to 20 miles per hour. One organization, the Farmers' Anti-Automobile Association, attempted to set a list of unreasonable rules and regulations on drivers, including one stating that if a horse refused to pass a car, the vehicle must be taken apart and hidden from view.

But the horse and carriage were eventually put out to pasture and automobile traffic became more common with each passing day. Most early motorists did not use the Lincoln Highway to get from one place to another, but rather for entertainment. The entire coast-to-coast route could reportedly be covered in approximately one month.

Through the years, the highway experienced a host of changes. Even the name started to fade into memory when the road was numbered U.S. Route 30 and sections received the U.S. Route 1 designation.

For many people, the route represents a link to the past and treasured childhood memories of the days before turnpikes and interstate highways became the roads to take. The Lincoln Highway symbolizes a time in our motoring history when speed was not the most important thing—just enjoying the ride was.

I have not attempted to assemble this book as a guide to the highway, as such texts already exist, nor is it meant to be an exhaustive history. Instead this is a look at the Lincoln Highway and its landmarks as many of us remember them. While some places shown here still survive, the majority have disappeared. One of the most noteworthy landmarks is the SS Grand View

Point Ship Hotel, which was destroyed by fire. Others were simply torn down, fell down, or now house other businesses and in some instances private homes.

It is my sincere hope that readers will look at the images contained here with fond memories of trips made along the highway, or plan future trips to see the remnants. Enjoy the ride.

One

The Highway

One of the most striking aspects about early views of the Lincoln Highway is the primitive condition of the road surface. In many places along its route through Pennsylvania and elsewhere, the highway was badly rutted and it was not uncommon for early motorists to get bogged down in the mud. Often horses from a nearby farm were used to free automobiles from the road's grip.

The highway was never designed as a single entity, but was made up of existing roads, many of them little better than cow paths. Through the years, as improvements were steadily made, the highway went from dirt to gravel and eventually concrete and blacktop. In many cases, the original route was bypassed in order to provide better and safer driving conditions. And the highway was relocated to skirt larger towns and cities as the years progressed.

The Lincoln's route took travelers through many miles of beautiful Pennsylvania scenery, especially in the central and western portions of the state. Even today, the original highway passes through woods and farmland and beside lakes and rivers.

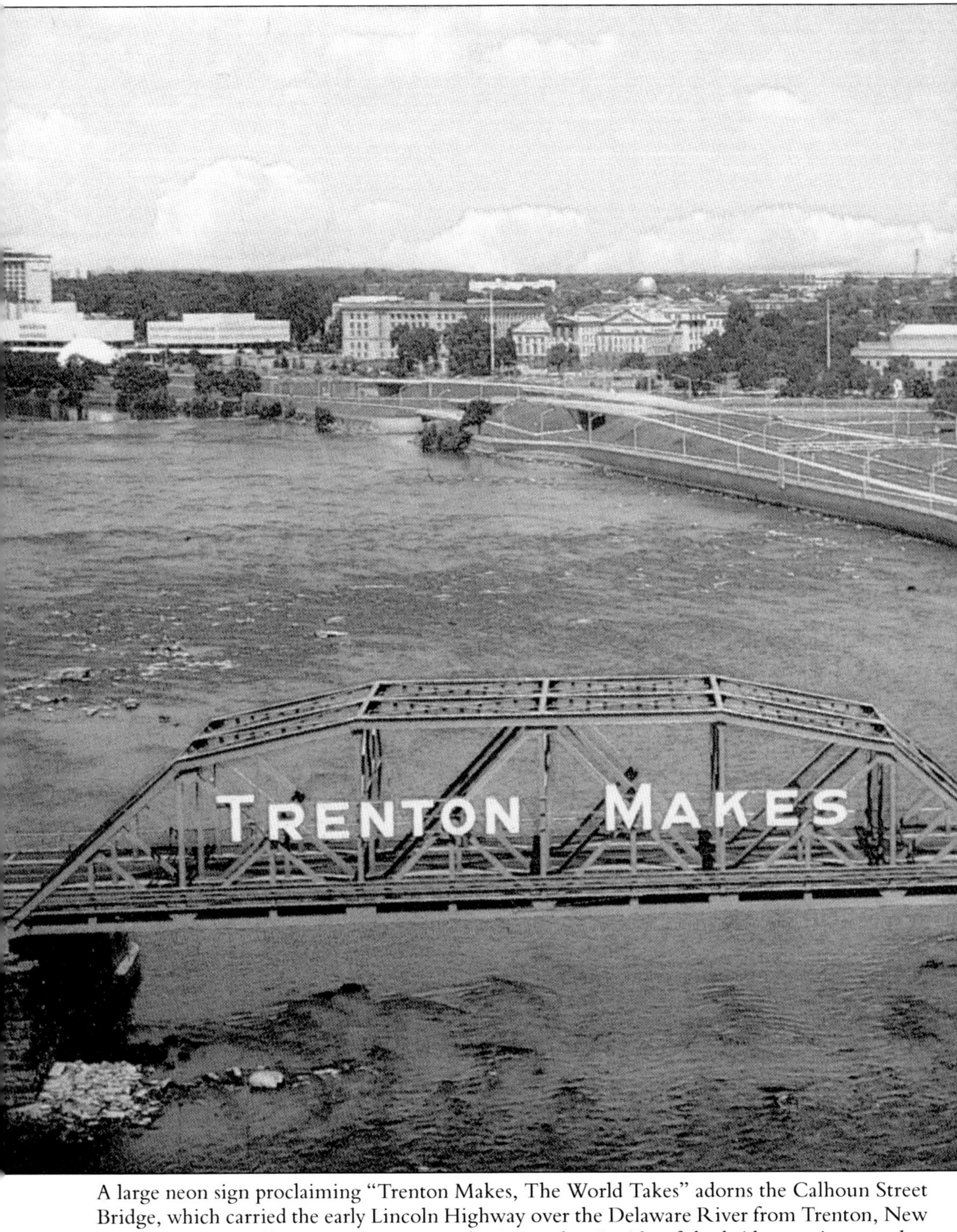

A large neon sign proclaiming "Trenton Makes, The World Takes" adorns the Calhoun Street Bridge, which carried the early Lincoln Highway over the Delaware River from Trenton, New Jersey, to Morrisville, Pennsylvania. On the Pennsylvania side of the bridge, an iron marker points the direction to New York City and San Francisco, the cities where the cross-country highway begins and ends. The original span to cross the river here was called the City Bridge

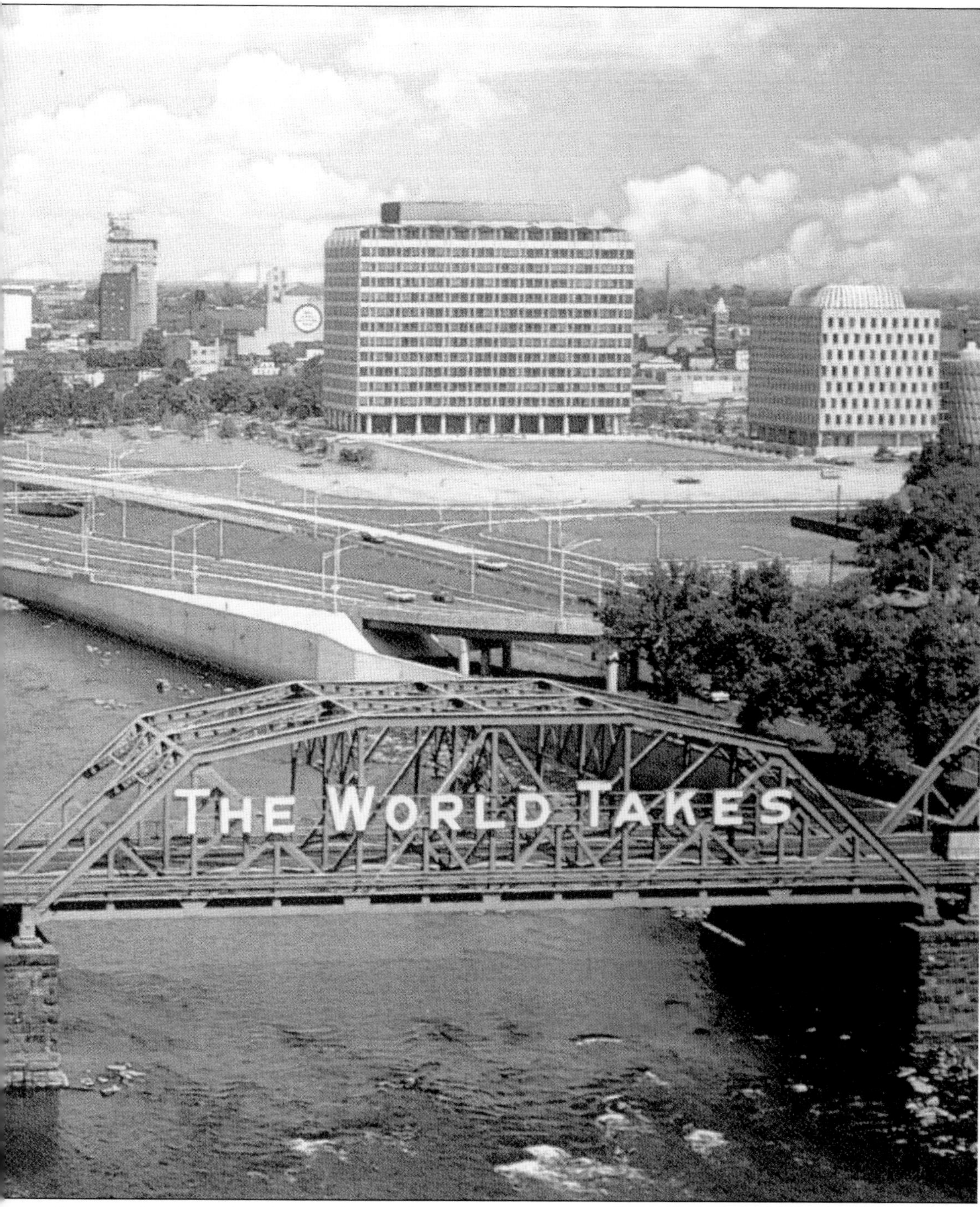

and was made of wood and opened to traffic in 1860. It was destroyed by fire 24 years later, and the present Pratt Truss bridge was completed in 1885. In 1920, the highway's route was changed, and those following the Lincoln crossed the river on the Lower Trenton Free Bridge, so named because, unlike the Calhoun Street Bridge, motorists did not have to pay a toll to cross.

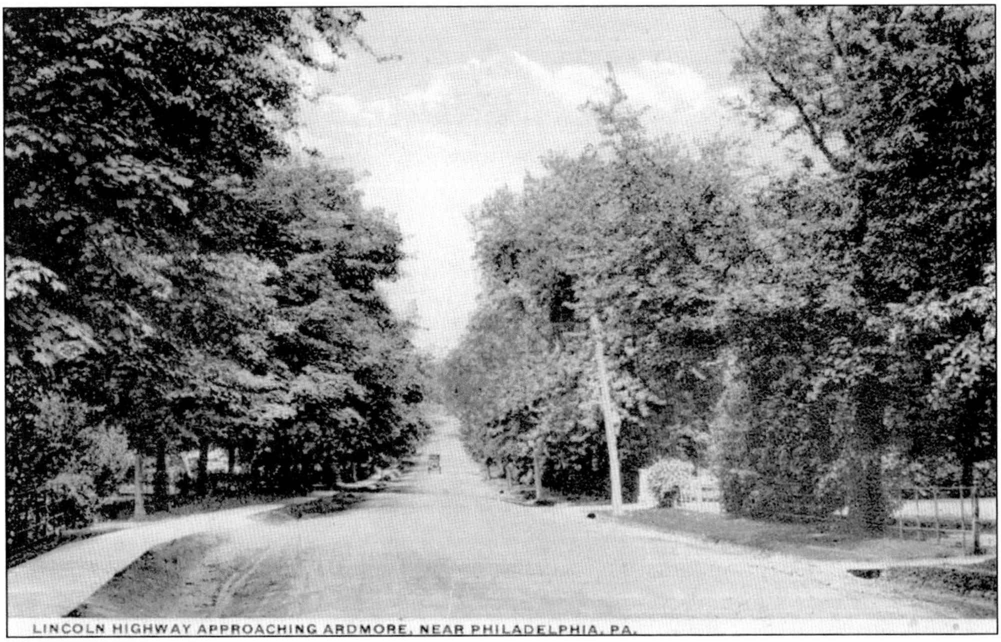

Looking more like a country road than a major transcontinental highway, the Lincoln Highway approaches Ardmore, west of Philadelphia. Ardmore was home to the Autocar truck manufacturing plant, and in 1920 the firm donated two of its trucks to travel the highway and mark the route with steel signs.

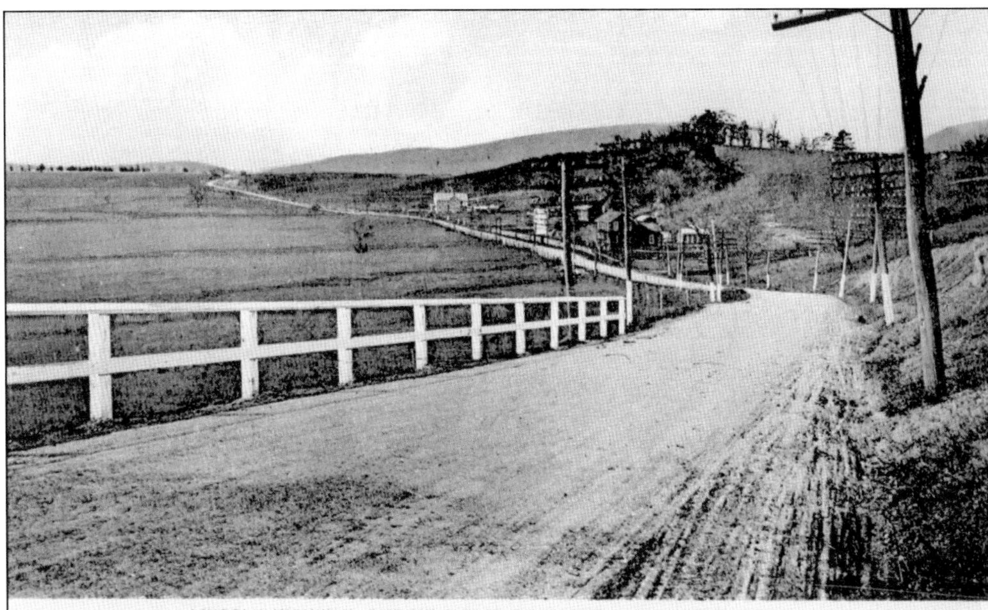

The Lincoln Highway, one mile east of Everett, appears to be a dirt or stone road in this view, likely taken before 1920. As traffic continued to increase through the years, the entire route was constantly being improved and upgraded to handle larger volumes. Due to this, many portions of the highway were bypassed.

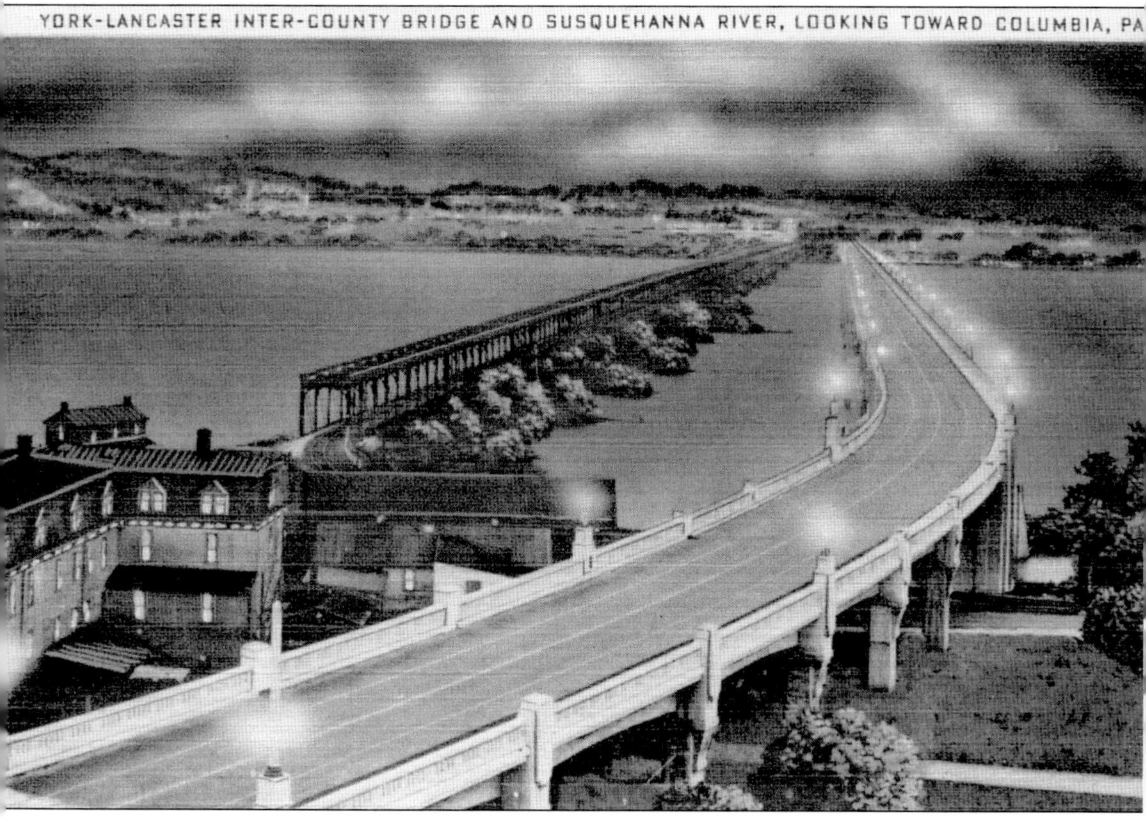

The York-Lancaster Inter-County Bridge, often called the Columbia-Wrightsville Bridge, is also known as the Veterans Memorial Bridge. Built at a cost of $3 million, the span opened to traffic in 1930 and was once the longest concrete arch bridge in the world. Although the bridge still carries the Lincoln Highway (Route 462) over the wide Susquehanna River, this section of the route was bypassed in 1970 by the U.S. Route 30 Wright's Ferry Bridge to the north. To the left is the steel Pennsylvania Railroad bridge, once used by both the Lincoln Highway and the railroad.

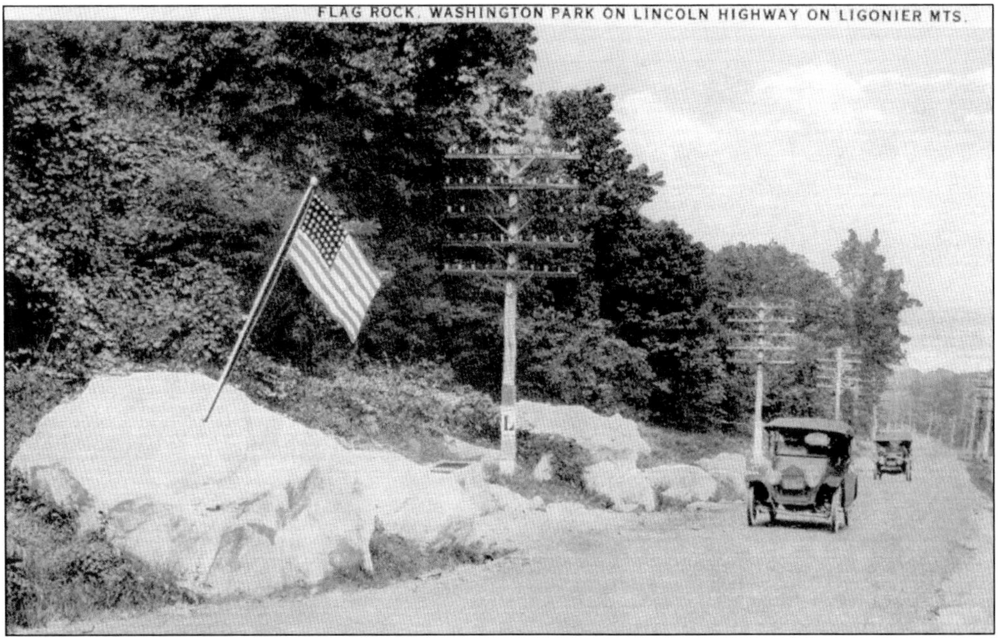

In the early days of the Lincoln Highway, the route was often marked on utility poles in red, white, and blue with a large "L" on the white background. This early signage is clear in the foreground on a pole at Flag Rock, near an area called Washington Park. A large part of the landmark rock was blasted away during a project to widen the road.

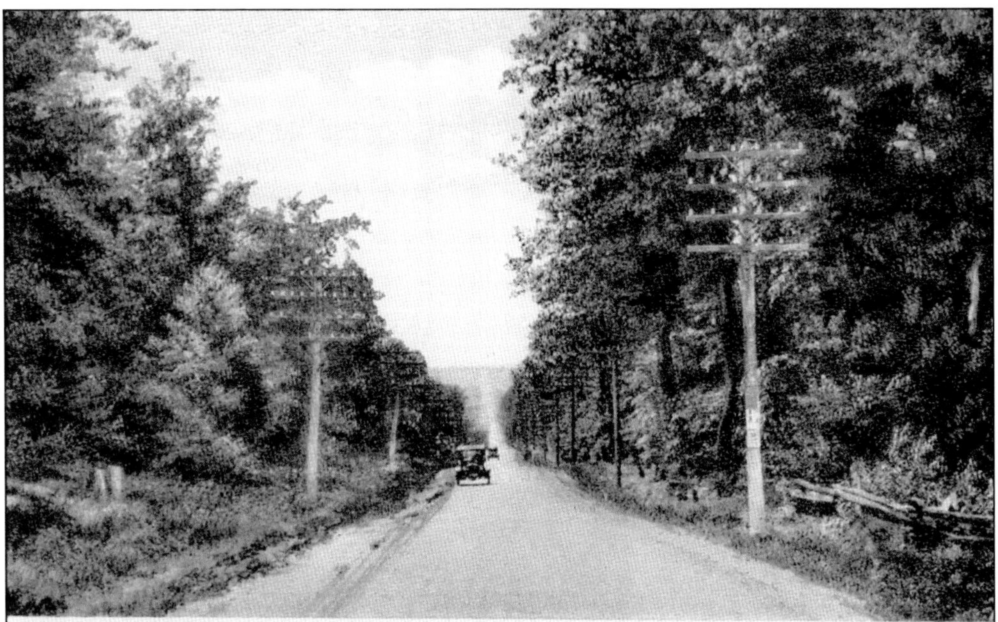

The Lincoln Highway is identified on the utility pole at right, along the famous Seven Mile Stretch, sometimes called the Seven Mile Straight. This section of the route is between Bedford and Ligonier and west of Grand View Point. The crossroads hamlet of Reels Corners is located along this part of the highway.

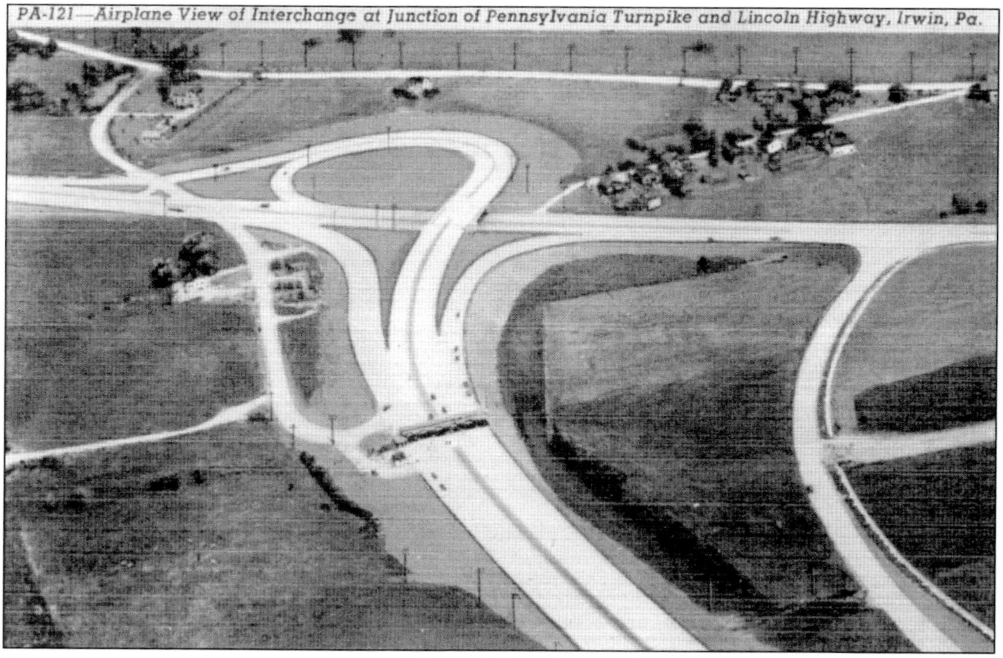

At the time of its construction, the Pennsylvania Turnpike started at Irwin, 21 miles east of Pittsburgh. The Lincoln Highway was four lanes wide in this area. However, it could not compete with "America's Super Highway," as the new toll road was often called. After the turnpike's completion in 1940, traffic began to decrease on the Lincoln Highway, a situation that led to the closing of many roadside businesses.

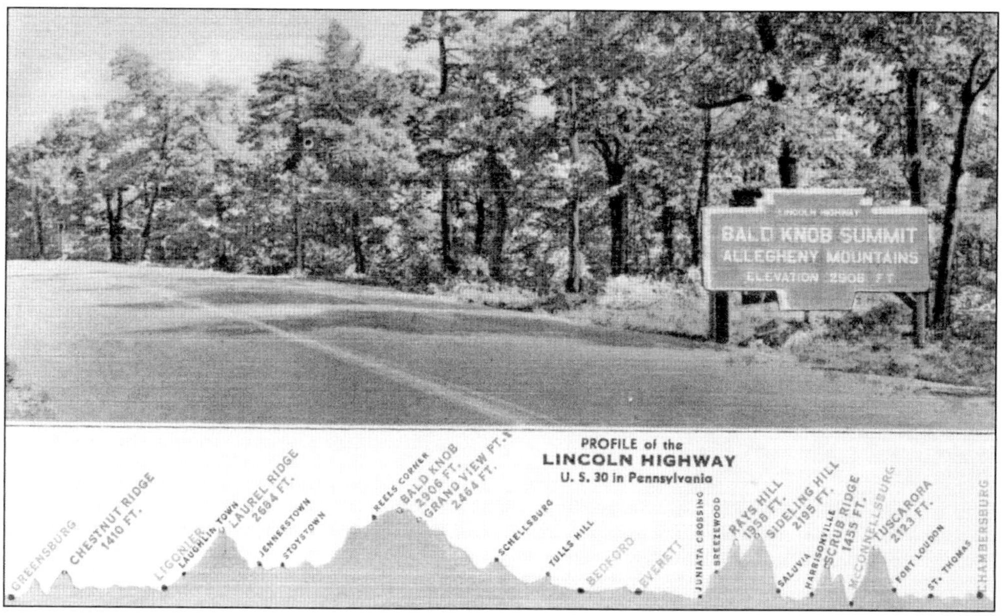

At 2,906 feet above sea level, Bald Knob Summit in the Allegheny Mountains is the highest point on the Lincoln Highway's route through Pennsylvania. As shown in this 1940s profile postcard, Bald Knob Summit lies between Grand View Point and Reels Corners. Profile cards were a popular means of demonstrating the route's many elevations and valleys.

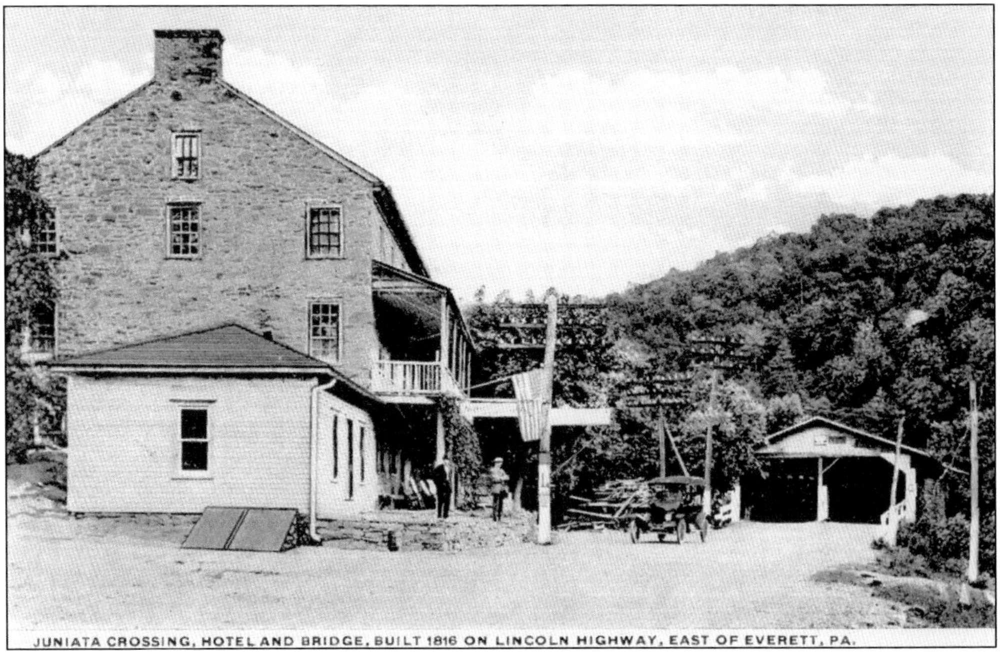

An early Lincoln Highway marker is visible on the utility pole in front of the Juniata Crossings Hotel. The Juniata Crossings Bridge, the covered span to the right, carries the highway over the Raystown Branch of the Juniata River. This historic wooden bridge was replaced in the 1930s by a modern concrete bridge. Built around 1816, the stone hotel is listed on the National Register of Historic Places and once hosted notable people such as Abraham Lincoln and Zachary Taylor. Before the Lincoln was routed through here, the area was an important stagecoach stop, with many taverns operating nearby.

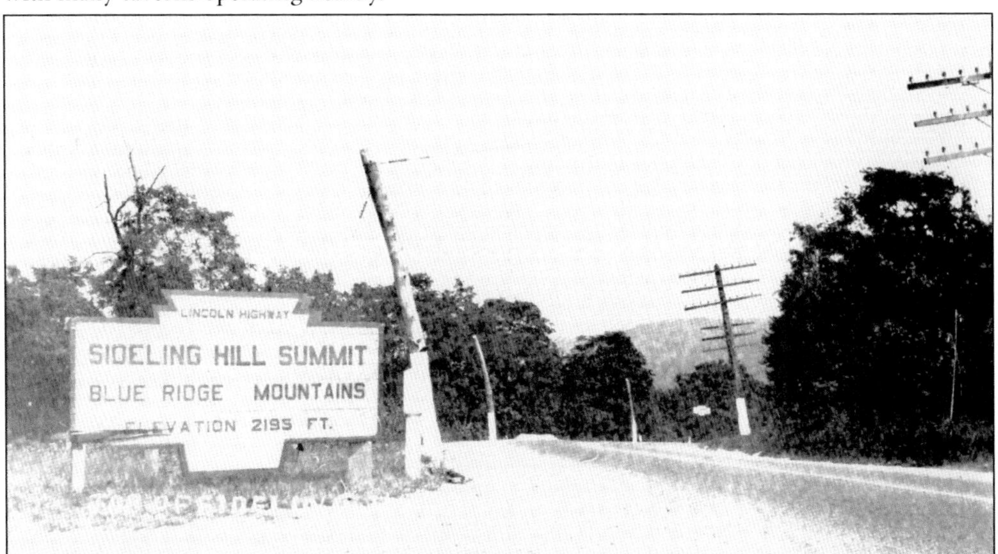

The large sign shown in this *c.* 1930 real-photo postcard tells Lincoln Highway travelers that they have reached Sideling Hill Summit, 2,195 feet above sea level in the Blue Ridge Mountains. As was common at many mountaintops along the route, several roadside businesses set up shop in this area to serve the needs of motorists.

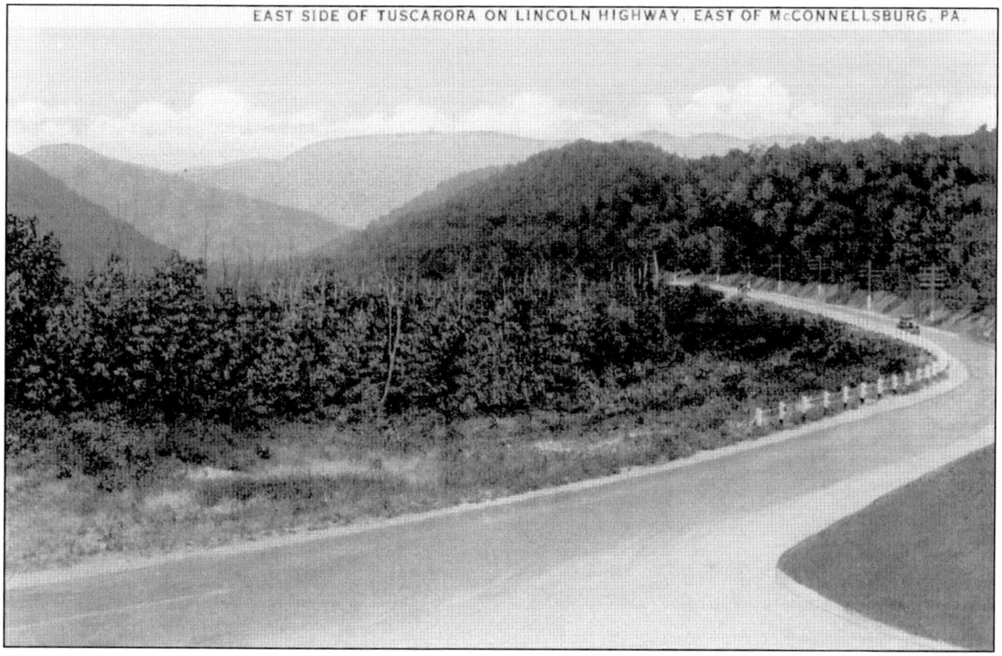

One of the major climbs on the highway's route through Pennsylvania was the trip to Tuscarora Summit high in the Blue Ridge Mountains. At 2,123 feet above sea level, the mountain offered scenic views, along with places that furnished water to cool early automobile engines.

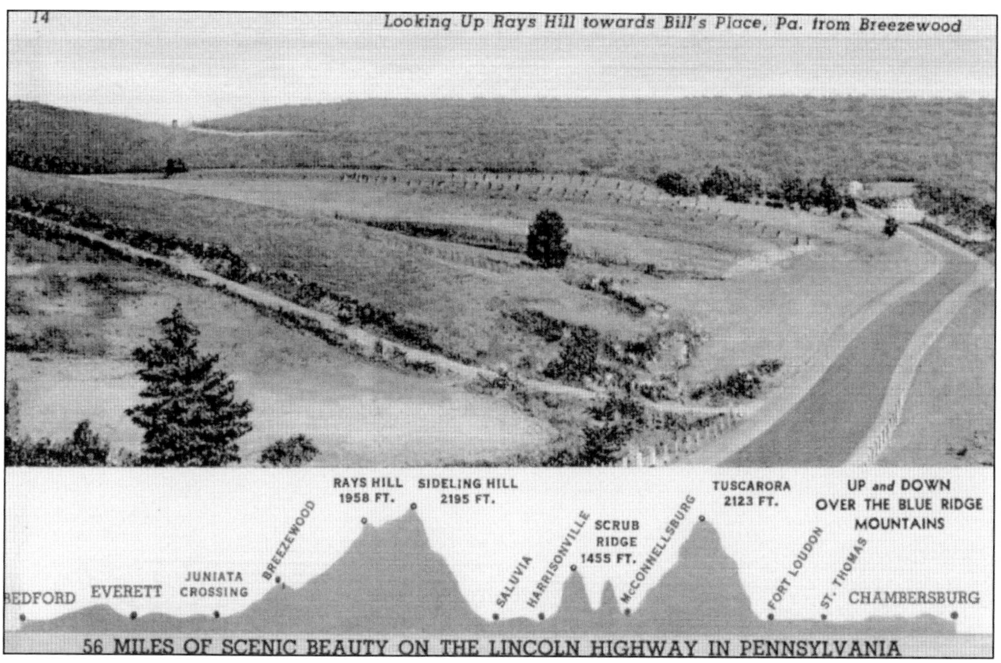

Calling the stretch "56 miles of scenic beauty," this early-1940s profile postcard shows the mountains and valleys between Chambersburg and Bedford. This view looks east from Breezewood toward Bill's Place, once a popular roadside stop at the top of Ray's Hill, which rises 1,958 feet above sea level.

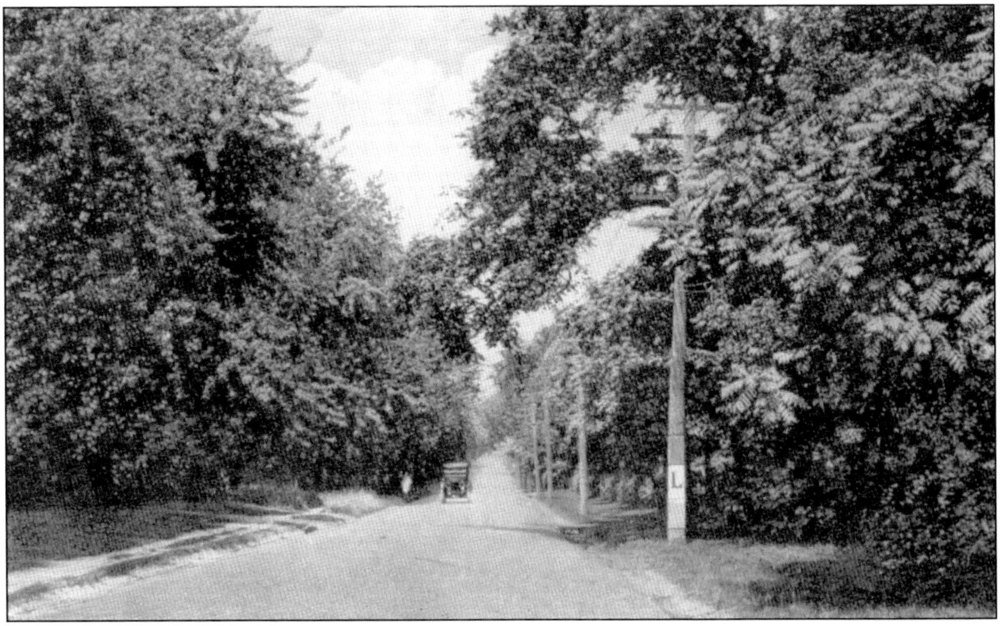

Although the exact location of this Lincoln Highway view near Philadelphia is unknown, it is a certainty that the landscape has changed drastically over the years. In the time since this view was published, likely in the early 1920s, growth has exploded in the entire area, sometimes wiping out all traces of the original route.

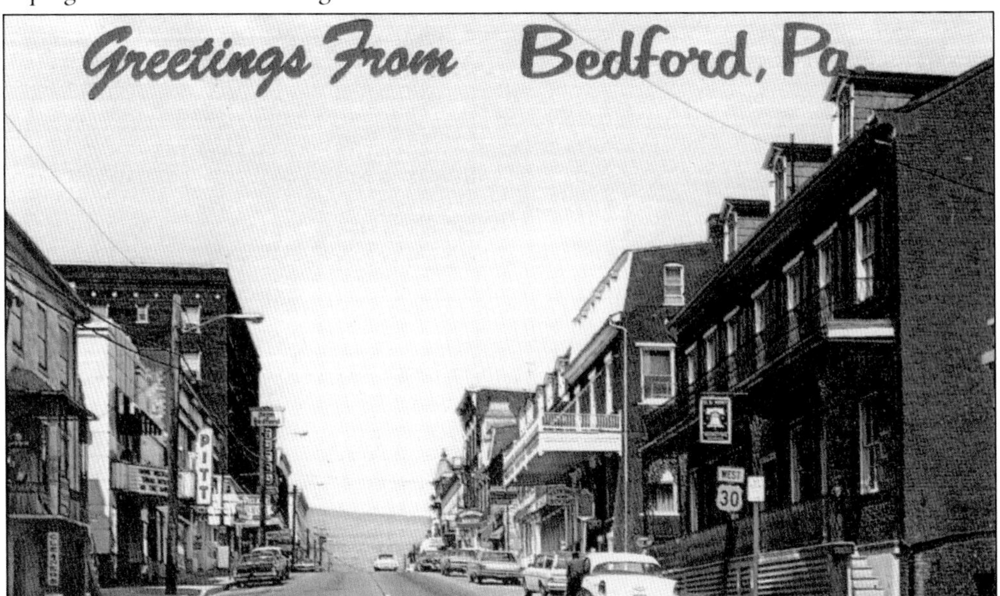

Like almost all other major roads of an earlier motoring era, the Lincoln Highway often passed directly through the business districts of towns along its route. As the automobile grew in popularity and traffic increased, many—if not most—of the towns were bypassed. Here the Lincoln Highway (U.S. Route 30) passes through Bedford's main downtown business district. During the highway's early days, most travelers' needs could be satisfied in the downtowns, but as years progressed, they were more often found on the edges of towns.

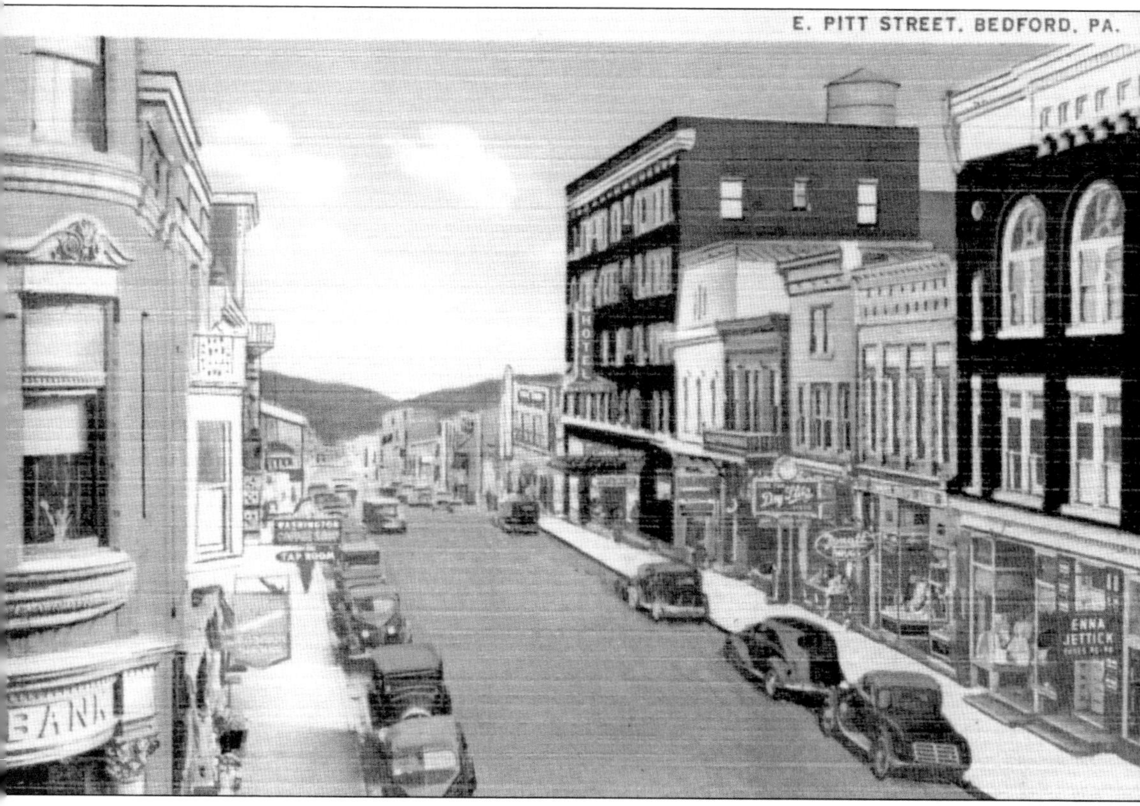

This 1930s view of Bedford's Pitt Street shows an active business district featuring shops, hotels, and garages in which Lincoln Highway travelers could store their cars overnight. Today Pitt Street continues to be the town's main business district and contains several antiques shops.

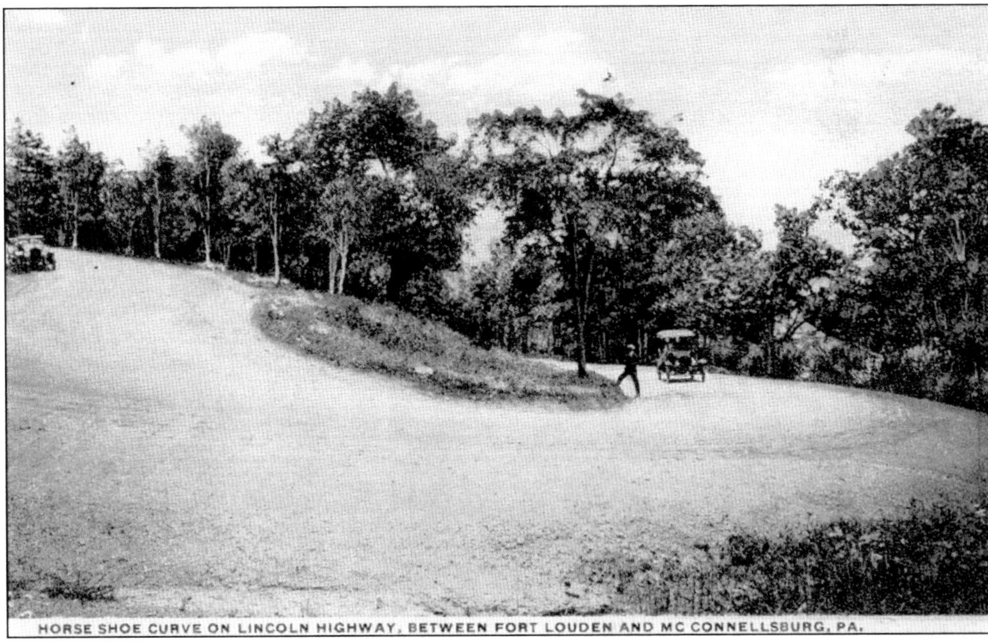

Early travelers of the road had to negotiate this very sharp bend, known as Horseshoe Curve. The dangerous curve, located near McConnellsburg, was in later years eased a bit and later still bypassed by U.S. Route 30.

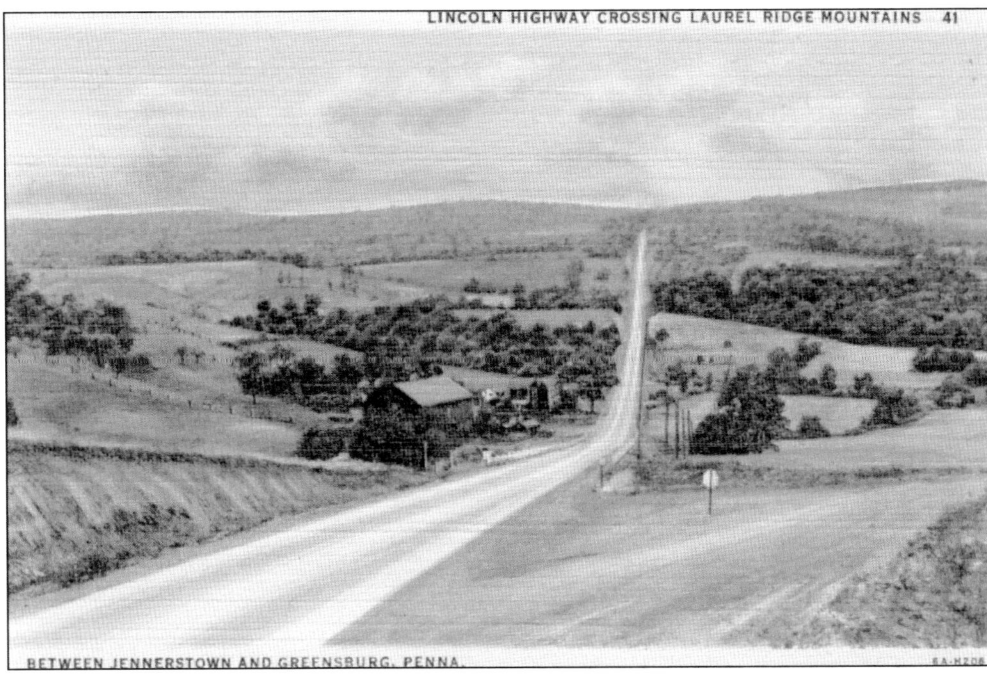

The highway follows rolling terrain through farmland on its route between Jennerstown and Greensburg. In the distance rises Laurel Ridge Mountain. Although the Pennsylvania Turnpike made the trip quicker through the western part of the state, travelers on the new road sacrificed scenery for speed.

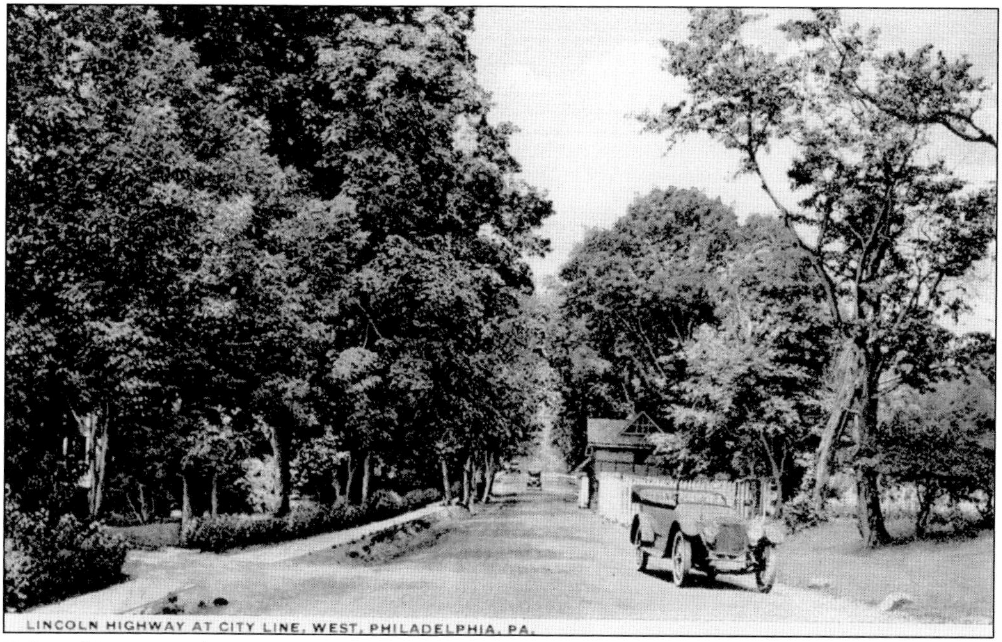

When this postcard was published, around 1920, the Lincoln Highway was a dirt surface at the western edge of Philadelphia. It is likely that a hotel known as Green Hill Farms stood nearby. As the years passed, the land west of the city grew to meet the demands of an increasing population and lost the rural look that was so common a little over 80 years ago.

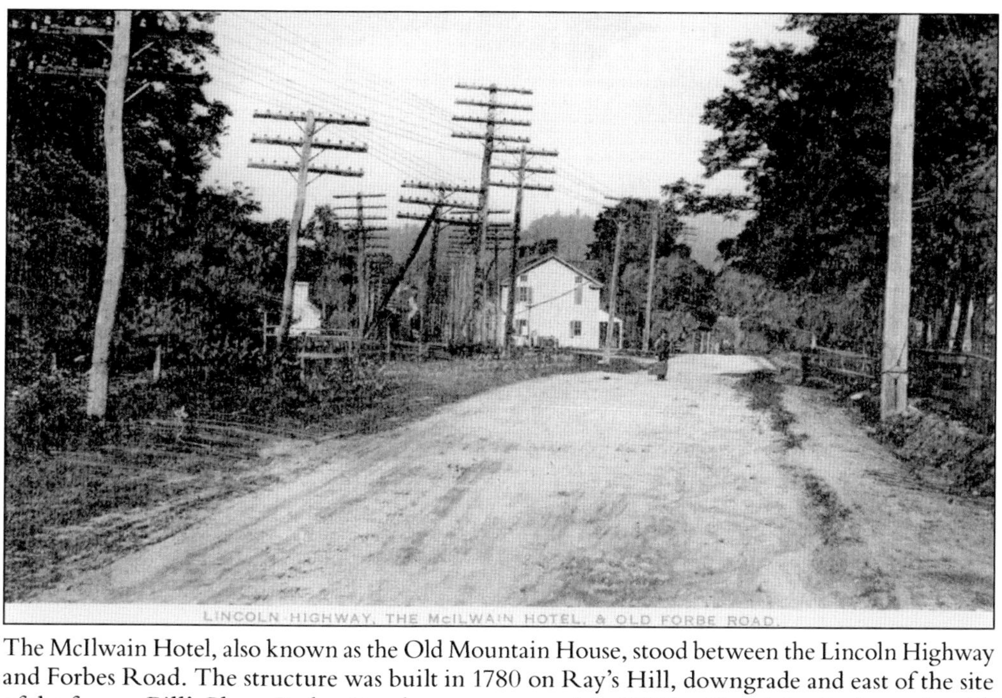

The McIlwain Hotel, also known as the Old Mountain House, stood between the Lincoln Highway and Forbes Road. The structure was built in 1780 on Ray's Hill, downgrade and east of the site of the former Bill's Place. Forbes Road was constructed in 1758 by Gen. John Forbes and, with the exception of an American Indian trail, was the earliest route across this part of the state.

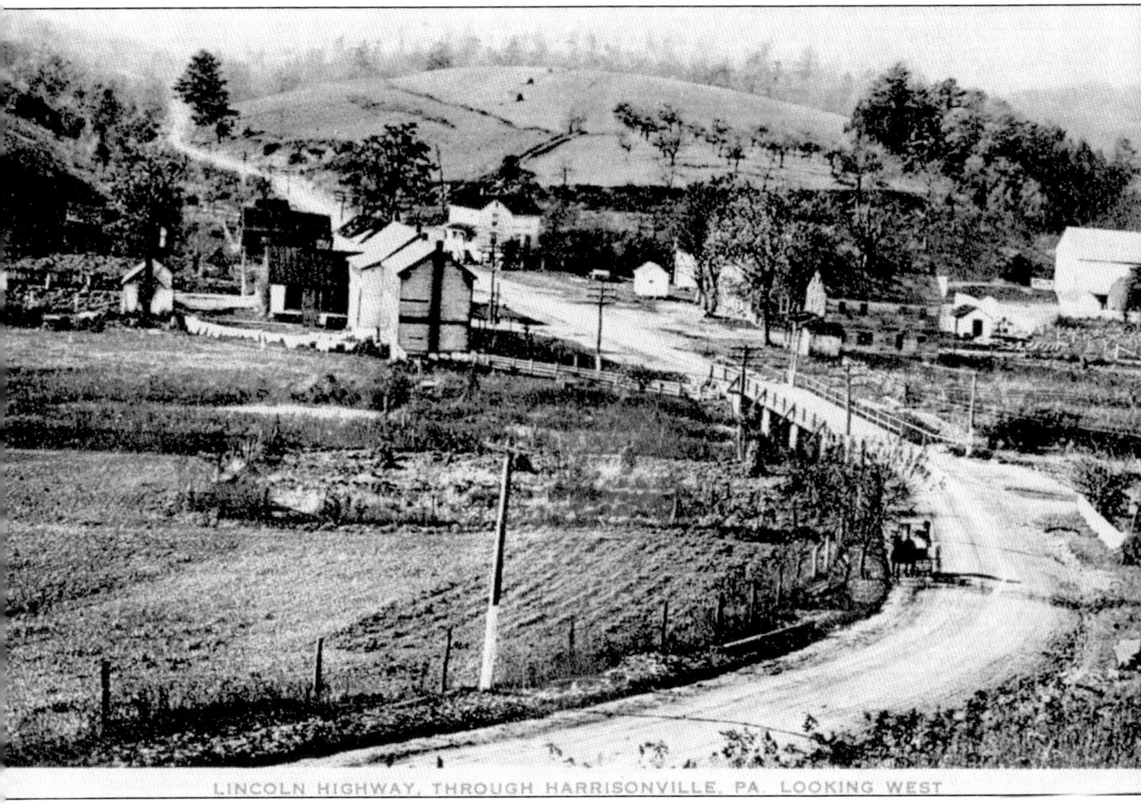

The Lincoln Highway winds through the rural village of Harrisonville, which is approximately midway between McConnellsburg and Breezewood. At least one roadside amenity, the White Cottage Inn Cabins, once operated near here at the foot of Sideling Hill. The highway passed through many similar areas of farmland on its path through the state.

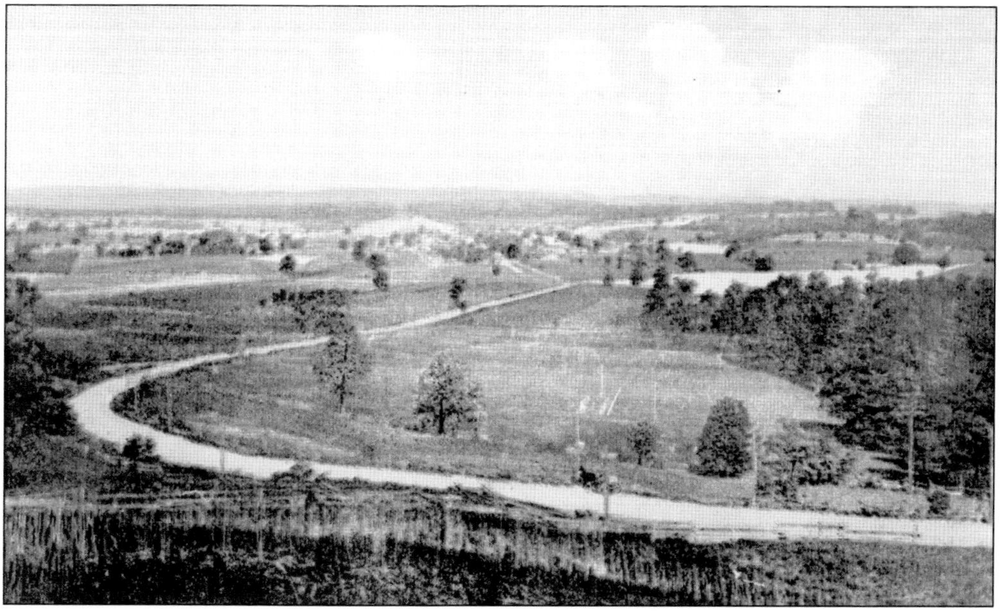

The highway looks like a country road as it approaches Schellsburg in the foreground of this view. The town, 11 miles west of Bedford, dates to 1808 and includes at least one garage operating from the route's early days. The area remains very rural.

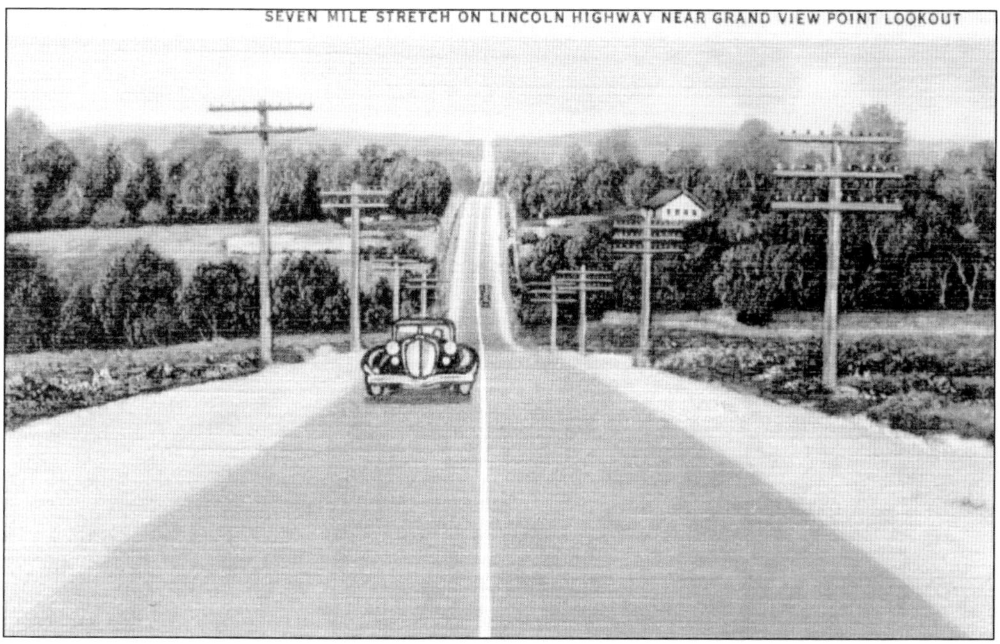

As was common in the late 1930s and 1940s, this postcard provides a rather stylized view of the route's famous Seven Mile Stretch. This rolling section of the Lincoln Highway passes through areas where coal mining was the major industry. Some people refer to this part as Long View Stretch.

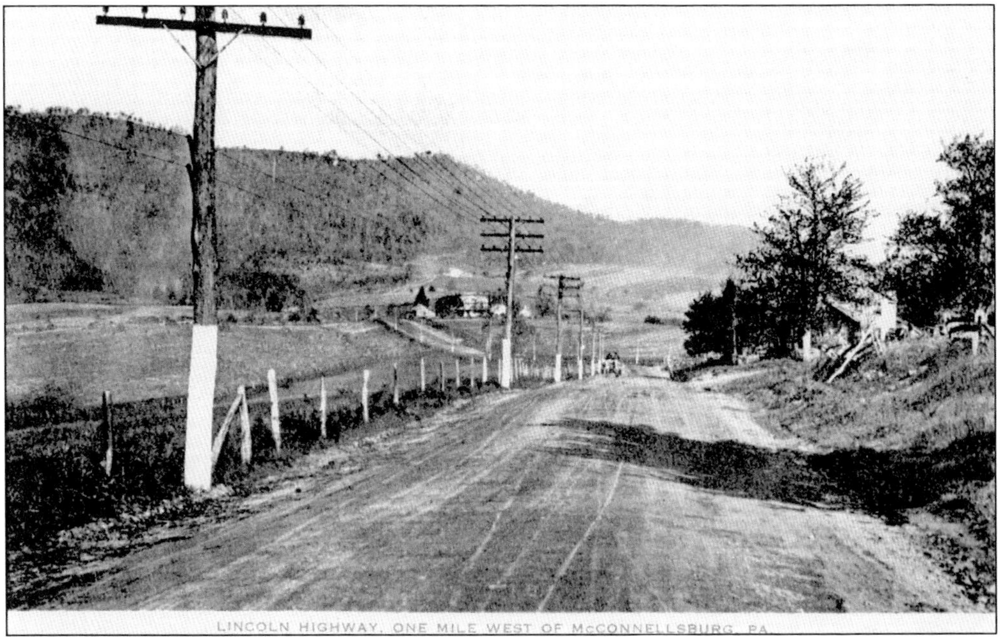

Shallow ruts are apparent in this *c.* 1920 view of the dirt or gravel surface of the Lincoln Highway, one mile west of McConnellsburg. Early travelers heading west next encountered the climb to Scrub Ridge Summit, 1,455 feet above sea level.

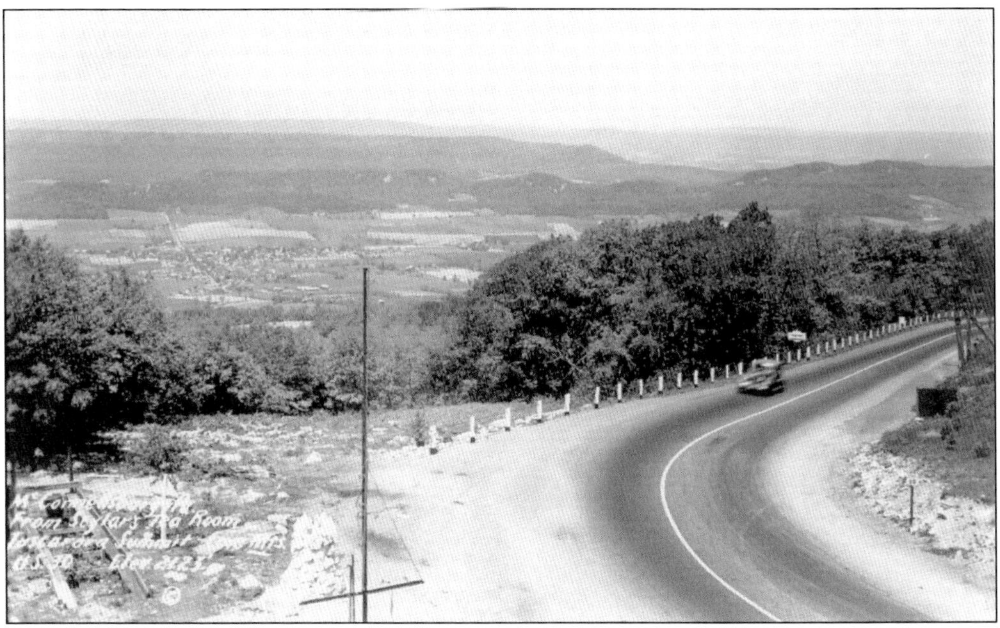

McConnellsburg and the Lincoln Highway are seen from Leslie "Doc" Seylar's establishment at Tuscarora Summit. According to this real-photo postcard, the popular roadside stop was known at that time as Seylar's Tea Room. Other businesses in the area included the Cove Mountain Tea Room and Tuscarora Summit Inn.

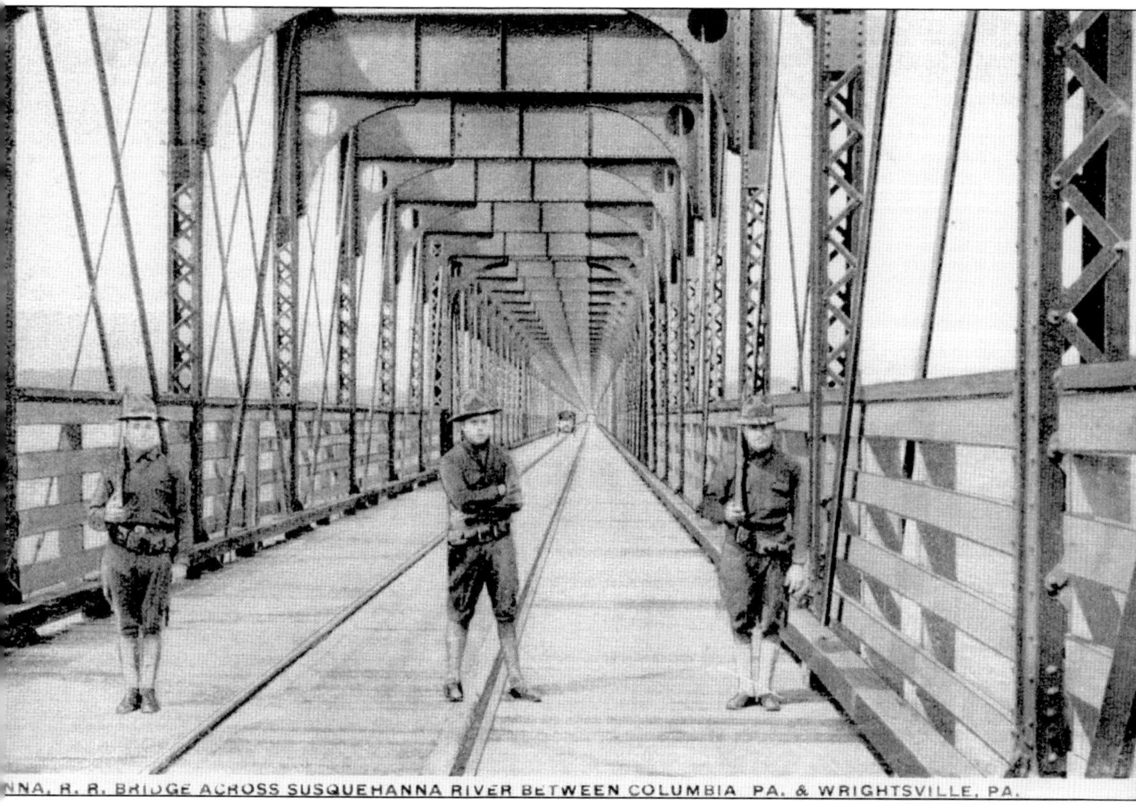

A trio of soldiers guards the Pennsylvania Railroad's Susquehanna River Bridge, between Columbia and Wrightsville. This could easily date the card to the World War I era, when officials were concerned that significant bridges and other structures could be sabotaged. In the years before the construction of the York-Lancaster Inter-County Bridge, this one-mile span carried the Lincoln Highway across the Susquehanna for both trains and automobiles.

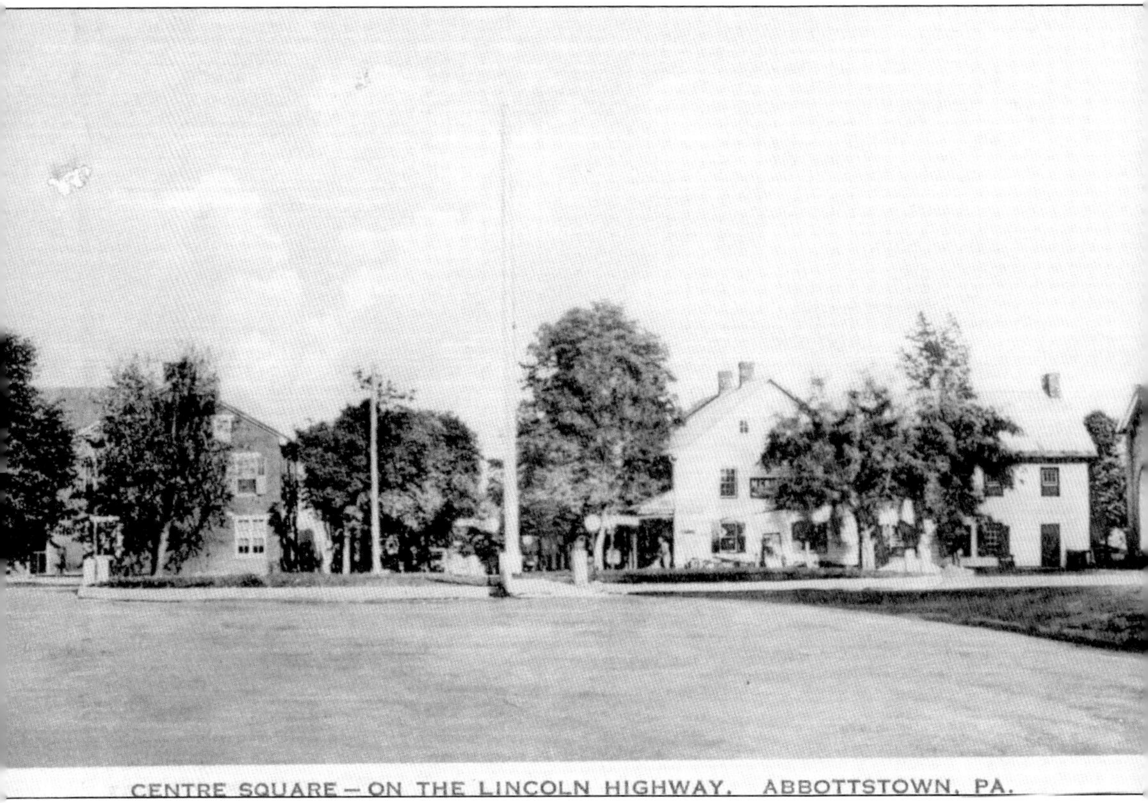

The Lincoln Highway passes through the Adams County borough of Abbottstown, whose Centre Square is shown here. Although many refer to the highway by today's U.S. Route 30 designation, the Lincoln name remains popular in the Abbottstown area, as evidenced by the nearby Lincoln Speedway south of the route. In the past, many businesses drew on the popularity of the highway for their names and continue to do so today.

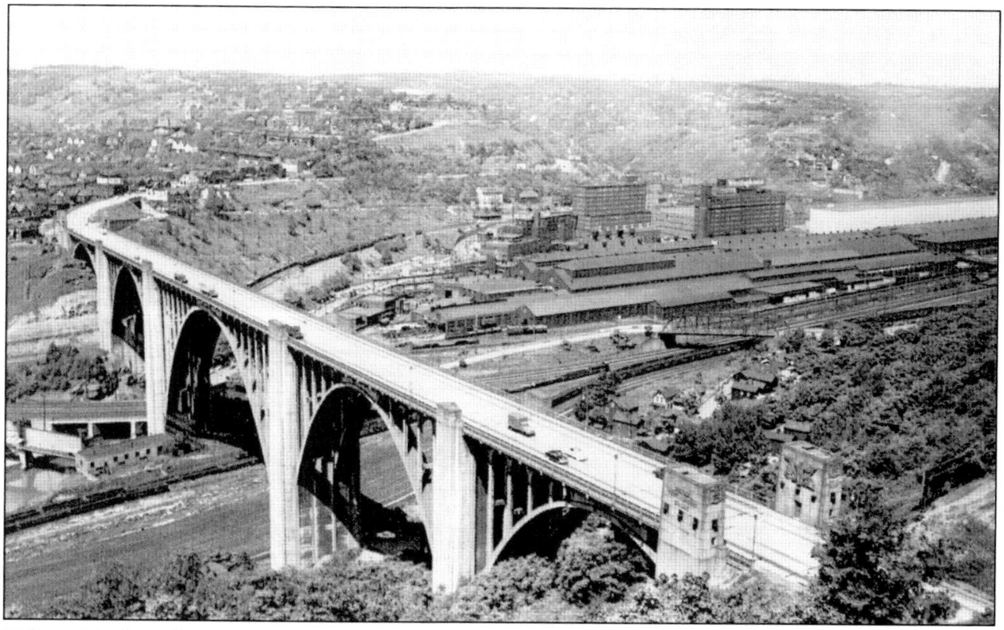

When Pittsburgh's Westinghouse Bridge was completed in 1932, it was the longest concrete span in the world. In the valley to the right of the bridge is the sprawling Westinghouse Electric Corporation plant. The bridge was constructed to bypass a busy section of the Lincoln Highway but still used the U.S. Route 30 designation.

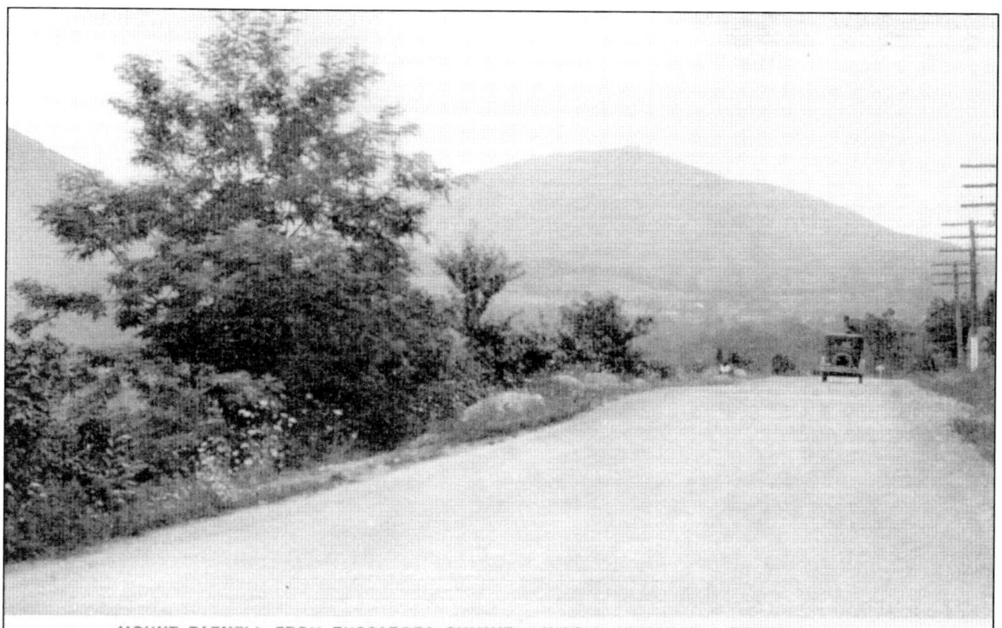

This early vehicle has made the trip to Tuscarora Summit, seen here with Mount Parnell in the distance. Although buildings were usually landmarks along the route, many mountains, rivers, and streams also became known to Lincoln Highway travelers.

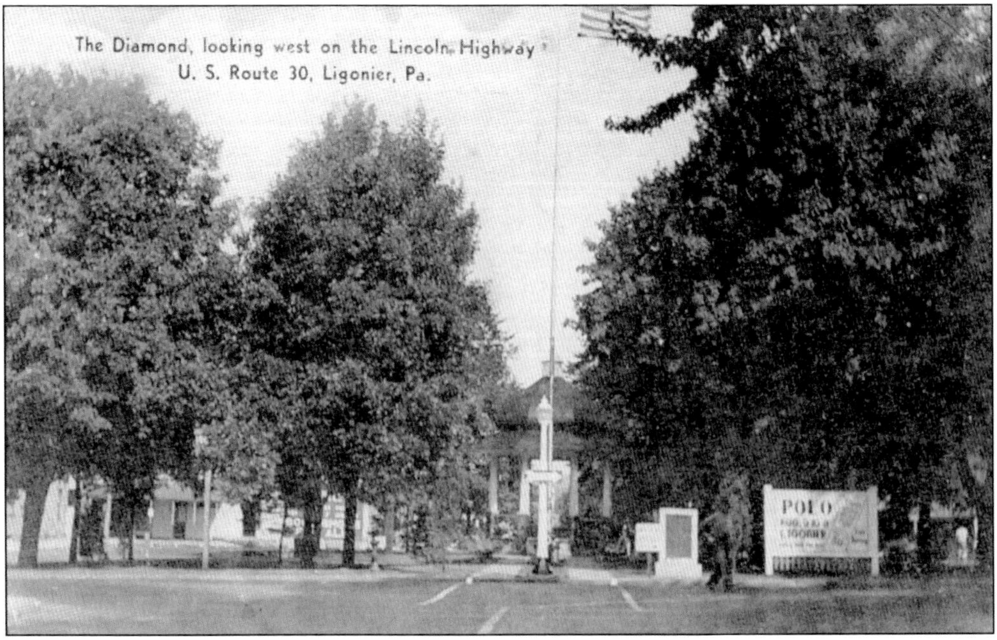

The original route of the highway went around the Ligonier Diamond, which in most other towns would be called a square. Tracing its history as a town back to 1817, Ligonier was named after nearby Fort Ligonier, built during the French and Indian War.

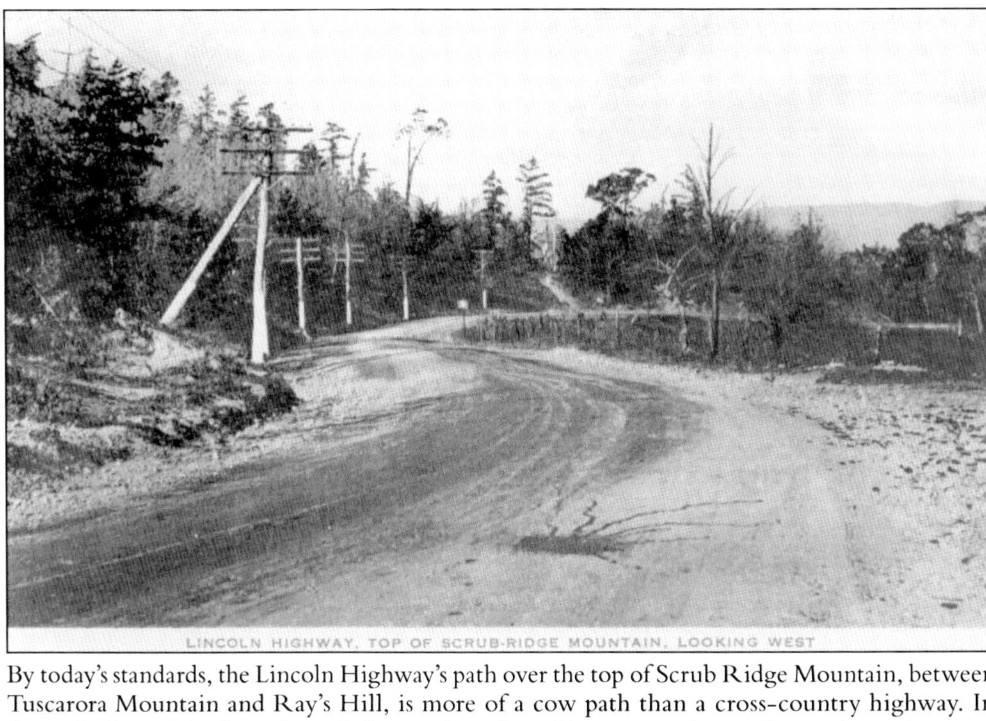

By today's standards, the Lincoln Highway's path over the top of Scrub Ridge Mountain, between Tuscarora Mountain and Ray's Hill, is more of a cow path than a cross-country highway. In the early days of the Lincoln, existing roads such as this were used to make up the entire route across the nation.

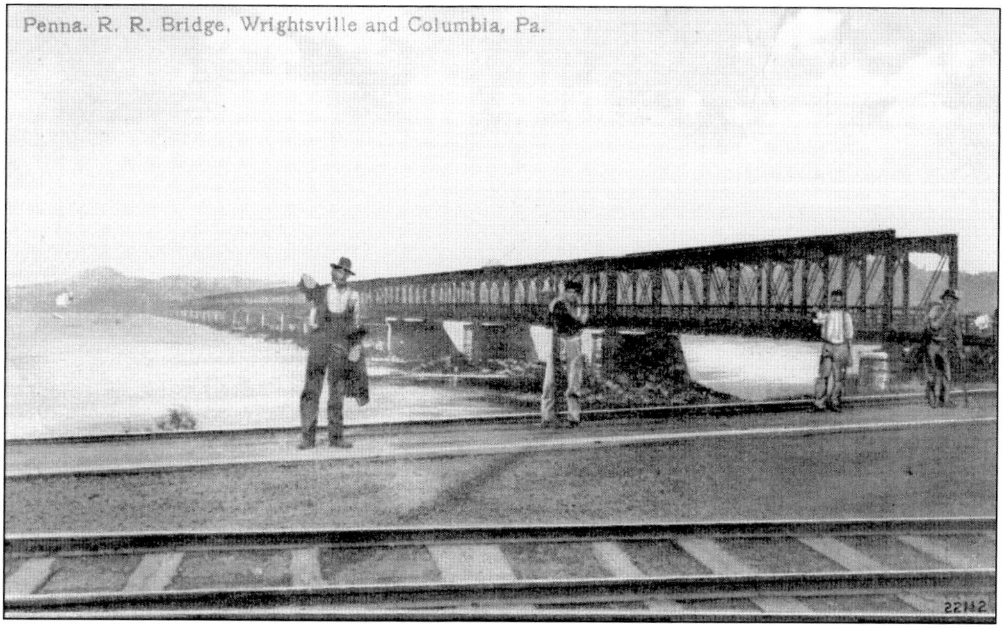

This *c.* 1909 side view of the Pennsylvania Railroad bridge connecting Columbia and Wrightsville shows the length of the steel span across the Susquehanna River. Several years after this postcard was published, the bridge was shared by the Lincoln Highway, and signals were installed to prevent traffic from entering when it was in use by a train. The famous landmark was removed in 1964, but the piers remain, still jutting out of the river.

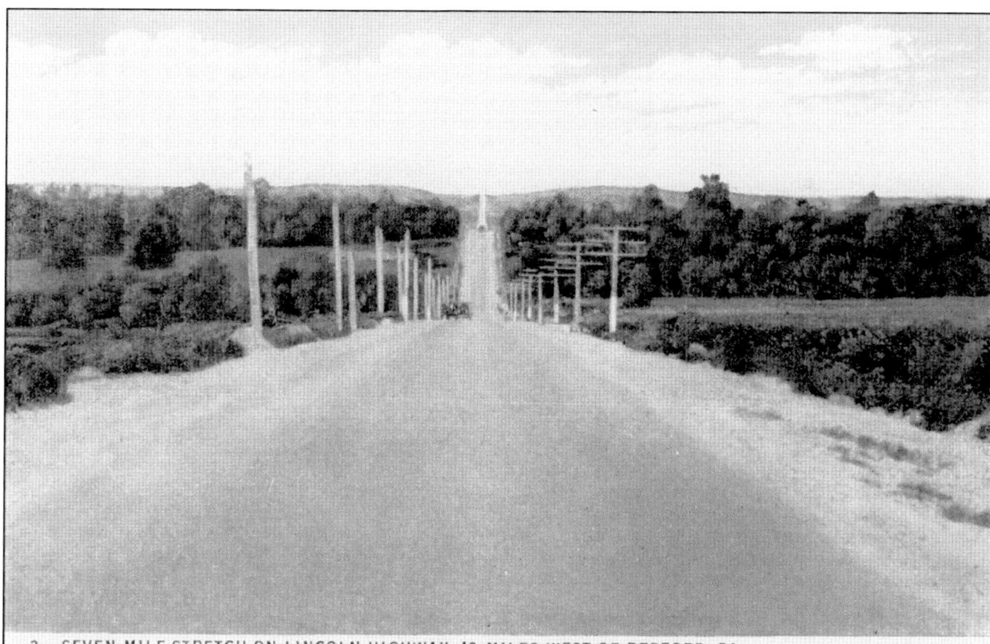

Almost the entire cross-country route was initially made of dirt or gravel, which led to slow, rough, and sometimes dangerous travel. By the 1930s, progress was being made. In this *c.* 1934 postcard view of the Seven Mile Stretch, the highway has either a paved or concrete surface.

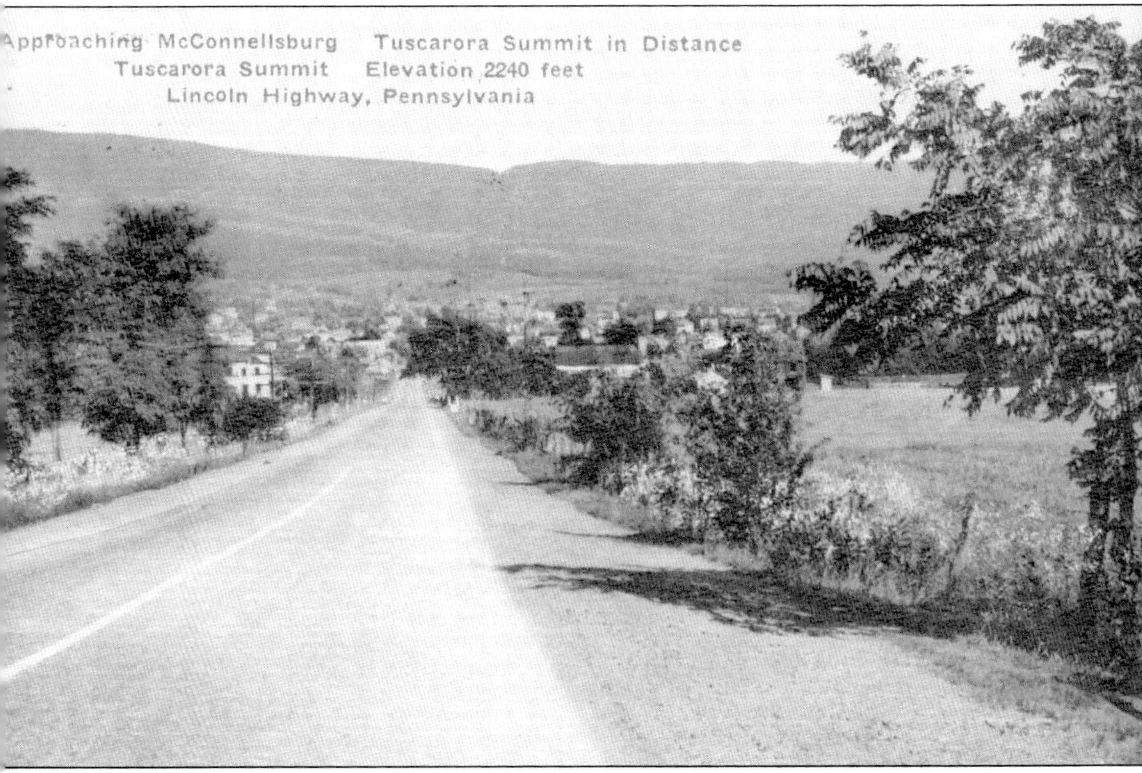

The Lincoln Highway approaches the Fulton County borough of McConnellsburg from the west, with Tuscarora Summit in the distance. Although the town has been bypassed by U.S. Route 30, the original route is still named Lincoln Way, which is rather common in several communities. The town was named for Daniel McConnell, who in 1786 deeded the land on which the municipality, which is the Fulton County seat, was built. McConnellsburg, already an important stop on the route west from Philadelphia, grew when the Lincoln Highway was established. Listed on the National Register of Historic Places today, its historic district contains 144 buildings, including taverns, inns, garages, and other structures related to travel.

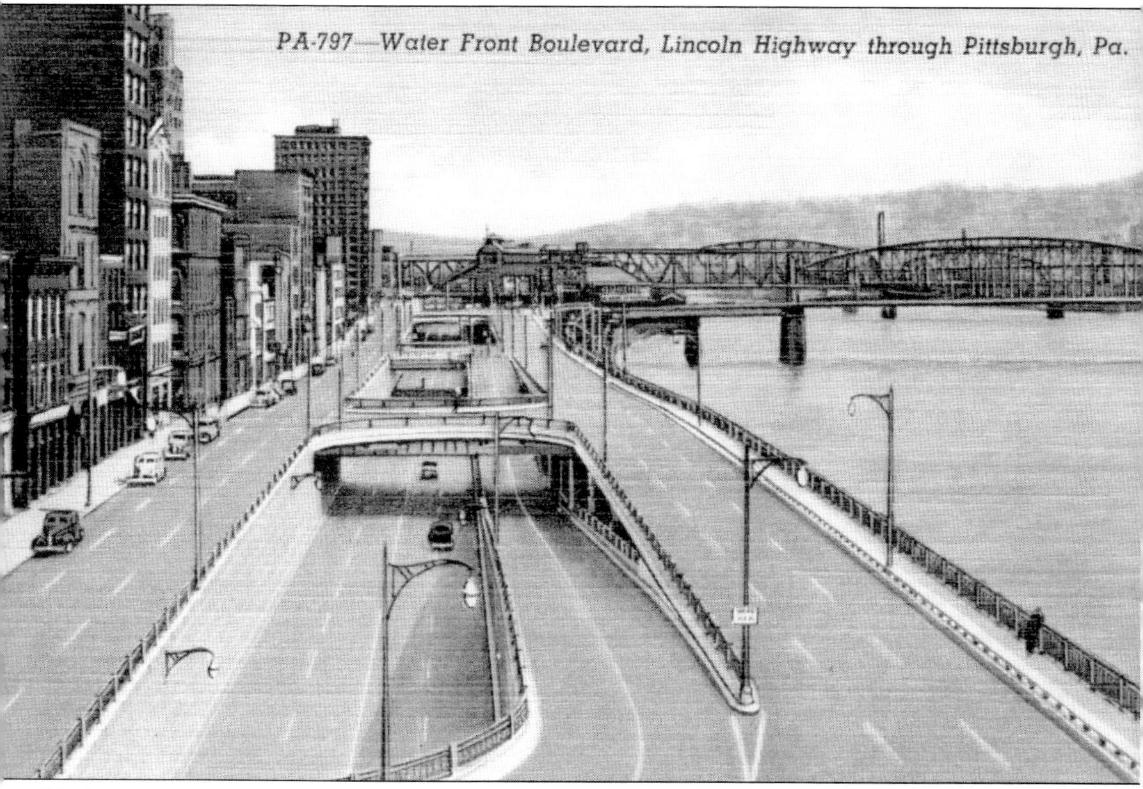

Pittsburgh's Water Street Boulevard was part of a $5 million improvement project designed to keep Lincoln Highway traffic moving through the city. In this view, the roadway has nine lanes built on two levels and is equipped with ramps to allow drivers easy entrance and exit.

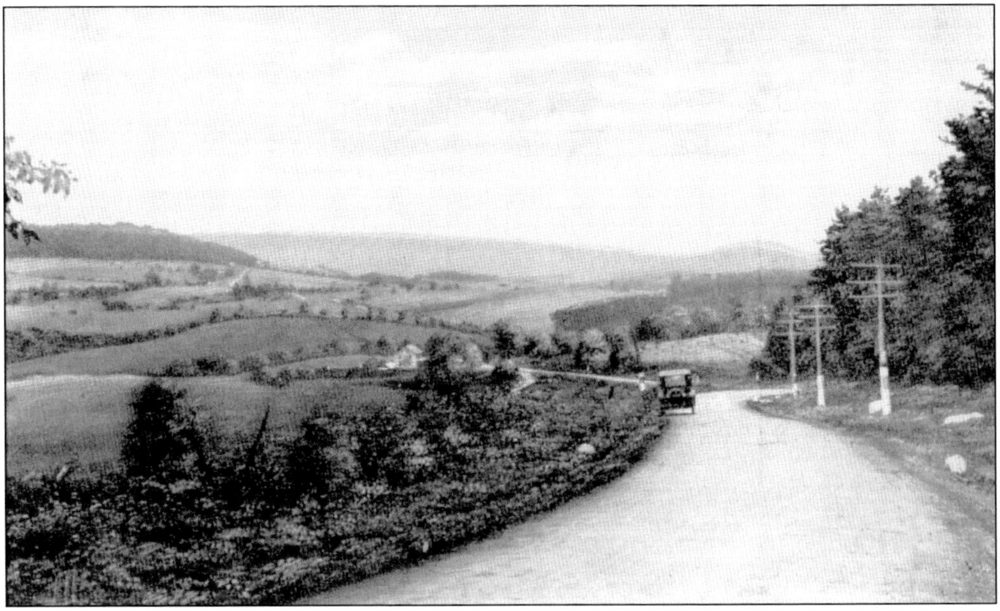

Surrounded by scenic Fulton County farms and woodland, the highway winds through the countryside two miles west of McConnellsburg. Travelers taking the route through this area encountered significant climbs, such as Tuscarora Mountain to the east and Scrub Ridge Summit to the west.

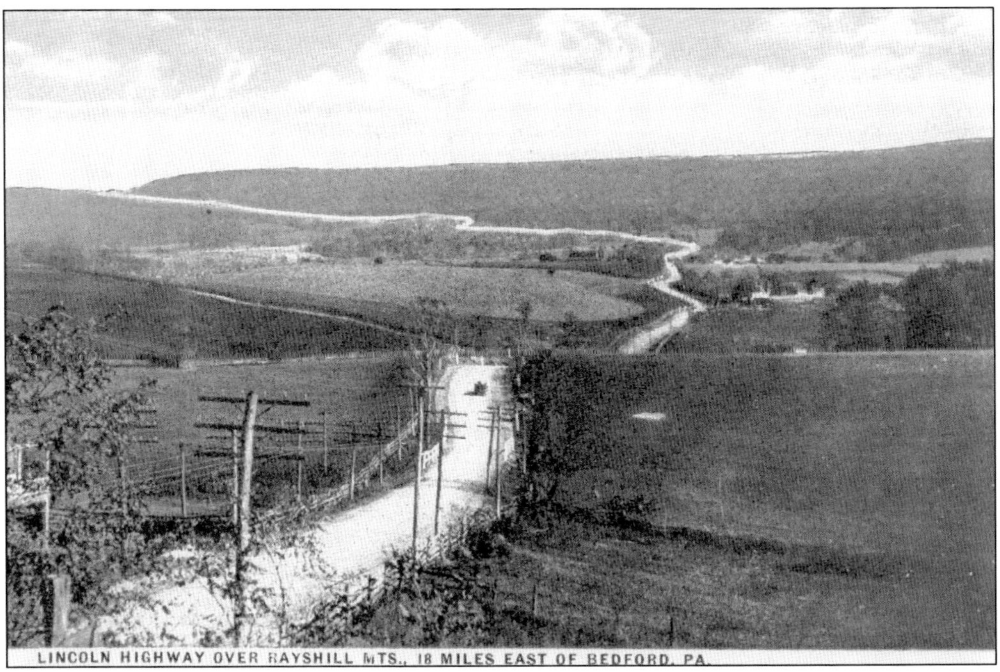

The Lincoln Highway winds through a valley and up Ray's Hill, once the site of Bill's Place, a popular stop along the route. When the Pennsylvania Turnpike was built, a tunnel was driven through this mountain. The Ray's Hill Tunnel was abandoned after the turnpike was rerouted through another cut made into the mountain.

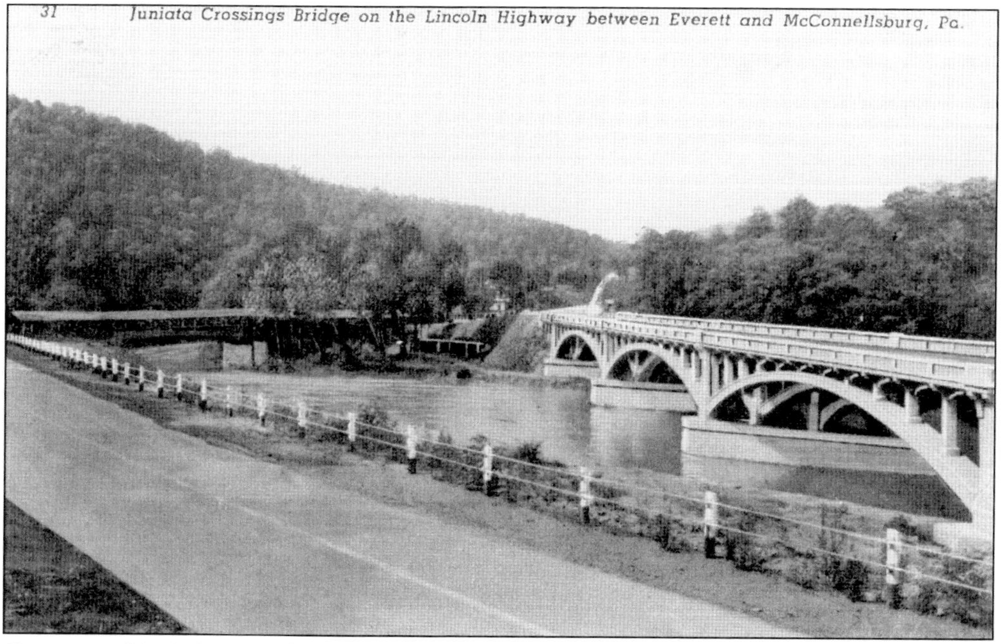

Constructed in 1934 to replace an 1818 covered bridge, the concrete Juniata Crossings Bridge sits just west of Breezewood. Although the covered bridge was not removed after the new span opened, it was destroyed in the St. Patrick's Day flood of 1936. Several tourist camps were located in the vicinity of the bridges.

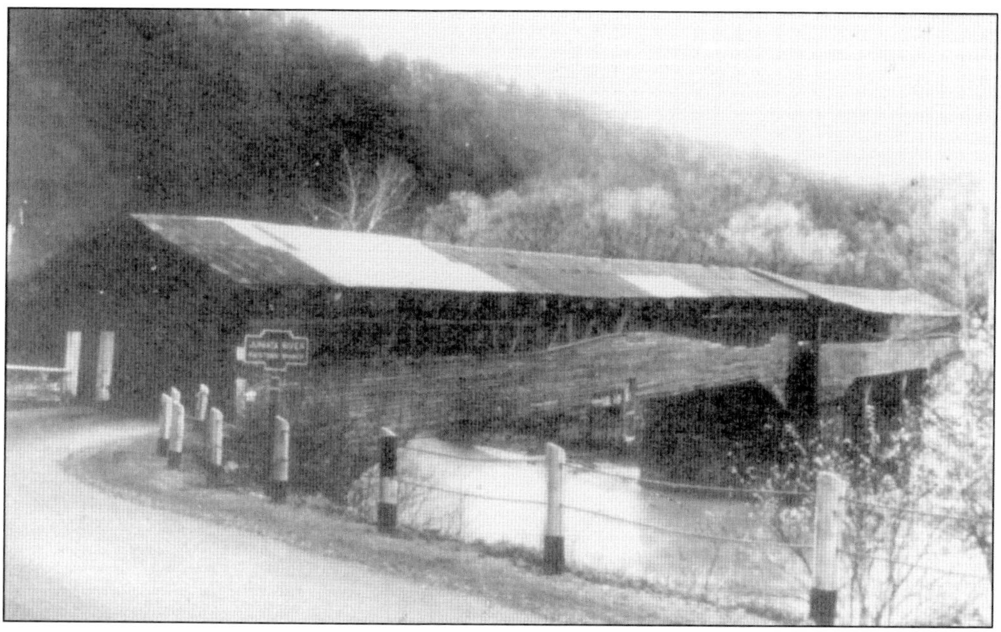

The Juniata Crossings Covered Bridge, west of Breezewood and in Bedford County, was a double-lane, 367-foot-long bridge built in 1818 that later carried the Lincoln Highway over the Raystown Branch of the Juniata River. Half of the bridge was made into a single-lane span before its destruction in the March 1936 flood.

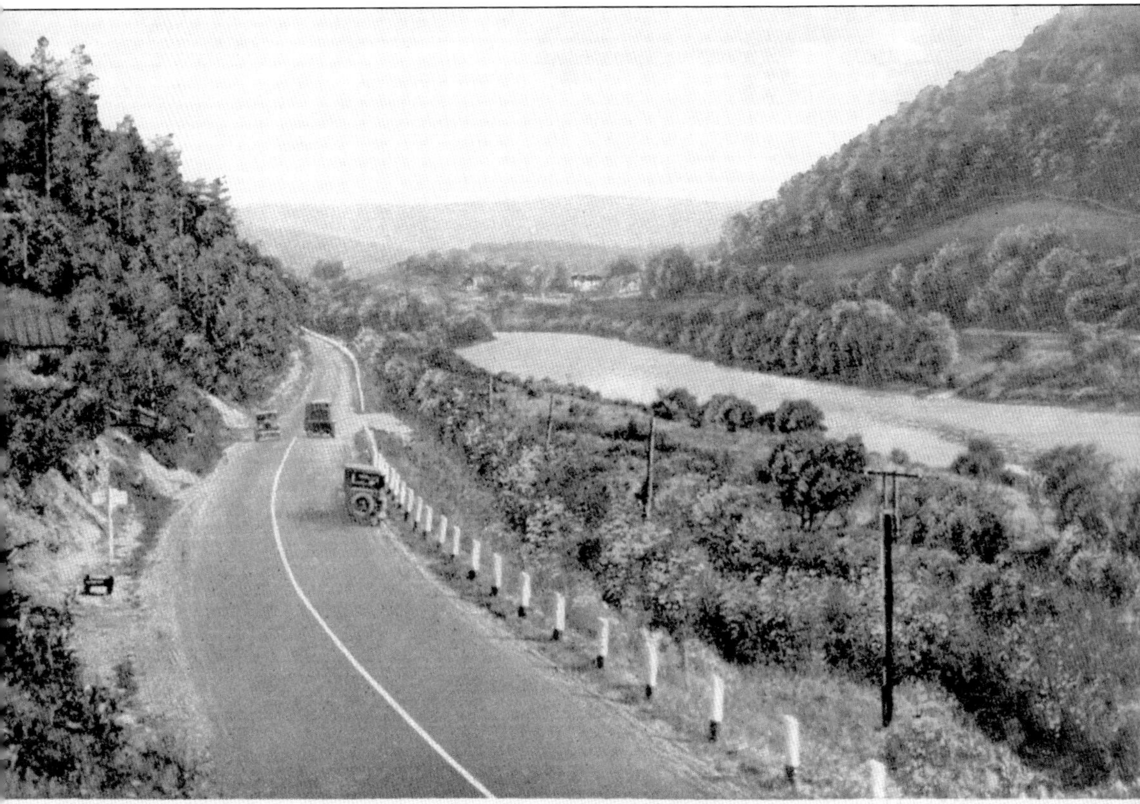

8 LINCOLN HIGHWAY AND JUNIATA RIVER EAST OF BEDFORD, PA. 117548

The scenery along the Raystown Branch of the Juniata River attracted the attention of many early travelers, and with that came businesses serving the motoring public. In this area could be found Bubbling Springs Camp and Rusty's Place, along with several others.

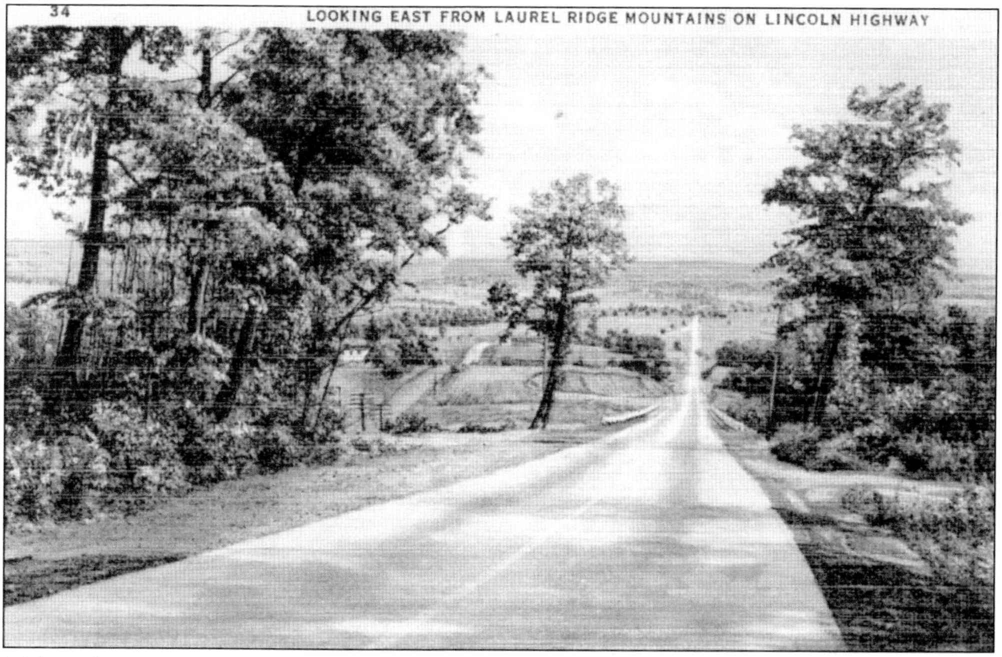

Although not a great distance from the city of Pittsburgh, the stretch of highway between Jennerstown and Ligonier is still very rural. This general area was home to a number of roadside businesses, including hotels and camps such as the Zeppelin Tourist Camp, which offered lunches in a blimp-shaped building.

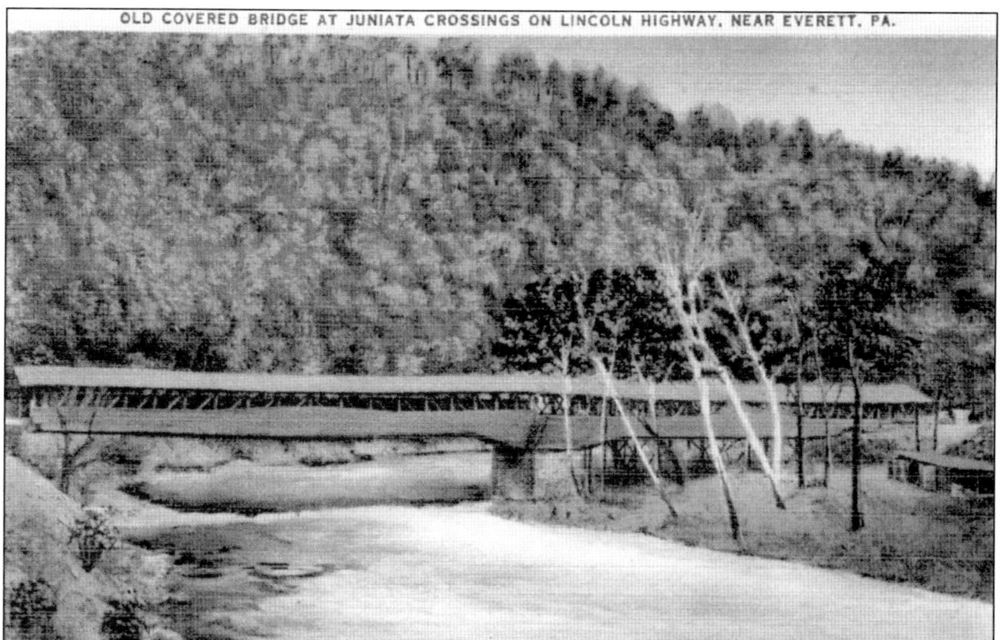

The Juniata Crossings Covered Bridge, east of Bedford, created a perfect country scene around 1940, when this card was published. This view was likely taken from the adjacent concrete span.

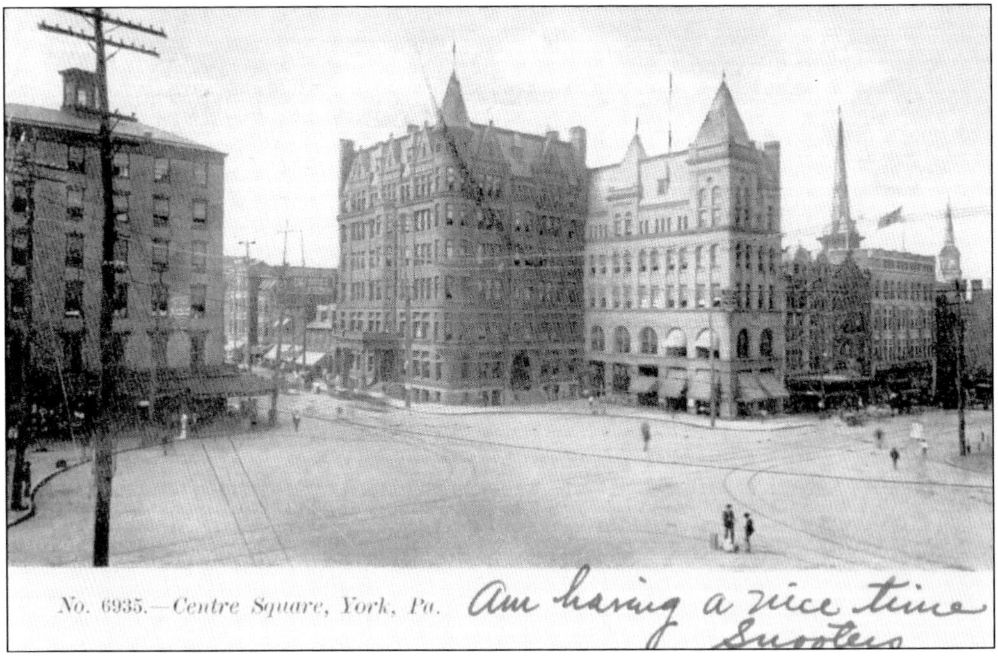

York's Center Square was already a busy place by the time the Lincoln Highway passed through it. In the foreground is the historic Colonial Hotel, which offered rooms to early travelers of the route.

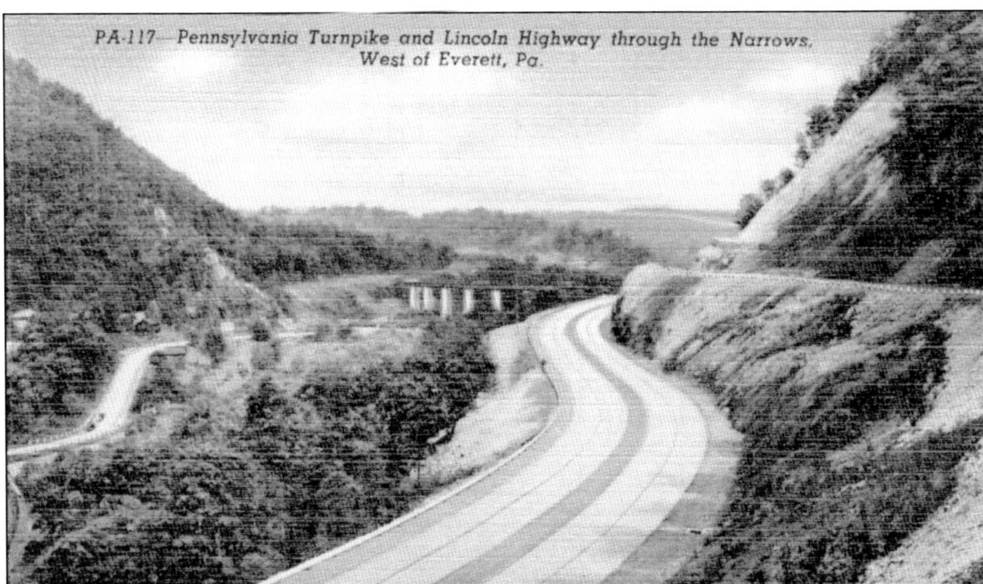

The Pennsylvania Turnpike crosses over the Lincoln Highway five miles west of Bedford. According to a description on the back of this 1940s postcard, the turnpike makes the two-lane Lincoln look "antiquated." After the turnpike's completion, much of the travelers that used the old route opted for the faster and straighter one, even though a toll had to be paid.

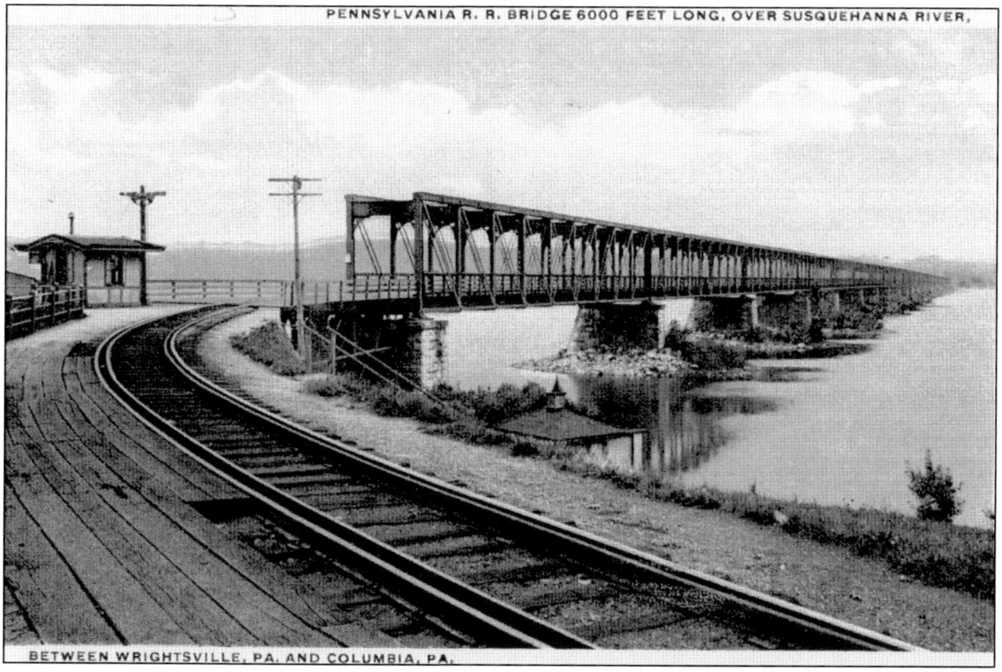

Spanning the mile-wide Susquehanna River is this iron Pennsylvania Railroad bridge, shared in early days by the Lincoln Highway. Before any bridge was built in this location, a ferry carried travelers across the river.

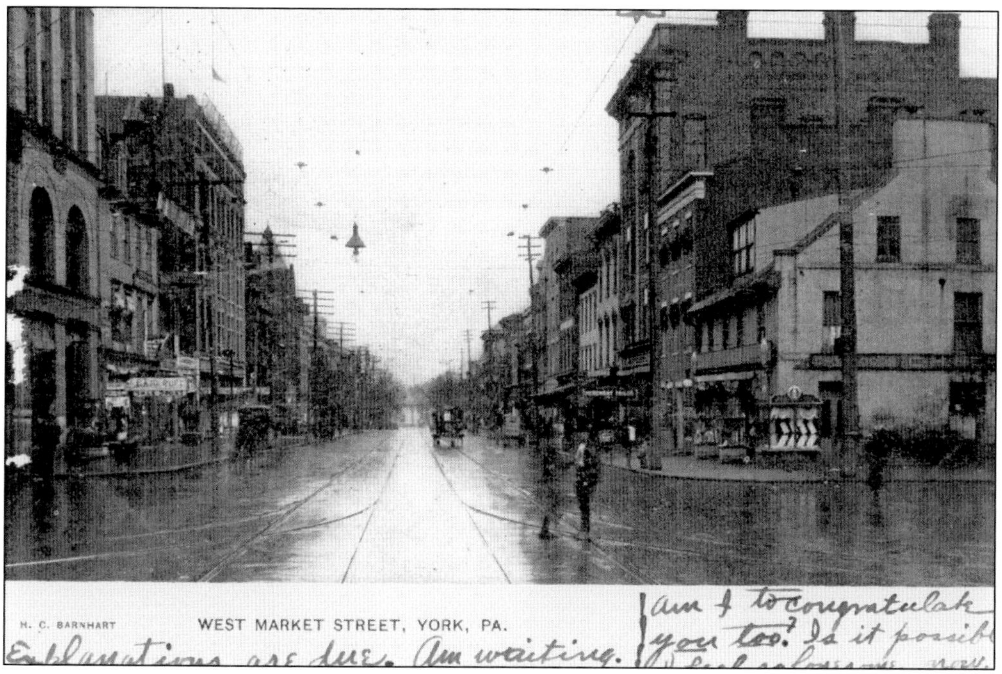

In later years, the Lincoln Highway's route through many towns was bypassed in an effort to speed transportation. One of those places was York, where the route ran directly through the city's business district along West Market Street.

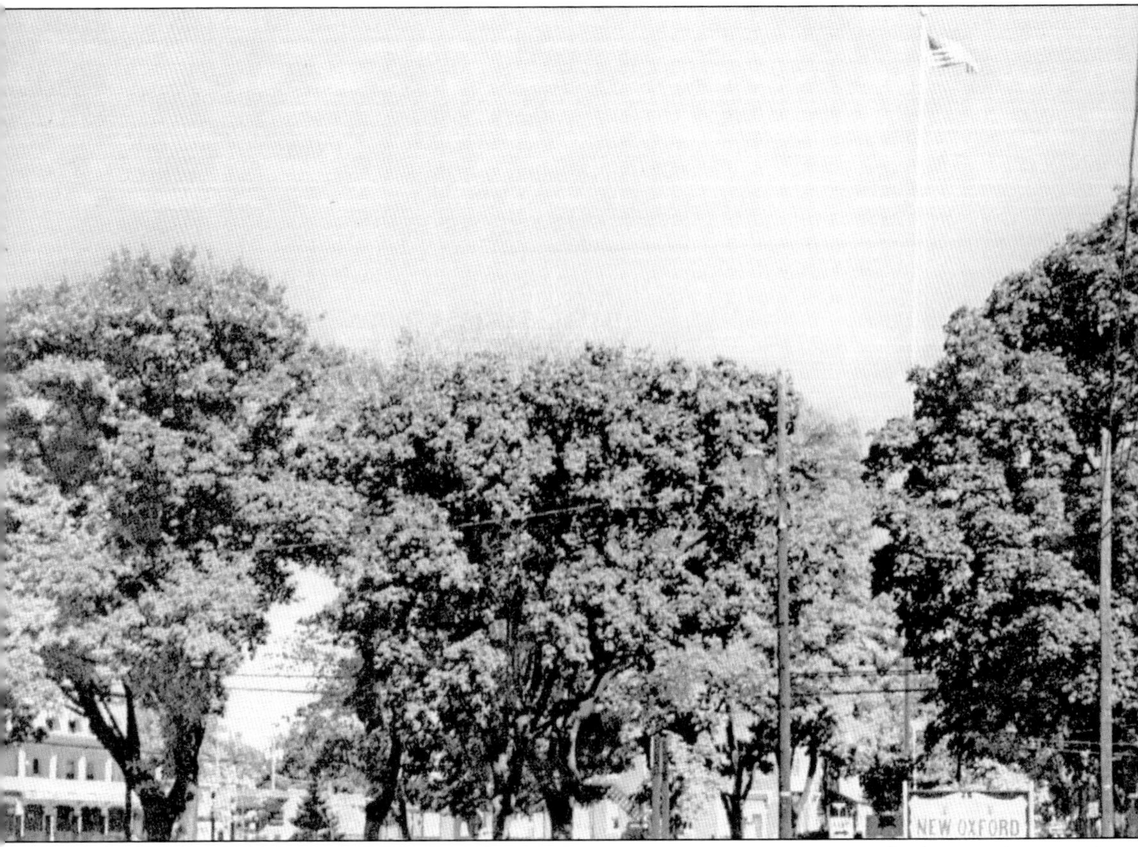

An American flag flies high above the town square in historic New Oxford, a south-central Pennsylvania community famous for its many antique shops. The Lincoln Highway passes directly through this Adams County town of just under 2,000 residents, and the square is actually a traffic circle. In fact, New Oxford is often called "the Little Town with the Beautiful Circle." The community, located east of Gettysburg, is surrounded by picturesque farmland.

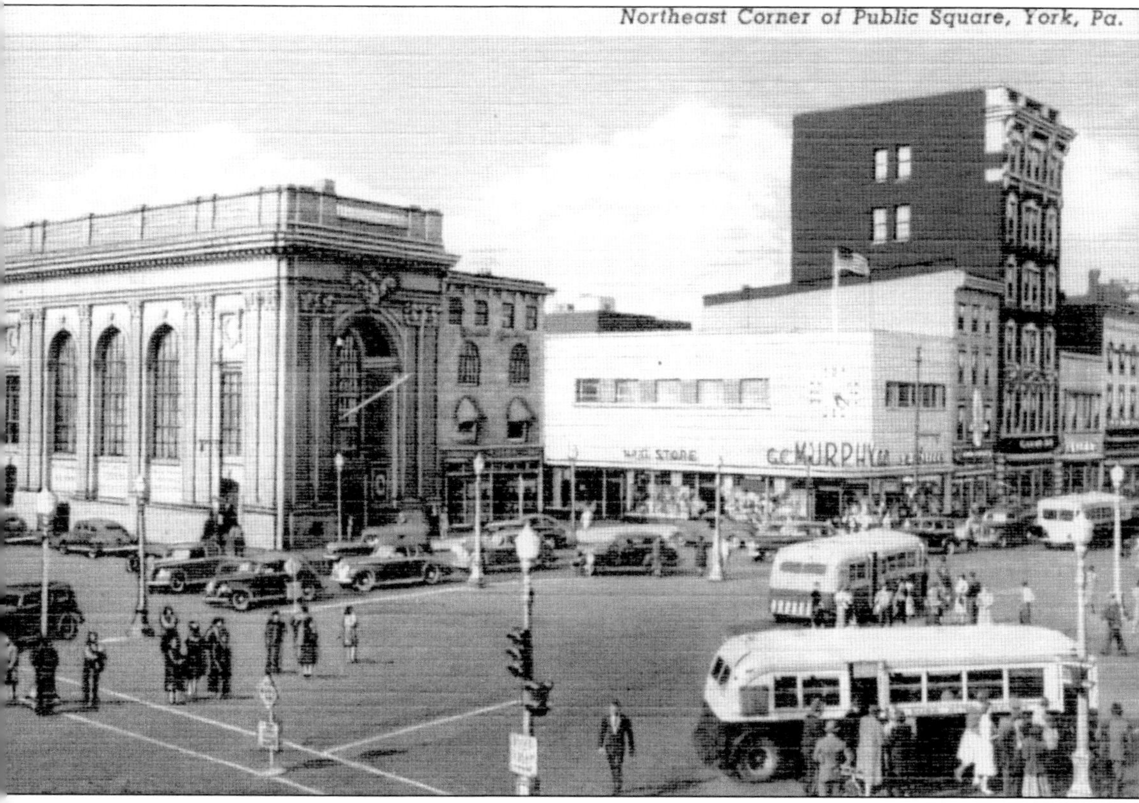

In the late 1930s and early 1940s, York's Public Square teemed with pedestrian traffic visiting any number of businesses nearby. Like many other towns and cities along the highway, York was bypassed in later years by U.S. Route 30. Today the Lincoln Highway through the city is marked as Route 462.

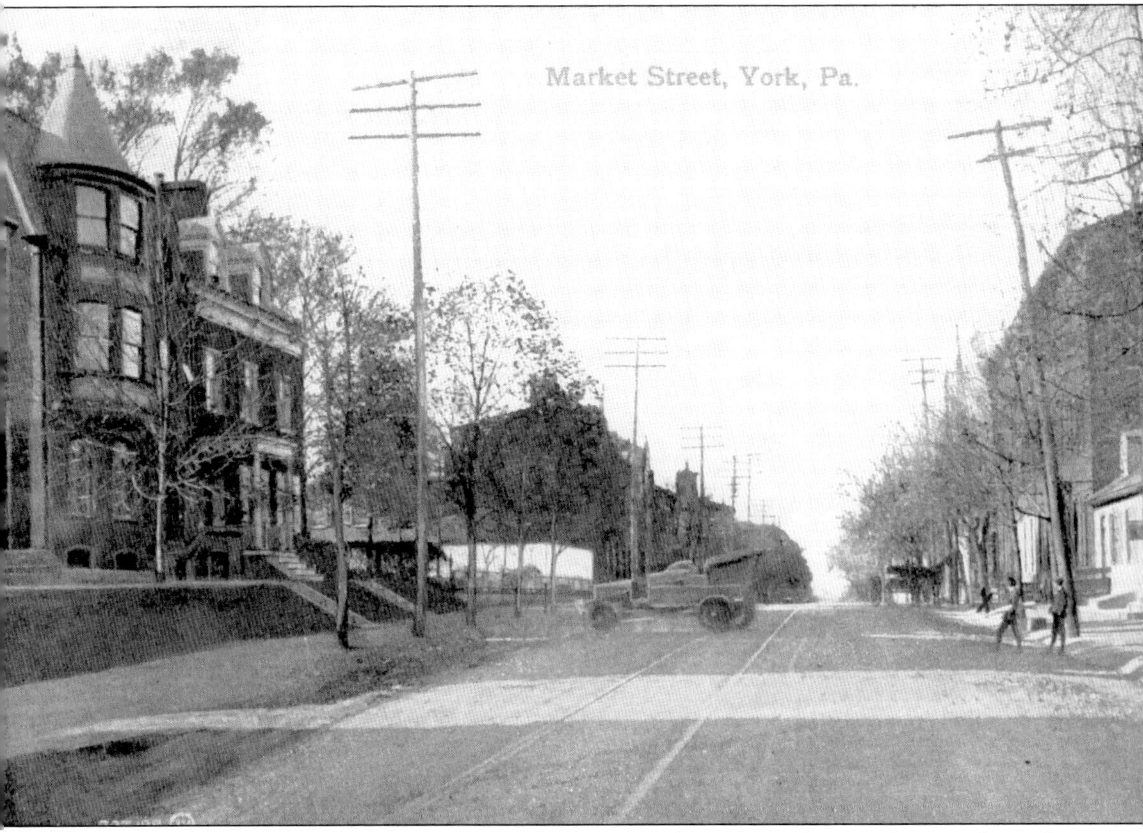

This view of York's West Market Street was likely published around the time the Lincoln Highway was routed through the city. After the highway was established, many larger towns and cities became oases along the road, as rural areas offered little to travelers in the early days. That era, however, was short-lived and many roadside businesses cropped up all along the cross-country highway.

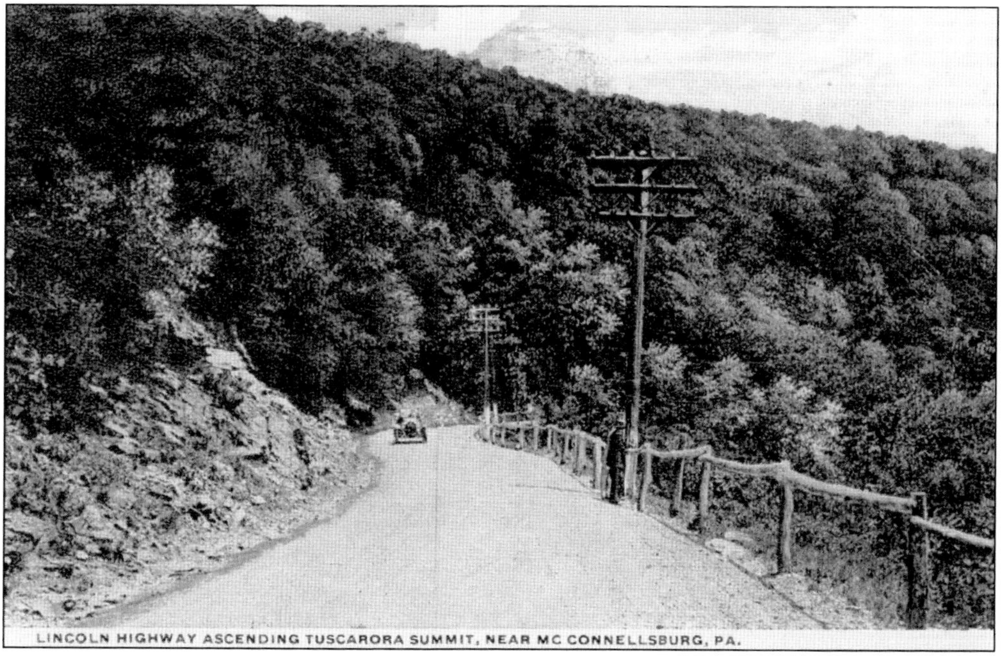

For today's vehicles, climbing to Tuscarora Summit is not considered hard, but in the early days, cars were prone to overheating and often had to crawl to the summit. Because of this, many roadside businesses located atop mountains offered free water in the hope that travelers would also buy food, fuel, or oil.

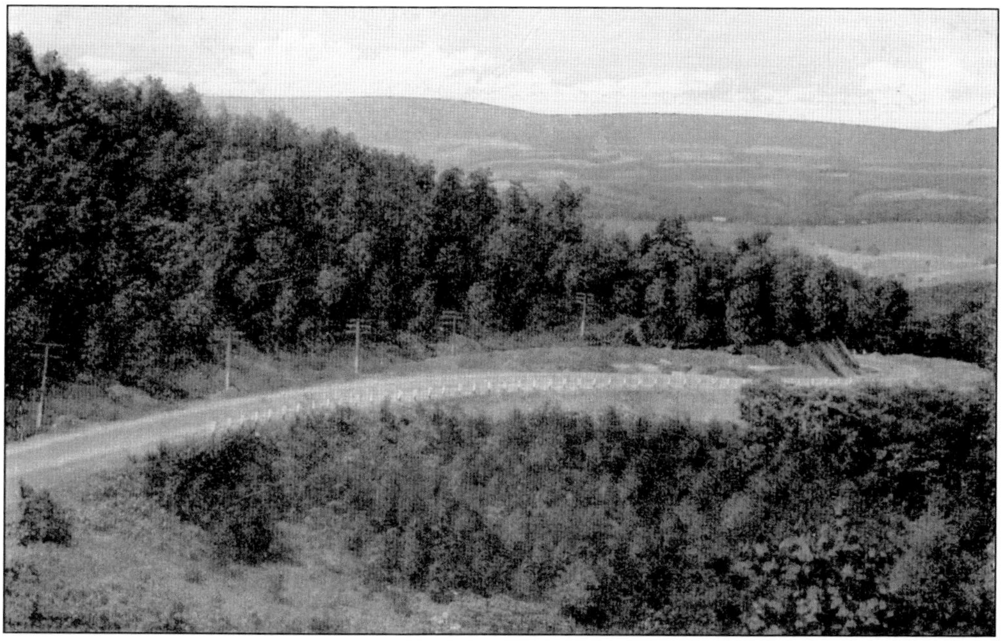

While the highway's route through the eastern part of the state is relatively flat, the opposite is true for the western section, portions of which are a series of ascents and descents. This early view shows the highway as it rises to Scrub Ridge Summit, between McConnellsburg and Bedford.

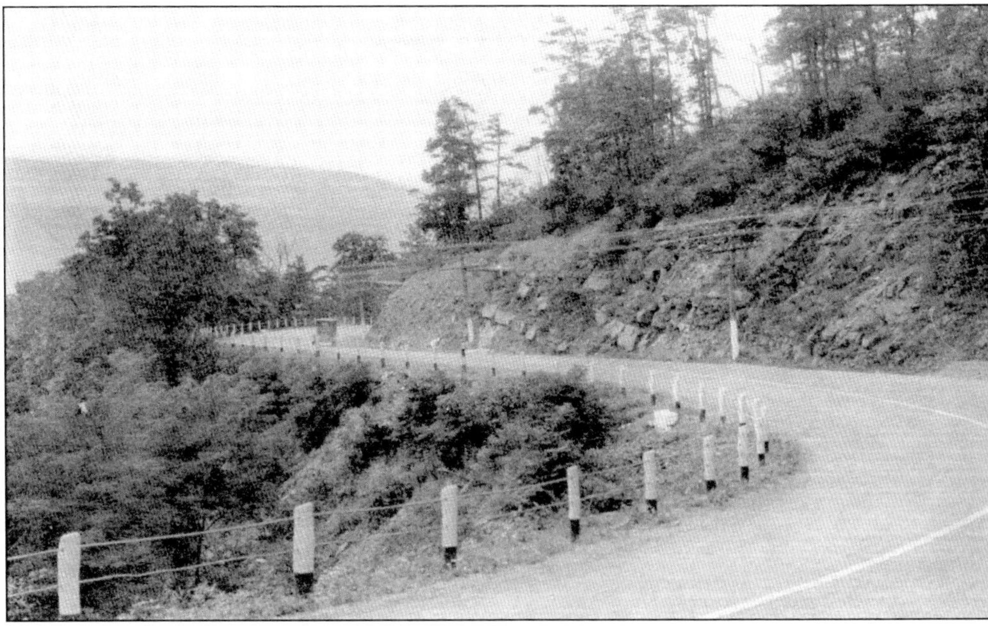

A single car climbs the western side of Tuscarora Mountain in this undated postcard view.

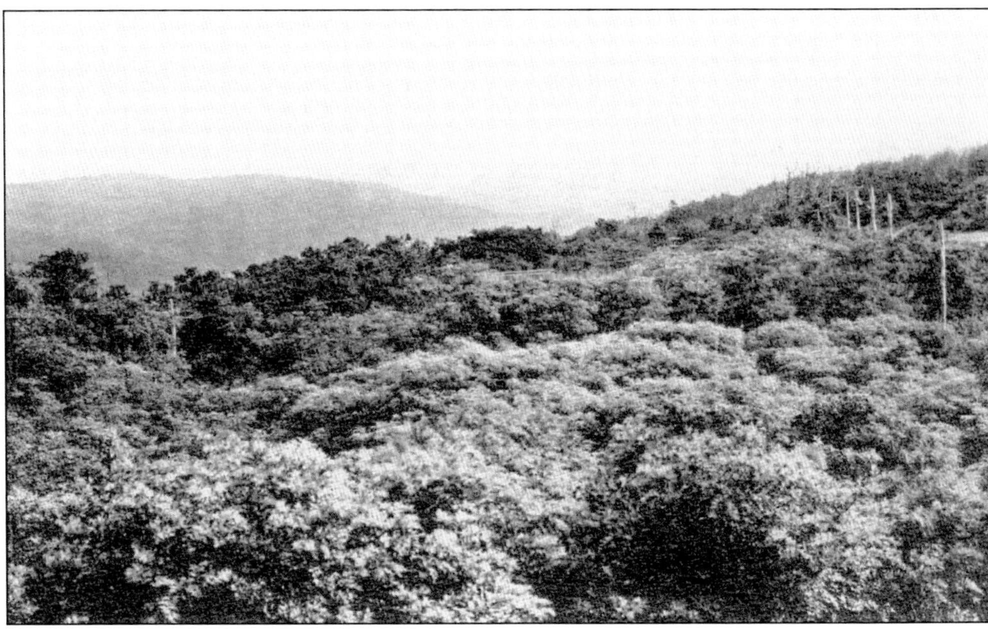

Vistas along the Lincoln Highway's route through Pennsylvania could be very urban or very rural in nature. The view from Tuscarora Summit was a popular subject for postcards due to its beautiful mountain scenery.

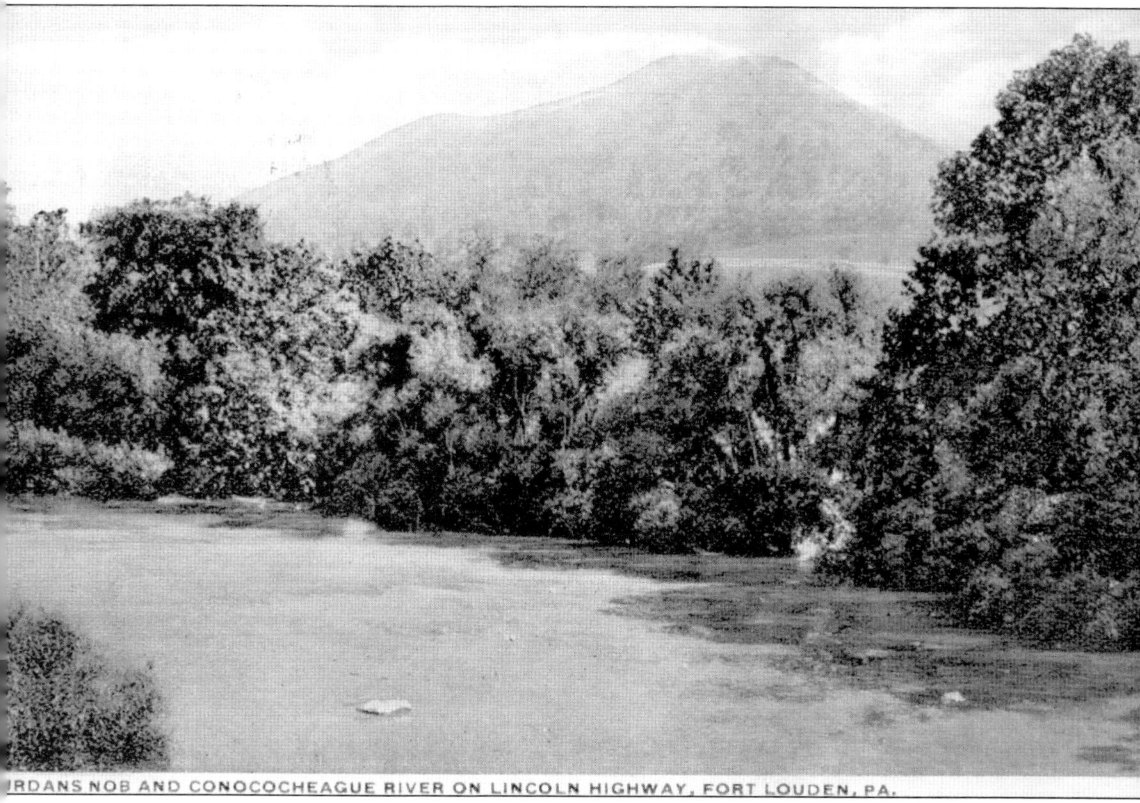

Jourdan's Nob and the Conococheague River were natural landmarks along the route in the vicinity of Fort Louden, along the old Chambersburg-Bedford Turnpike.

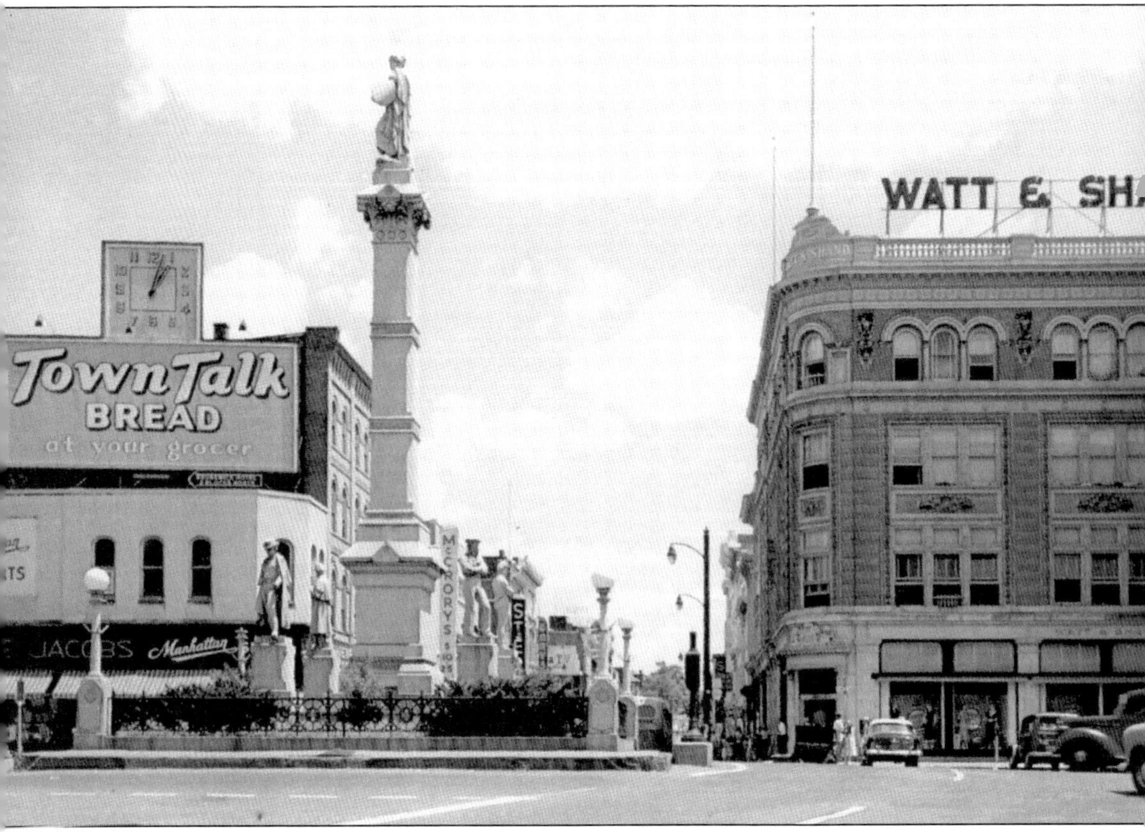

Lancaster's Center Square, also known as Penn Square, appears here during the early 1950s, when cars using the Lincoln Highway still had to pass through the city. As traffic became heavier, especially in areas of high tourist interest, bypasses were usually built to provide a faster, smoother trip.

Two

A Meal and a Place for the Night

Creature comforts were not always available to travelers in the earliest days of the Lincoln Highway, and it was not uncommon for various small roadside businesses to offer free camping, hoping that those who stopped would eat in their establishments as well. However, it was not long before entrepreneurs realized that they could build and offer small cabins for shelter, therefore making a higher profit from travelers while providing a necessary service. Although this became an added cost to travel, most motorists did not complain; they appreciated the opportunity to have dry, solid shelter.

These early facilities gave rise to roadside cabin courts, as they were commonly known. Early on, many of these cabins were unheated and without running water. Bathroom facilities were generally outhouses, shared by all who called the court home for the night. As a whole, the cabin court era did not last long. Owners soon understood that they could join the cabins under a single roof, a concept that gave birth to the now familiar motel, tourist court, or motor court.

When the Lincoln Highway was established, it consisted only of the route, without roadside amenities. Early travelers who did not wish to camp could spend the night in cities that had hotels catering to railroad travelers.

Dining was another necessity. While many travelers brought food from home, it was not always practical, especially on longer trips. Outside of establishments in towns or cities, the highway's first roadside eateries were often crude shacks, built at convenient places along the route. With travel increasing almost every day, most were quickly replaced by more substantial structures. As the years progressed, stainless-steel diners were located along the highway, though very few remain today.

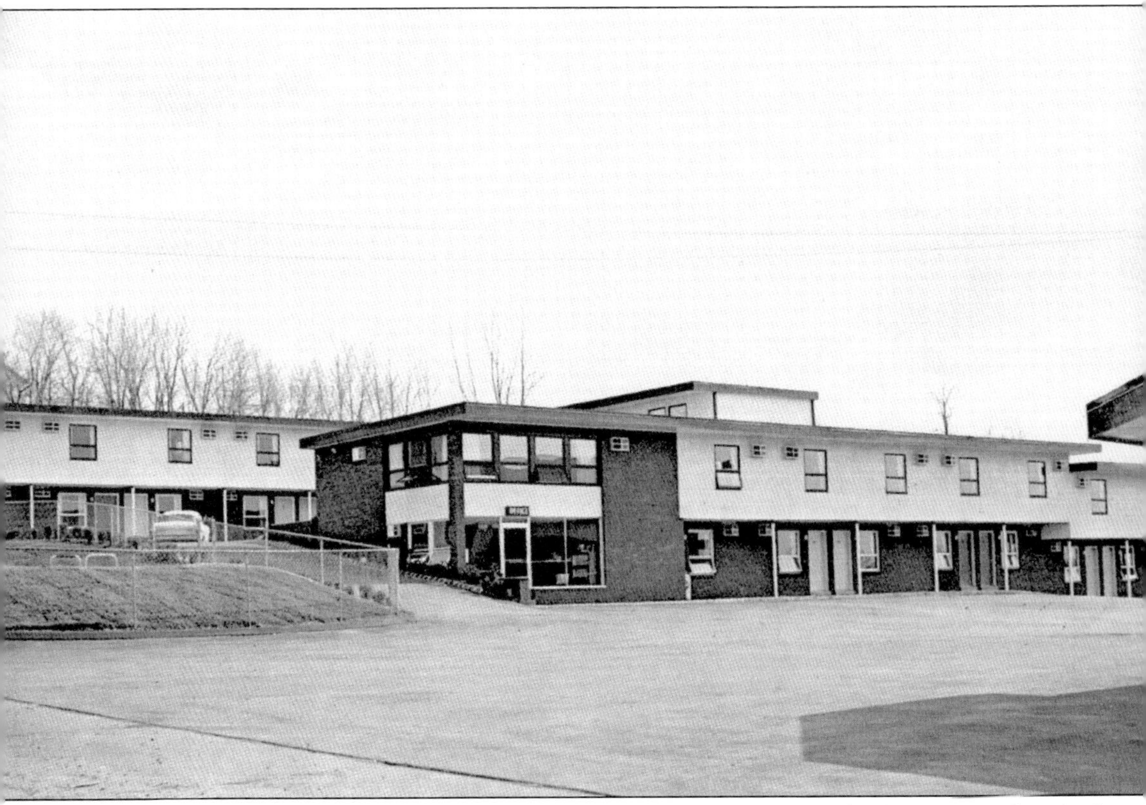

The Adrilee Motor Hotel and Supper Club, near Irwin in Westmoreland County, advertised 45 units, which included "luxurious" bridal suites, free television, telephone, and air-conditioning. The facility also offered a swimming pool, air-conditioned conference room, cocktail lounge, and dining room.

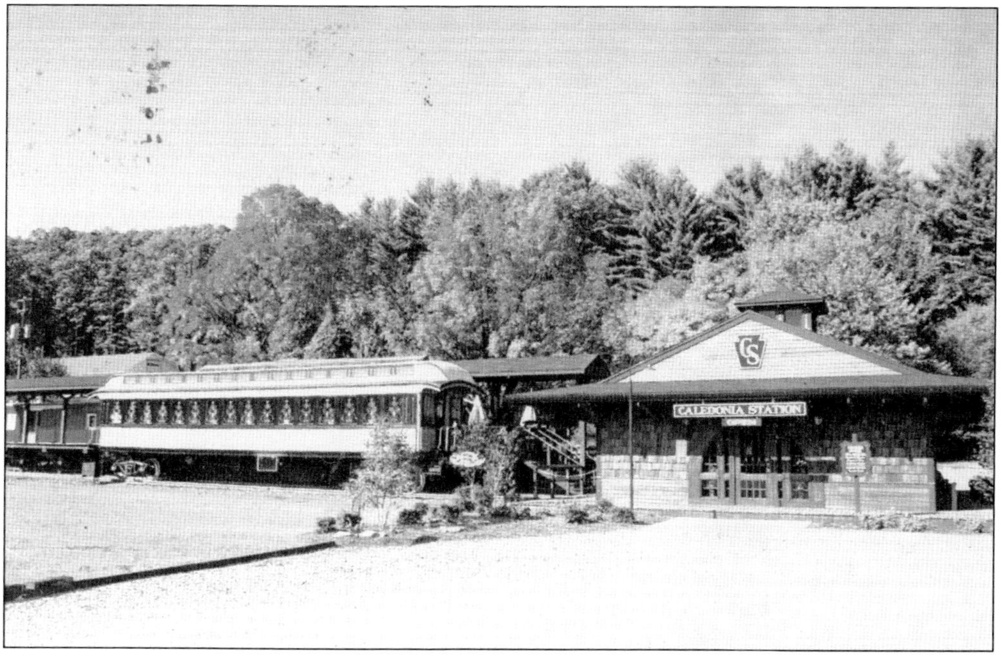

The Caledonia Station in Fayetteville was a roadside restaurant that offered a "unique dining experience," as meals were served in a refurbished railroad car dating to 1892. The business has since closed, and the old railroad car has reportedly been moved to nearby Chambersburg.

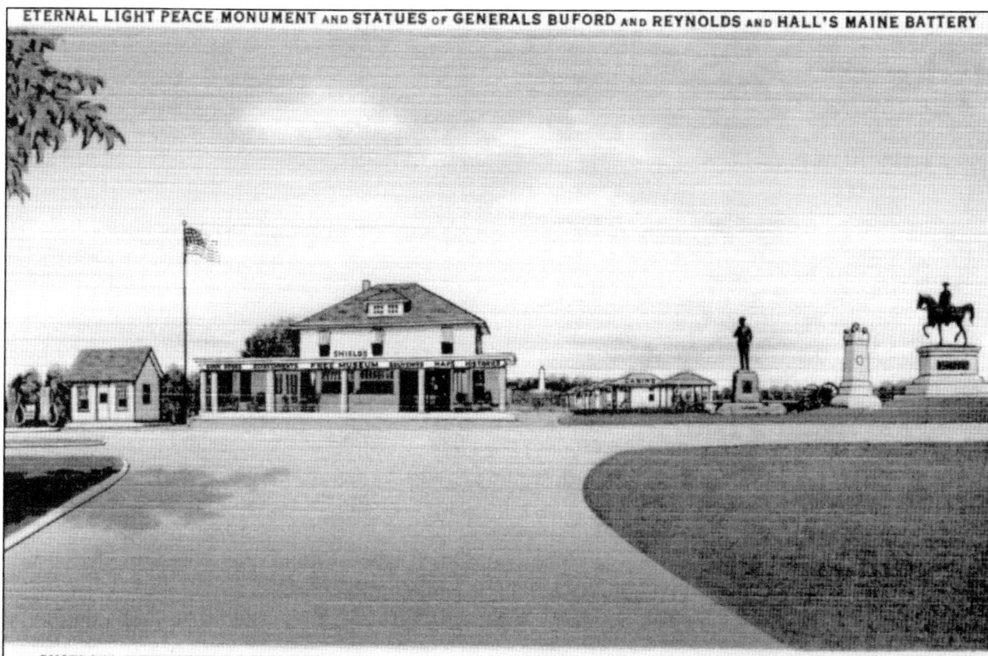

The scene of a historic three-day Civil War battle, Gettysburg was a tourist destination even before the Lincoln Highway existed. Shields' Gettysburg Camp Park, situated near several monuments commemorating those who fought, offered cabins, gas, oil, refreshments, souvenirs, and even antique guns. The establishment was closed in the 1980s and subsequently razed.

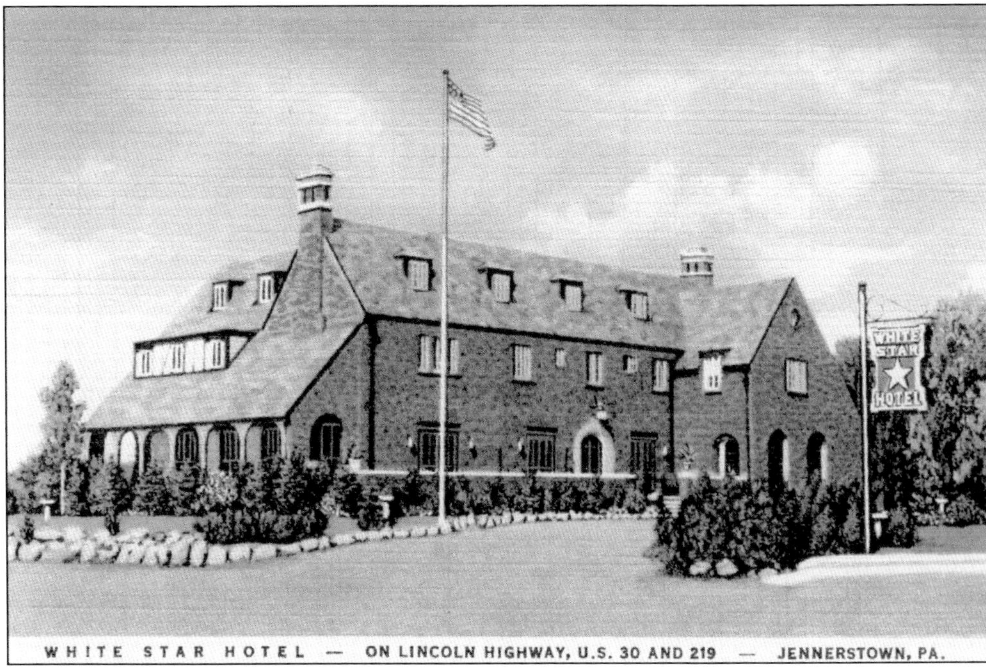

The White Star Hotel, at the intersection of Routes 30 and 219 near Jennerstown, was advertised as being "strictly modern." When this card was published, a room with running water was priced at $1.25 and up, while accommodations having private bathrooms cost $2 and up.

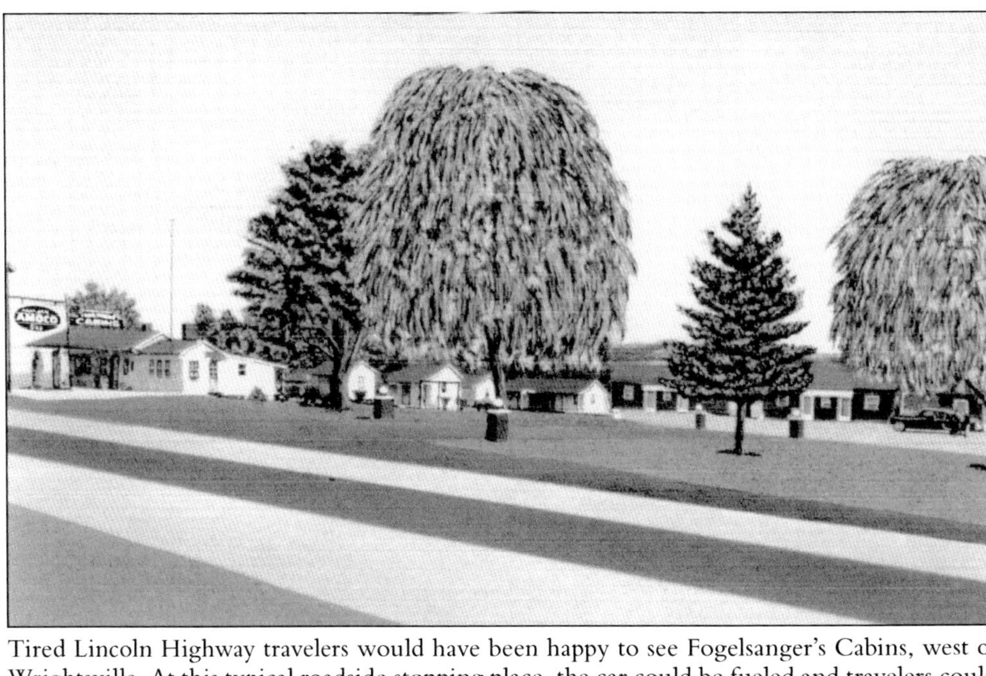

Tired Lincoln Highway travelers would have been happy to see Fogelsanger's Cabins, west of Wrightsville. At this typical roadside stopping place, the car could be fueled and travelers could enjoy a hot meal before retiring to a cabin, which had hot water and tile baths. Cabin courts such as Fogelsanger's were the predecessors to motels.

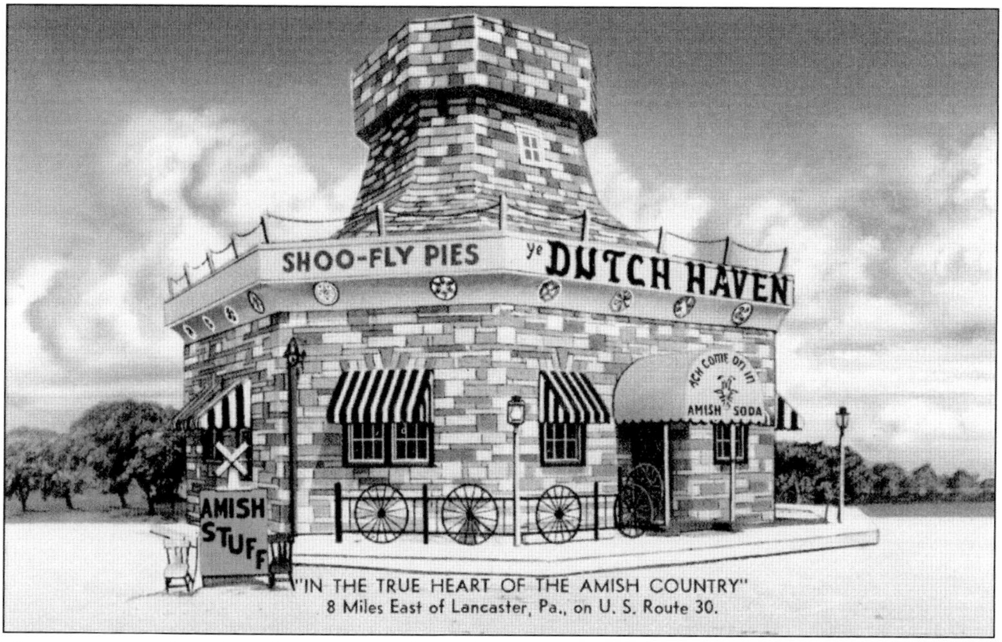

The area around Ye Dutch Haven, eight miles east of Lancaster, has changed greatly over the years and is today populated with other buildings. Published in the early days of the restaurant's history, this card advertises local food favorites like shoo-fly pie, Dutch made barbecue, and homemade soups. Along with the line of food products, the business offered toys and Pennsylvania Dutch gifts.

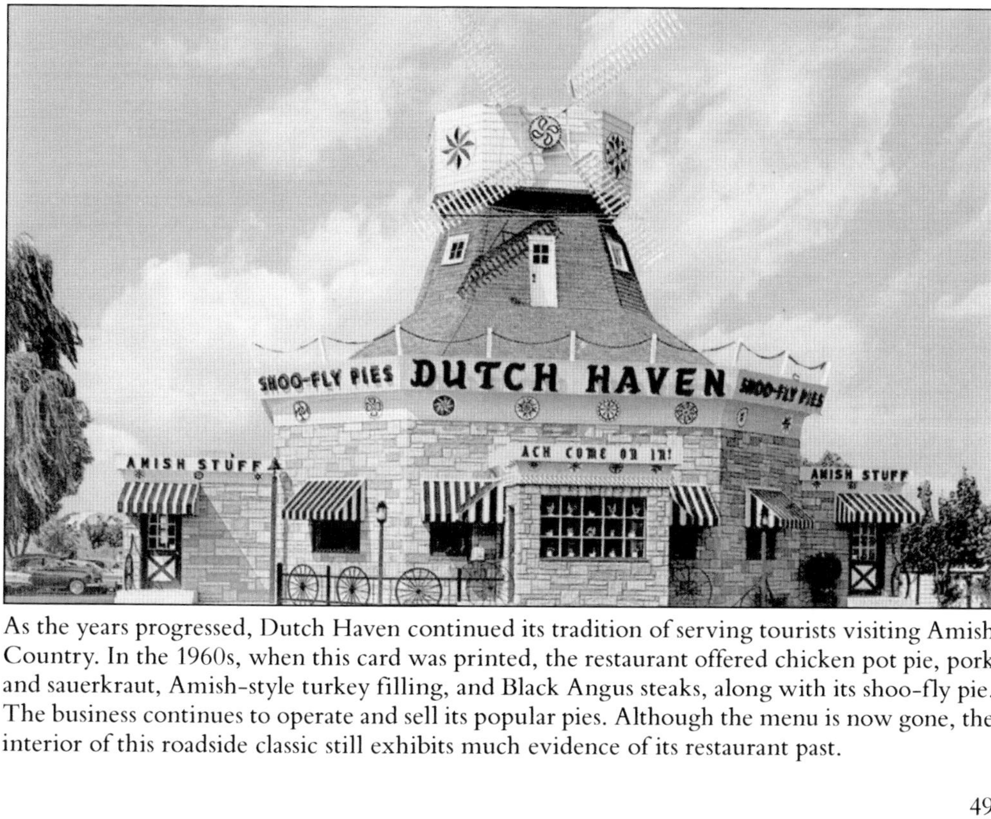

As the years progressed, Dutch Haven continued its tradition of serving tourists visiting Amish Country. In the 1960s, when this card was printed, the restaurant offered chicken pot pie, pork and sauerkraut, Amish-style turkey filling, and Black Angus steaks, along with its shoo-fly pie. The business continues to operate and sell its popular pies. Although the menu is now gone, the interior of this roadside classic still exhibits much evidence of its restaurant past.

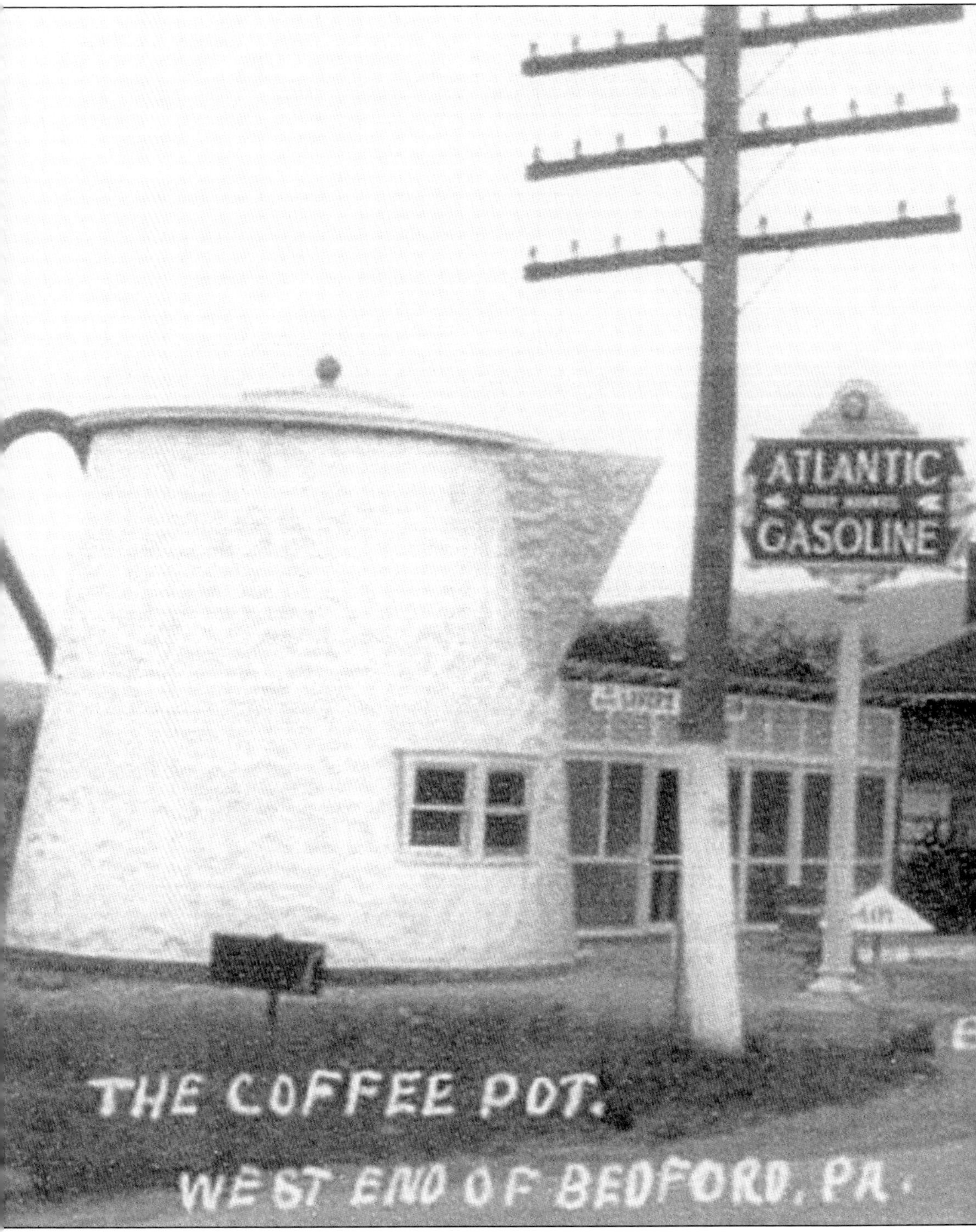

A Lincoln Highway landmark since 1927, Bedford's Coffee Pot was built by Bert Koontz to be a catchy roadside lunch stand at the west side of town. Over the years, the building has housed a Greyhound bus station, a bar, and even a beer distributor. Closed in the mid-1980s, the building fell into disrepair, but was saved through the efforts of the Lincoln Highway Heritage Corridor.

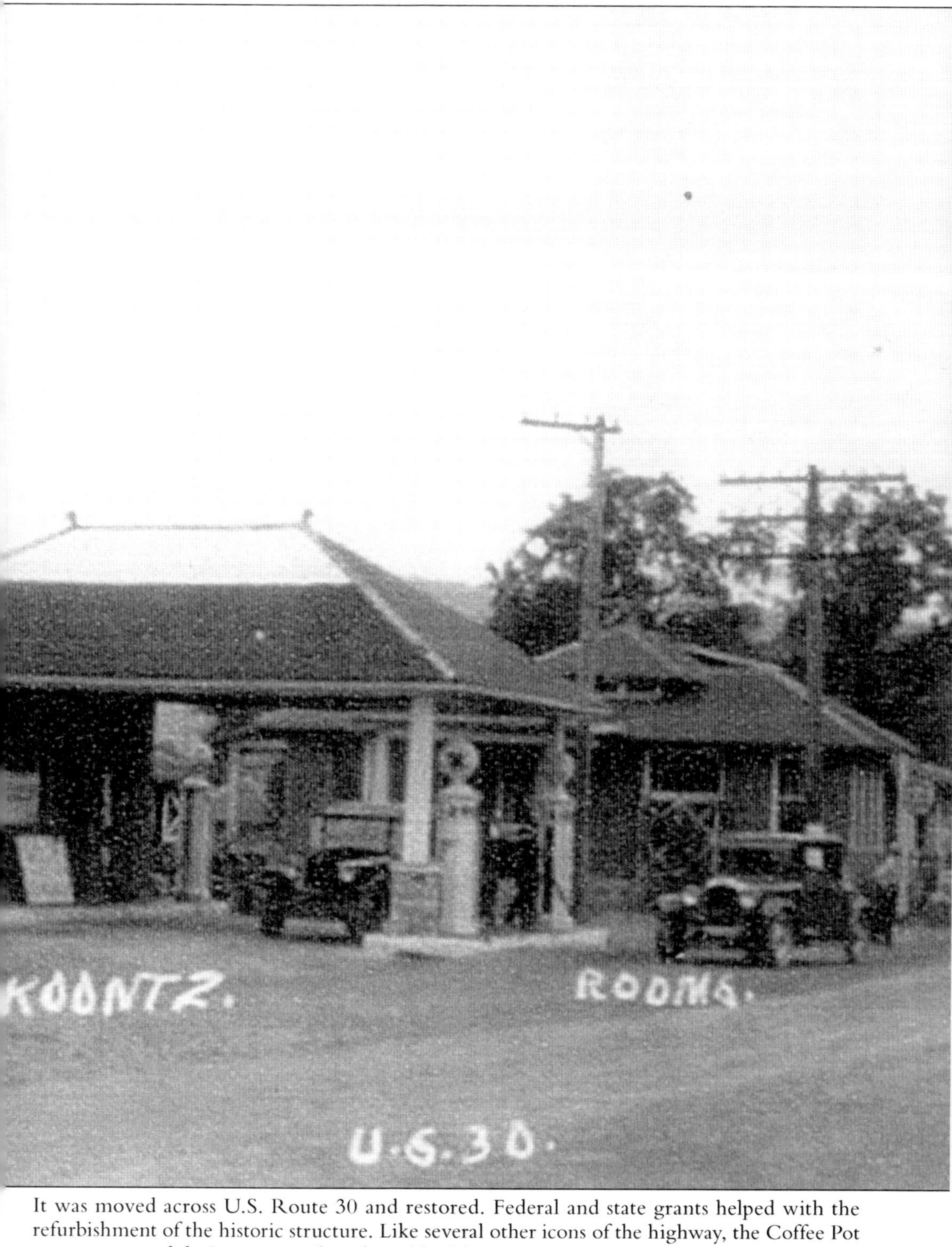

It was moved across U.S. Route 30 and restored. Federal and state grants helped with the refurbishment of the historic structure. Like several other icons of the highway, the Coffee Pot was constructed during an era when shaped buildings were a common form of advertising.

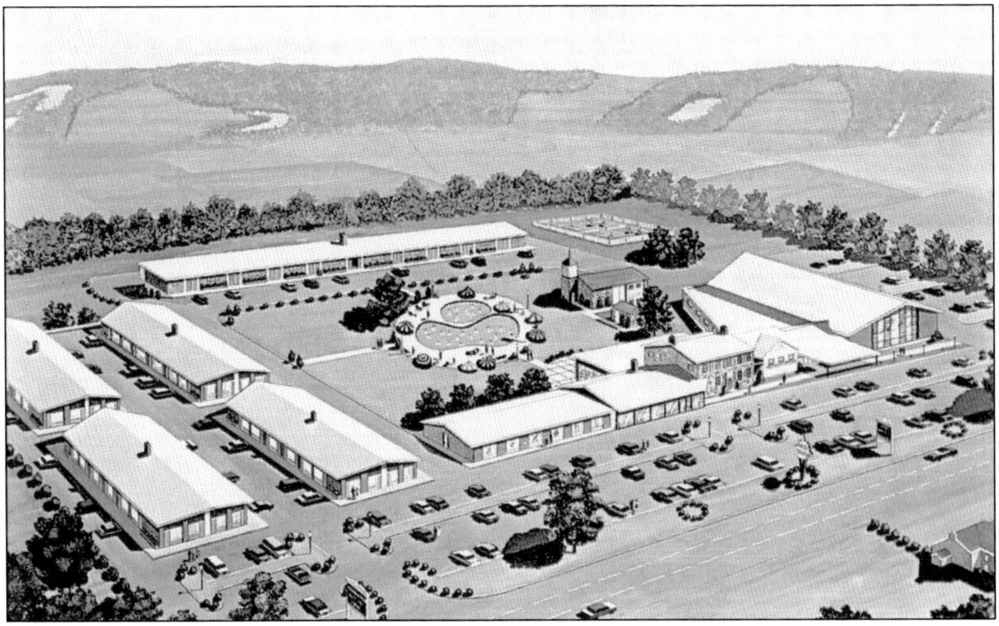

When this card was published in the early 1960s, the Downingtown Inn offered 150 air-conditioned, carpeted rooms with televisions, telephones, and Posturpedic beds. The facility, approved by the American Automobile Association, also provided an exhibition auditorium and grand ballroom. A message on the reverse reads, "God bless the Turnpike," a statement many Lincoln Highway business owners of the day would have opposed.

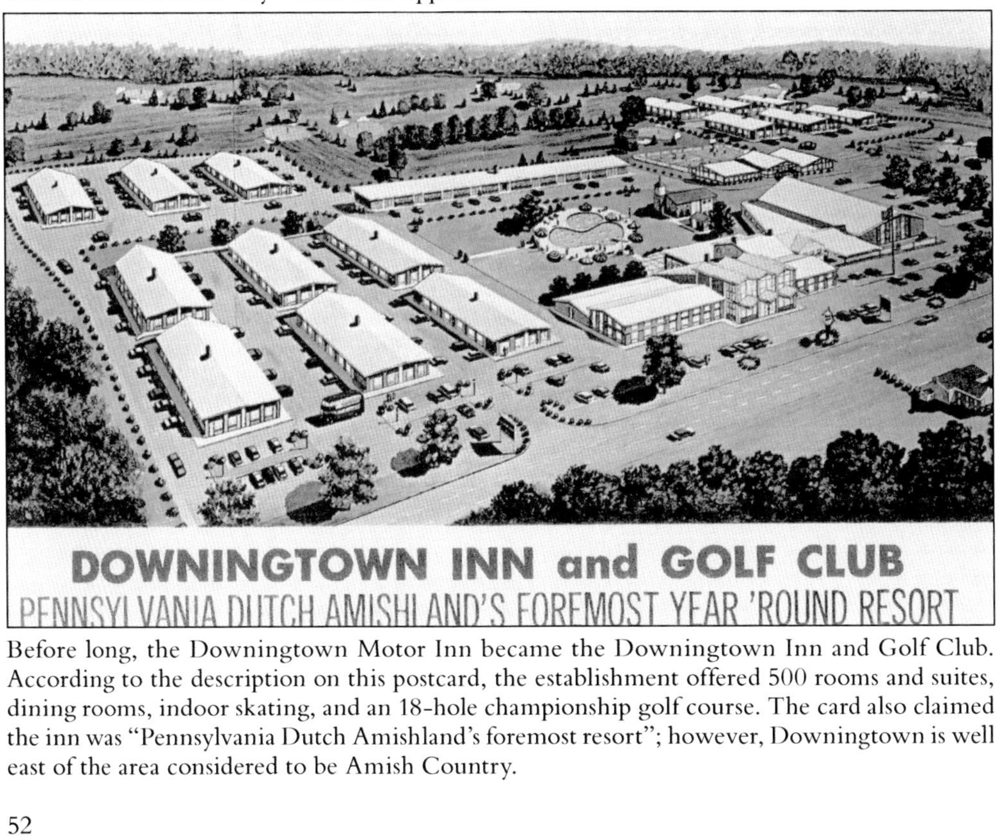

Before long, the Downingtown Motor Inn became the Downingtown Inn and Golf Club. According to the description on this postcard, the establishment offered 500 rooms and suites, dining rooms, indoor skating, and an 18-hole championship golf course. The card also claimed the inn was "Pennsylvania Dutch Amishland's foremost resort"; however, Downingtown is well east of the area considered to be Amish Country.

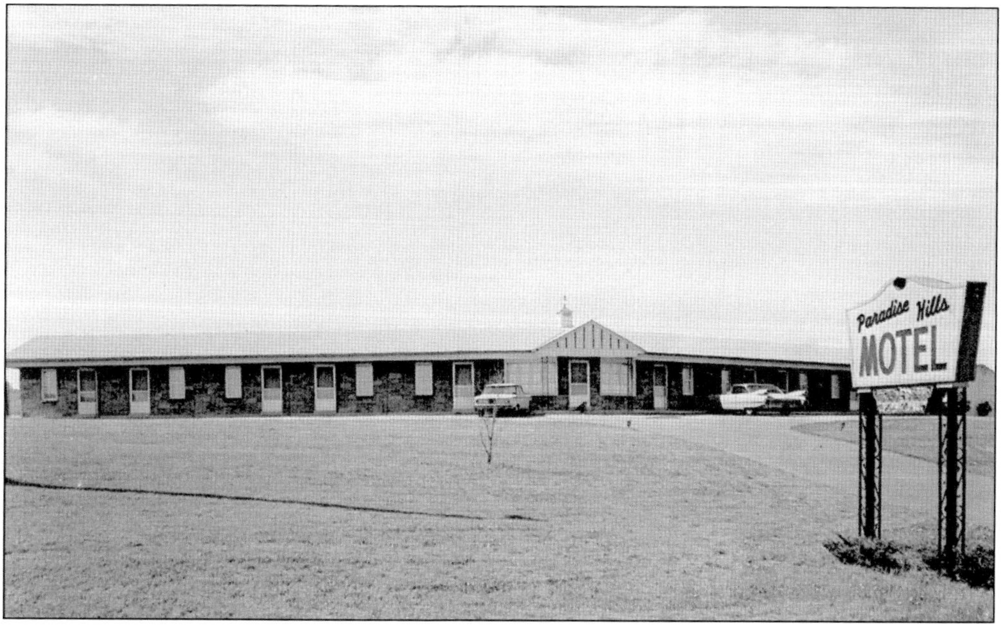

The Paradise Hills Motel, 14 miles east of Lancaster in the village of Kinzer, was advertised as being in the heart of the Pennsylvania Dutch tourist attractions. The advertisement on the reverse of this card states that a restaurant stood nearby the motel, which was owned by Chester Labeck.

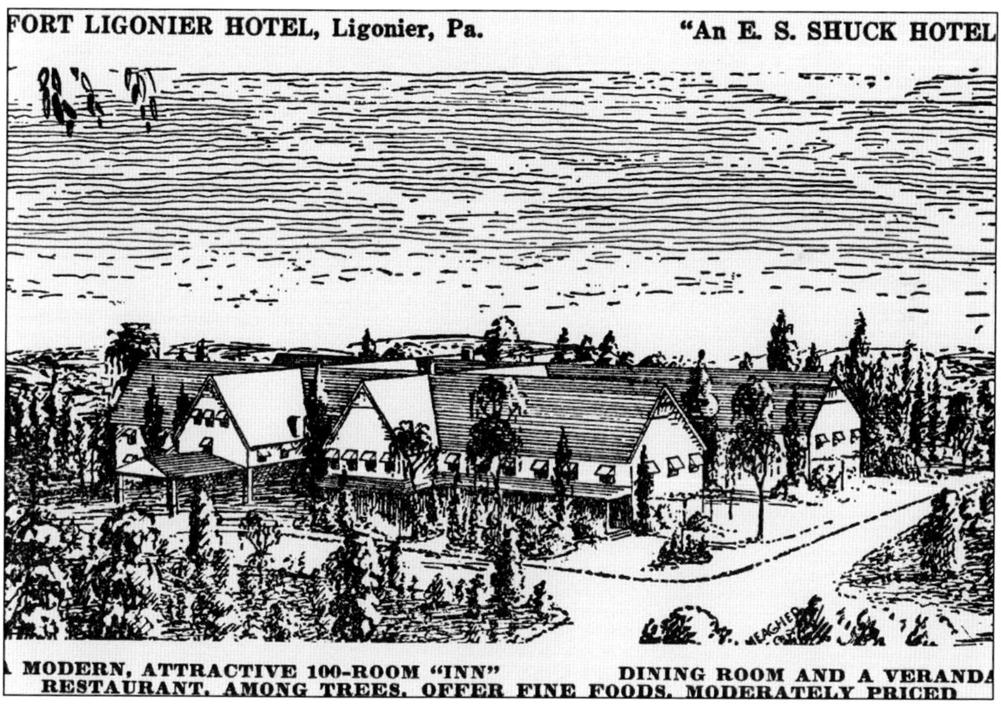

A popular spot along the highway was the Fort Ligonier Hotel. According to this *c.* 1937 promotional card, the hotel offered travelers 100 rooms and two "famous" restaurants. The establishment also featured modern bathrooms, a dining room, and veranda restaurant that served moderately priced meals.

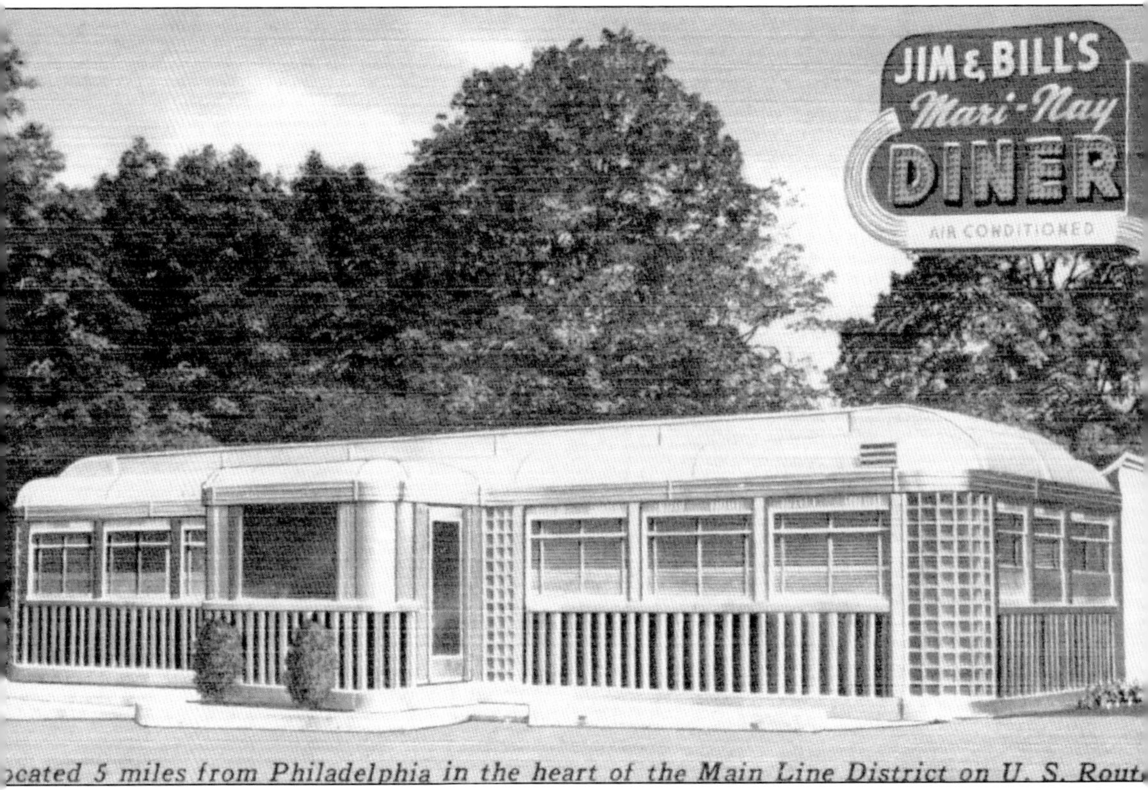

Jim and Bill's Mari-Nay Diner, at Lancaster and Norwood Avenues in Rosemont, was owned and operated by Jim Forsythe and Bill Shannon, who named their establishment for the military branches in which they served. Three different diners bearing the same name were located here over the years. But landmarks do not last forever, and the famous diner was razed in the 1990s to be replaced by a McDonald's. In this 1940s view, the diner was advertised as being near the King of Prussia interchange of the "Pennsylvania Super Highway," also known as the Pennsylvania Turnpike. The turnpike became so popular with travelers that many businesses along the Lincoln Highway closed, while those found near the new route's interchanges prospered.

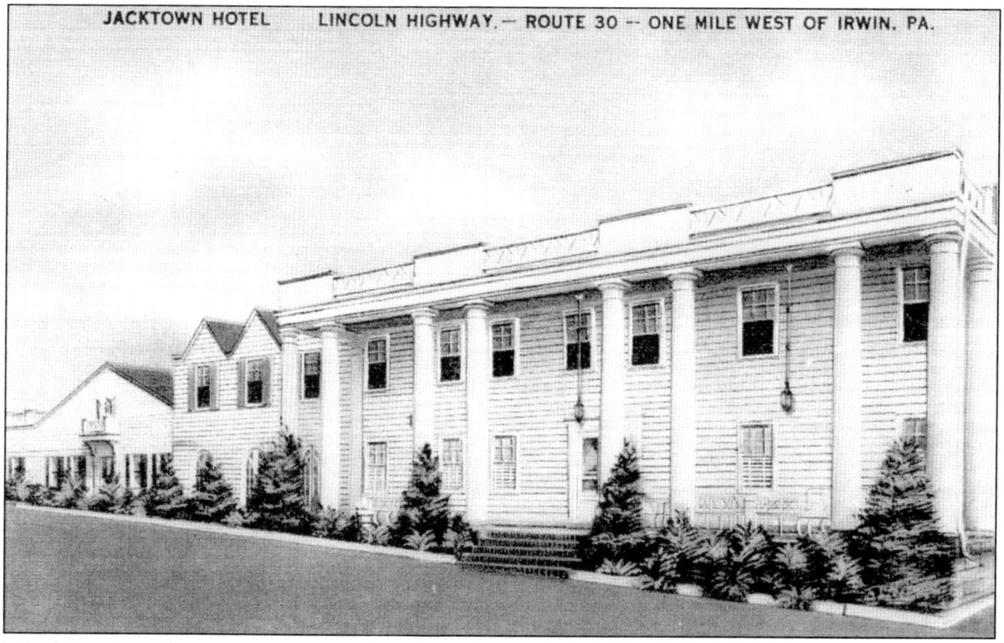

The historic Jacktown Hotel was located one mile west of Irwin in Westmoreland County. For part of its life, the Pennsylvania Turnpike ended here, and traffic on U.S. Route 30 (the Lincoln Highway) was quite high, giving rise to many roadside businesses in the area.

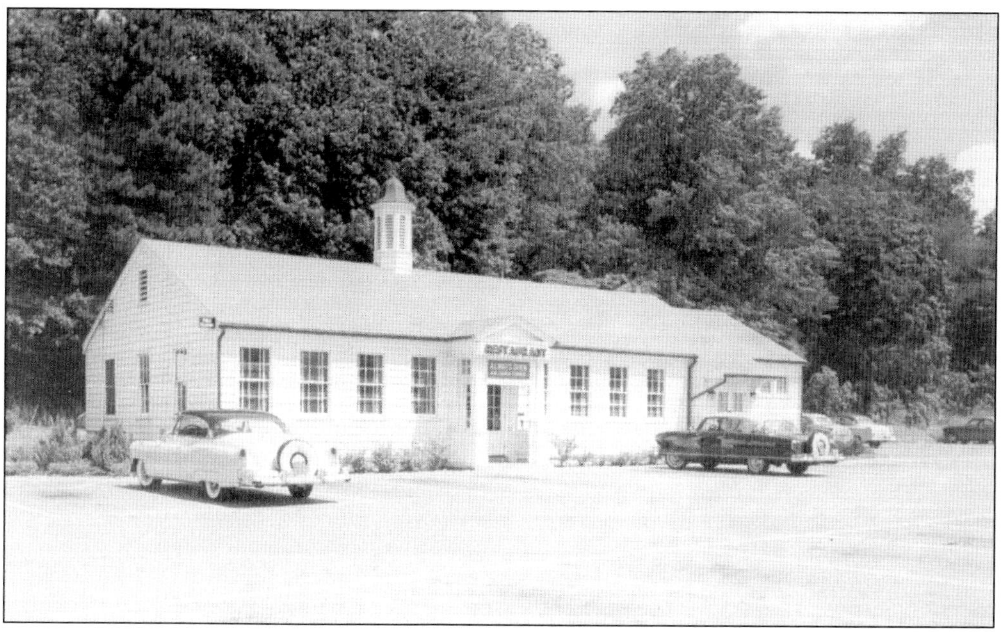

Although small, Hap Miller's Restaurant, located on the Lincoln Highway east of York, was a popular eating establishment in its day. The business was promoted as being "scientifically air conditioned" and offering customers everything they "expect in a good restaurant." Miller's eatery was also known as the Truck Town Restaurant.

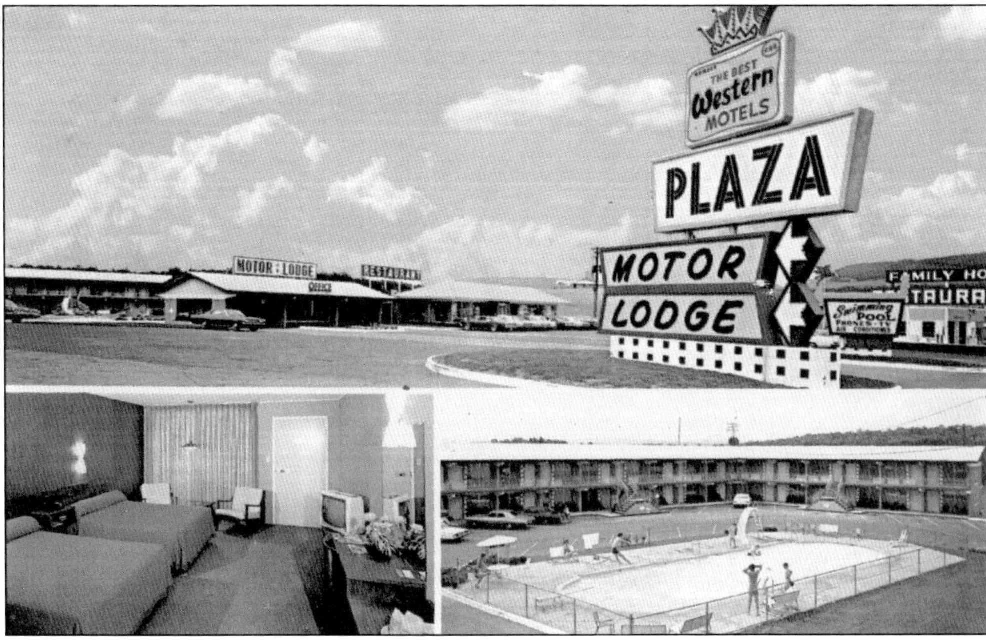

Breezewood's Plaza Motor Lodge was advertised as being 500 yards west of the Pennsylvania Turnpike interchange along U.S. Route 30. This early 1960s view was published before the Family House Restaurant was built next door. Prior to the turnpike constructing an interchange there in 1940, Breezewood was little more than a small country town. The interchange soon turned the quiet village into "the Town of Motels." Further growth was realized after the construction of Interstate 70, often referred to as "the Gateway to the South."

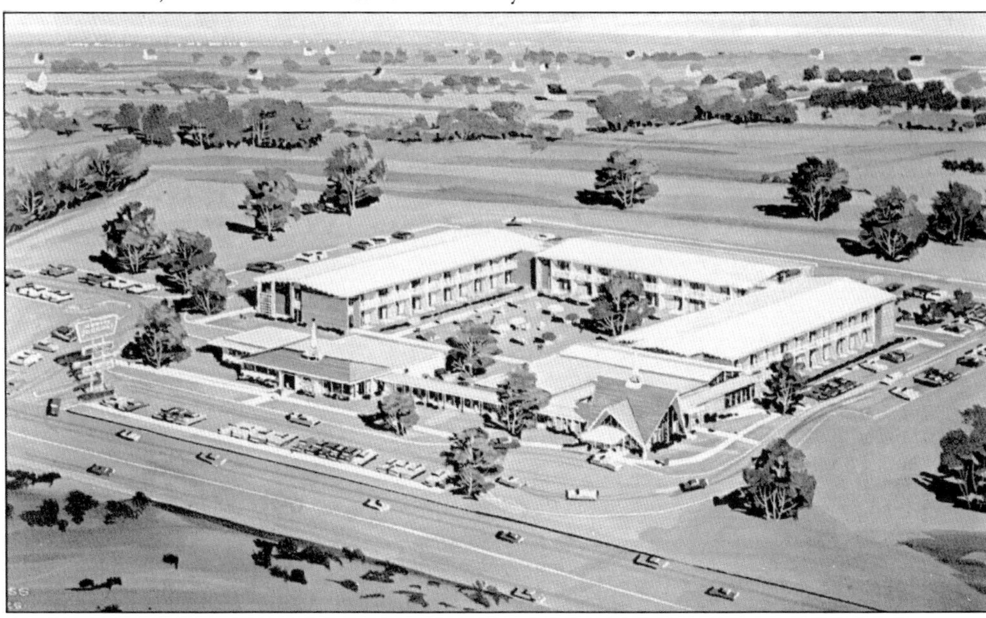

At 2100 Lincoln Highway East in Lancaster, the Howard Johnson's Motor Lodge continues to be a popular place with those visiting the area's numerous attractions. Today it offers a host of amenities, including a Quizno's Sub Shop and a Dominos Pizza outlet. In the mid-1960s, the motel promoted rooms for two at an in-season rate of $18 or $20 a night.

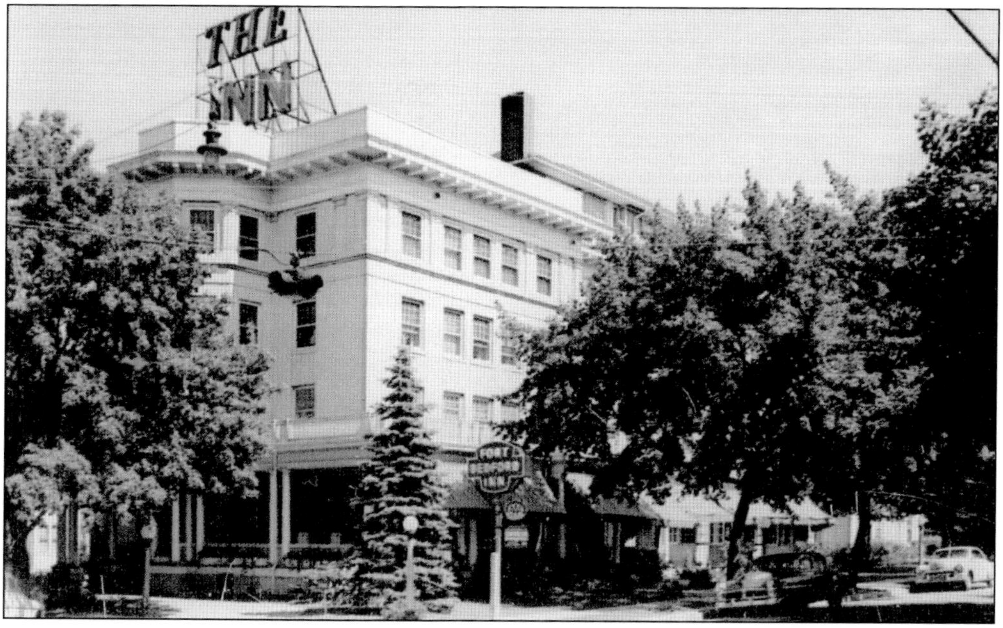

Once called "the Pride of the Lincoln Highway," the Fort Bedford Inn was actually one block off the route, which followed Pitt Street through town. As late as the 1960s, the inn advertised 100 rooms and a restaurant approved by Duncan Hines. The building is now used as senior citizen housing.

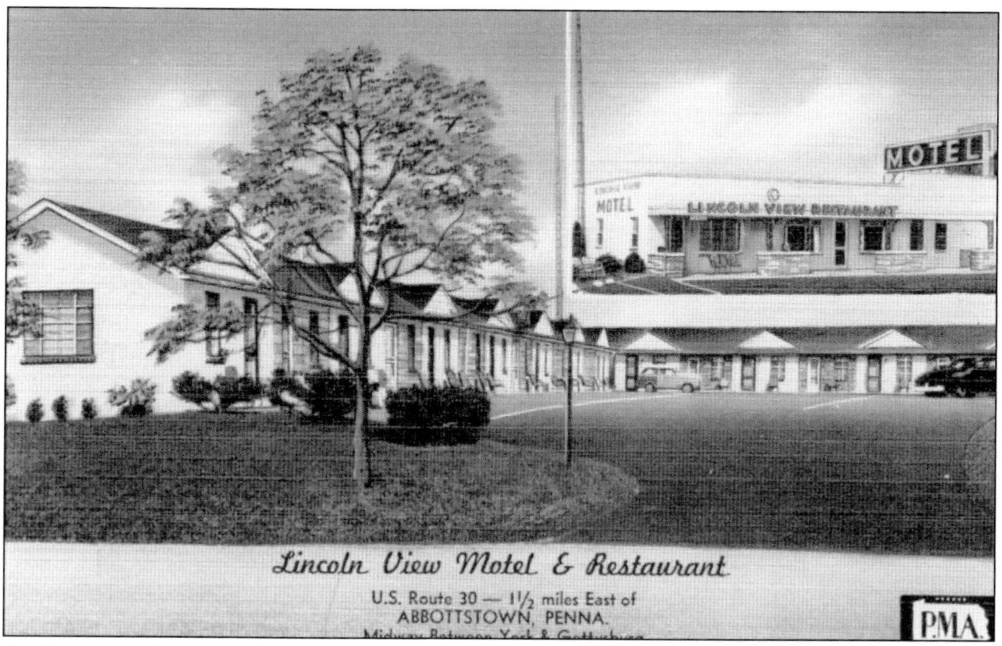

At the approximate midpoint between York and Gettysburg, and near Abbottstown, Lincoln Highway travelers could enjoy almost one-stop service at the Lincoln View Motel and Restaurant. Owned and operated by Mr. and Mrs. Kenneth Stauffer, the roadside establishment offered 23 modern rooms, central hot-water heat, air-conditioning, and free radio and television. In addition, the Lincoln View contained a gift shop and sporting goods store.

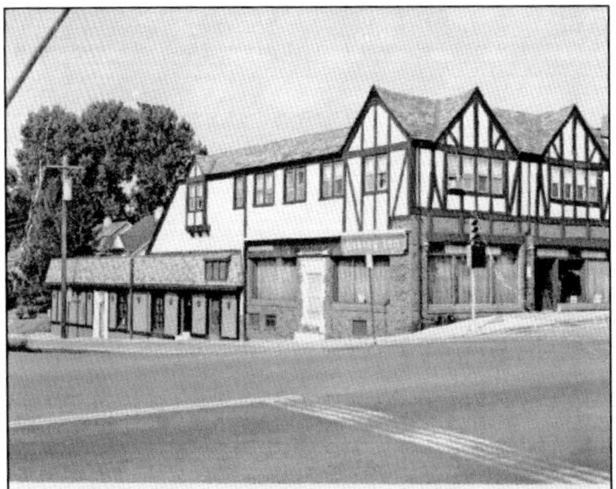

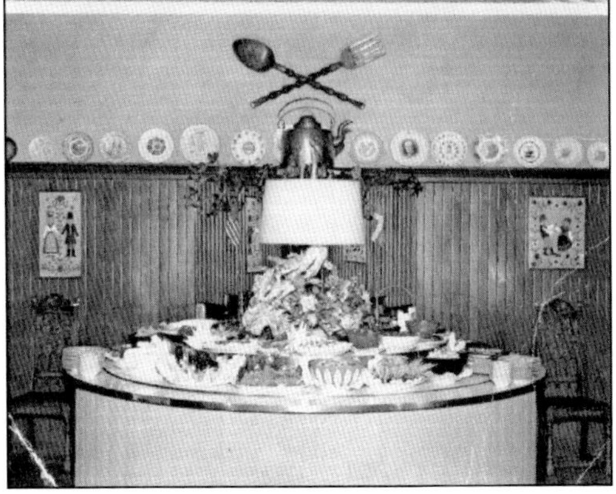

Established in 1931, Ardmore's Viking Inn was noted for its revolving smorgasbord and its status as the only Scandinavian restaurant in the Philadelphia vicinity. The inn featured a dining room for American à la carte dinners and hosted banquets, wedding parties, and other events.

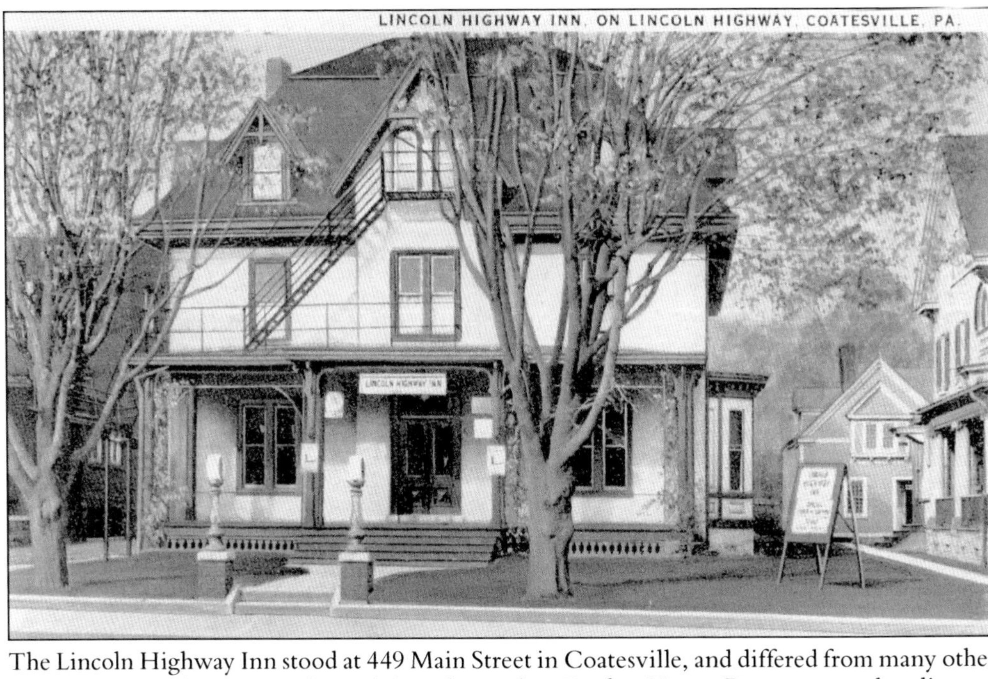

The Lincoln Highway Inn stood at 449 Main Street in Coatesville, and differed from many other establishments of its type in that it did not have a bar. Banker Henry Branson served as director of the inn, which was later razed. Today the site is home to the Coatesville Towers Apartments, a senior citizens' apartment building.

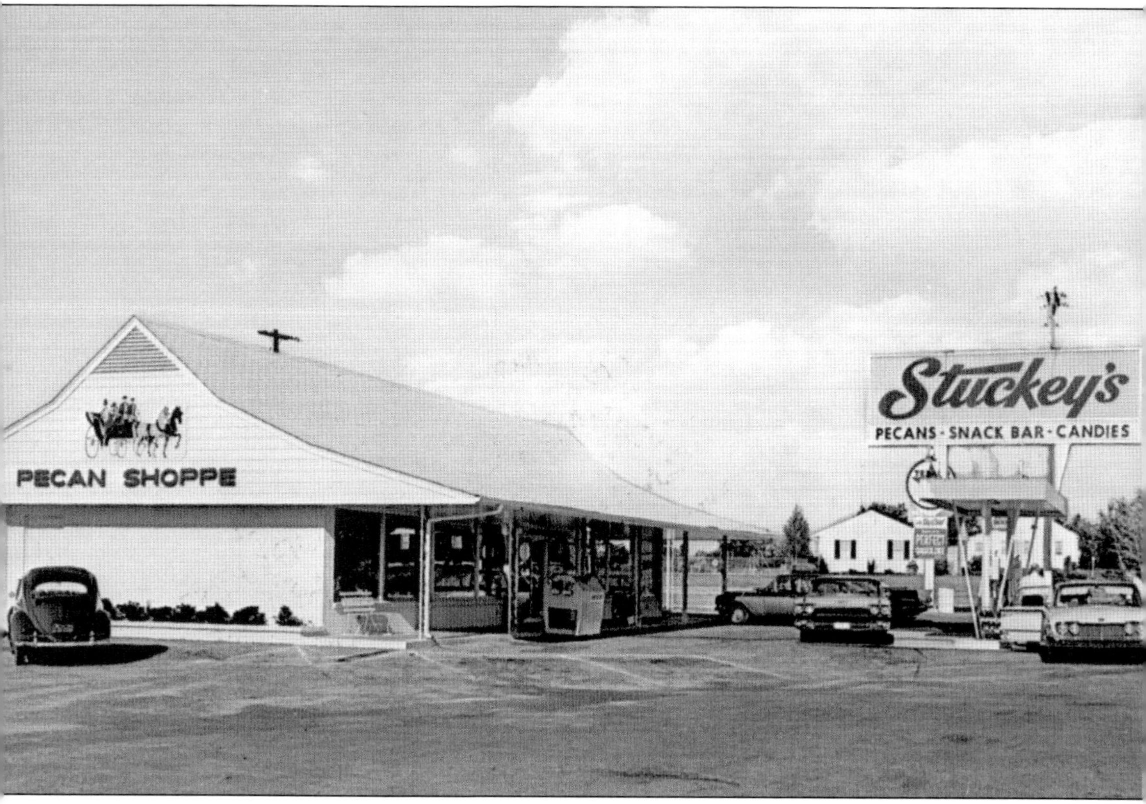

Stuckey's Pecan Shops were noted for setting up business along highly traveled routes, especially in areas that attracted the tourist trade. This outlet was in Ronks, seven miles east of Lancaster. Originating in 1937 near Eastman, Georgia, the chain sold candies, jellies, gifts, and souvenirs and was well known for its food offerings. The particular store in this 1960s view is closed, although Stuckey's products can still be found along the Lincoln Highway in Breezewood.

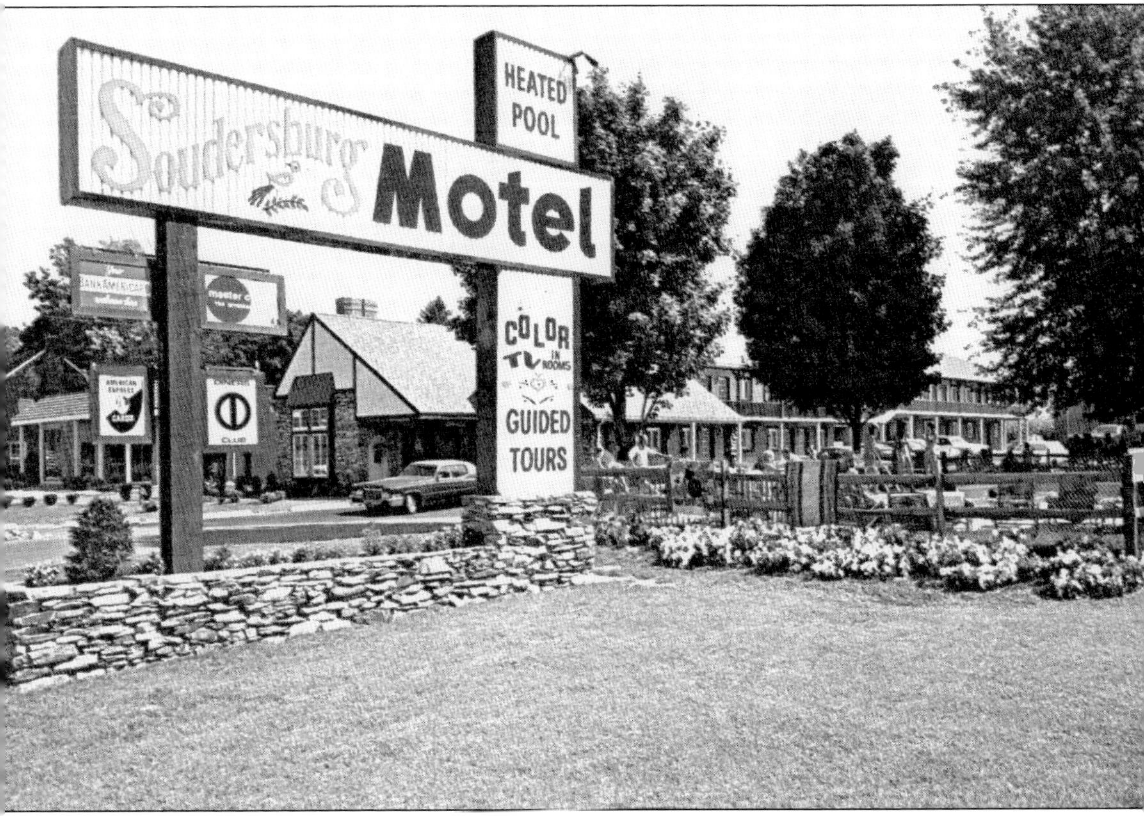

The route of the Lincoln Highway passes through a large part of Pennsylvania's Old Order Amish Country, fueling Lancaster County's tourist economy. The Soudersburg Motel, eight miles east of Lancaster, advertised 70 modern rooms, a heated pool, and tours of the area. In recent years, outlet stores have been built east of Lancaster, generating heavier traffic on U.S. Route 30. This motel continues to serve travelers and tourists.

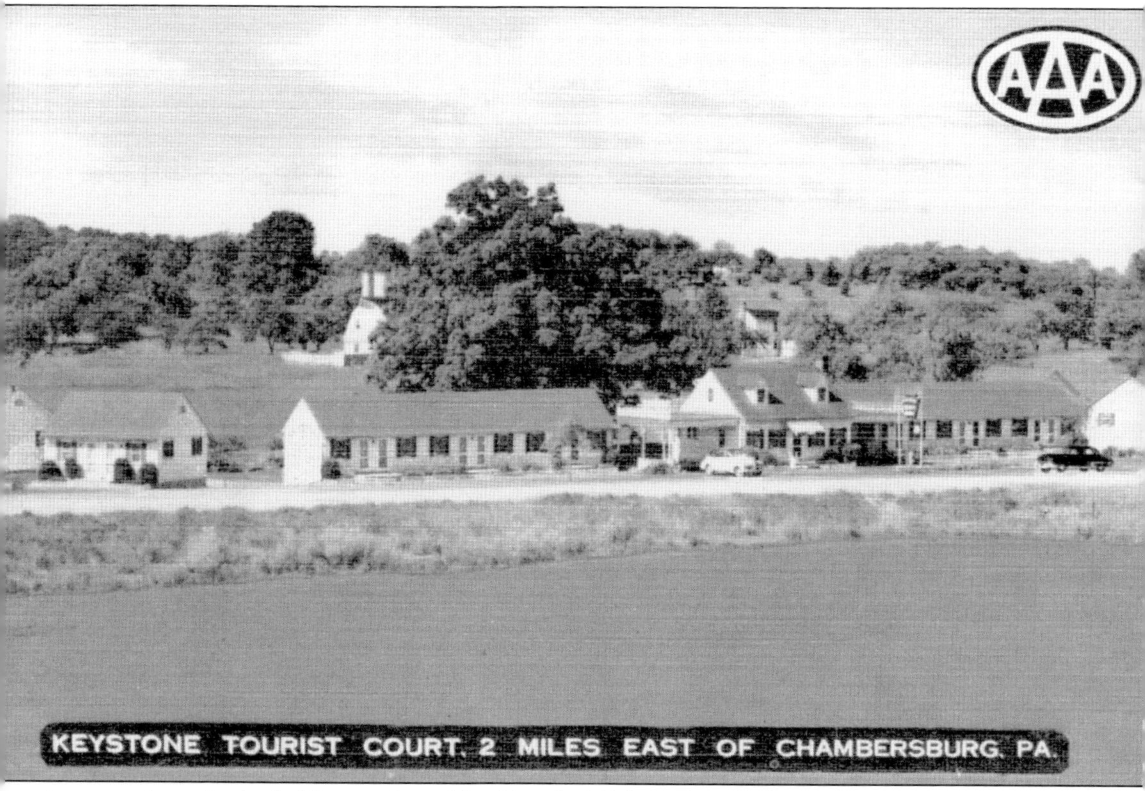

At approximately the halfway point of the Lincoln Highway's path through Pennsylvania and two miles east of Chambersburg in Franklin County, the Keystone Tourist Court was approved by the American Automobile Association when this view was printed, likely in the 1940s. The complex was typical of the era and advertised "20 modern rooms." Like many other roadside stops, the court was razed by developers in 1999.

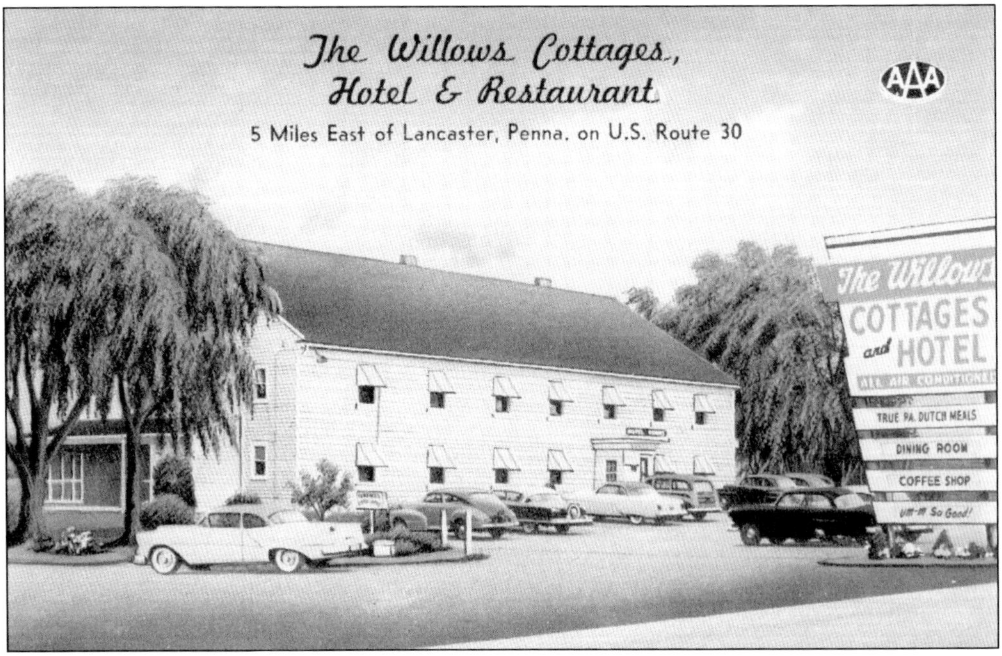

For many travelers, a trip to Lancaster County's Amish Country would not have been complete without a stop at the Willows Cottages, Hotel, and Restaurant. The Willows, one of the earlier tourist-oriented establishments in the area, was promoted as being "a good place to eat and sleep." The year-round hotel was "completely air conditioned."

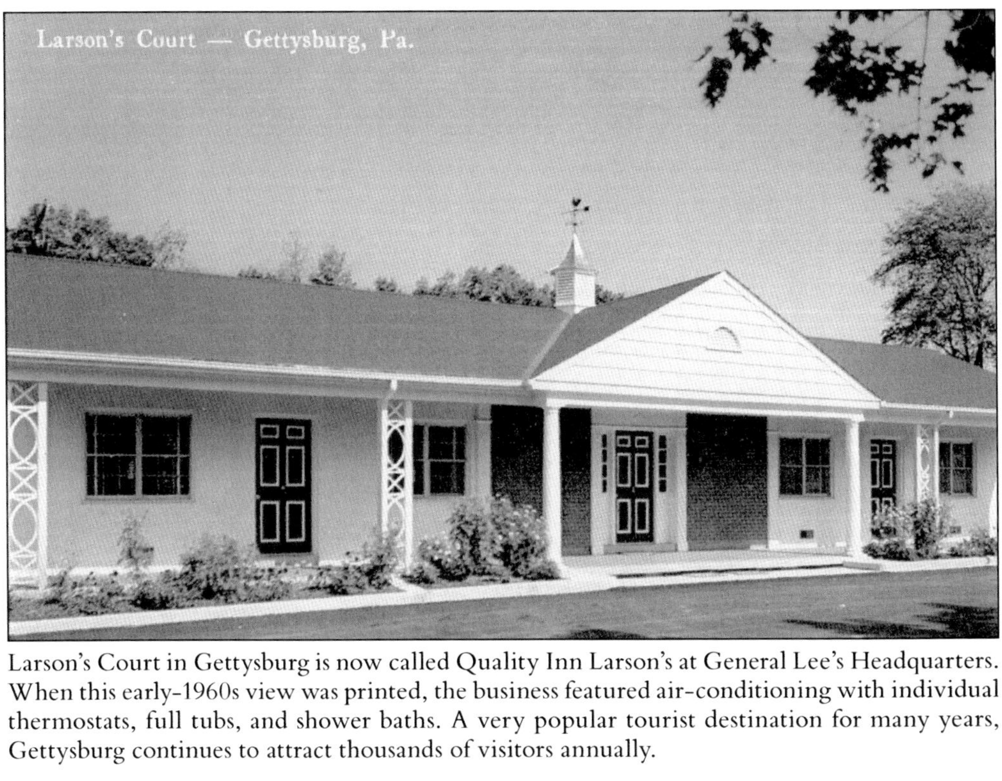

Larson's Court in Gettysburg is now called Quality Inn Larson's at General Lee's Headquarters. When this early-1960s view was printed, the business featured air-conditioning with individual thermostats, full tubs, and shower baths. A very popular tourist destination for many years, Gettysburg continues to attract thousands of visitors annually.

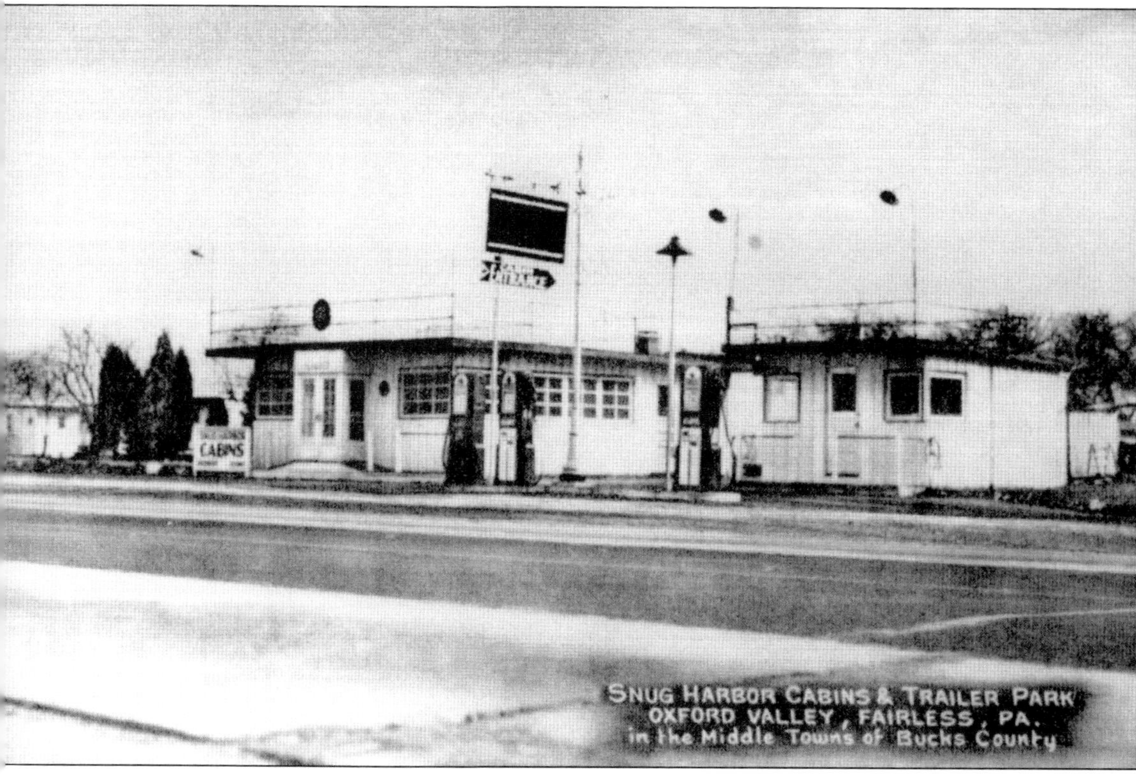

The Snug Harbor Cabins and Trailer Park was a perfect example of an early Lincoln Highway roadside business. Located in Fairless, Bucks County, the establishment stood seven miles west of Trenton, New Jersey. This section of the highway was designated as U.S. Route 1. In the early days of travel, many operators strived to offer travelers almost every need that could be imagined—everything from a meal to fuel and oil, rooms and cabins. Today very few places like this exist in the entire nation.

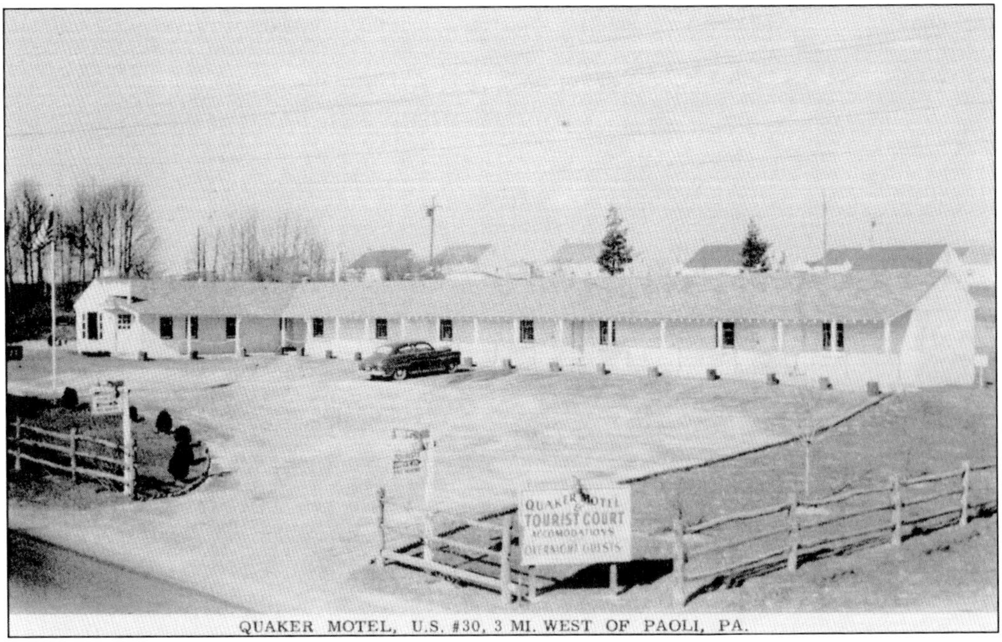

Dating to 1948, the Quaker Motel Tourist Court was located west of Paoli on a rather busy stretch of the Lincoln Highway. This Philadelphia suburb included other roadside businesses such as the Paoli Diner, which was located here to take advantage of the higher traffic flow around cities.

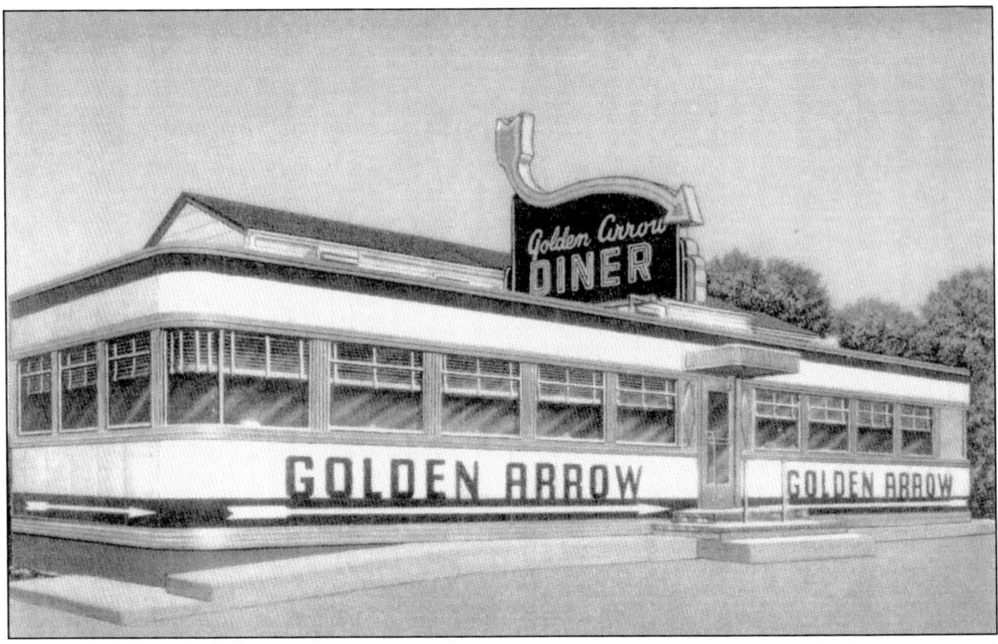

Those wanting to open a roadside restaurant often looked to diners, which were built in plants and transported to the site. Langhorne's Golden Arrow Diner was a true roadside classic. Since many diner manufacturers were located in New Jersey, eastern Pennsylvania had a large concentration of the mobile restaurants, but the numbers have diminished over the years.

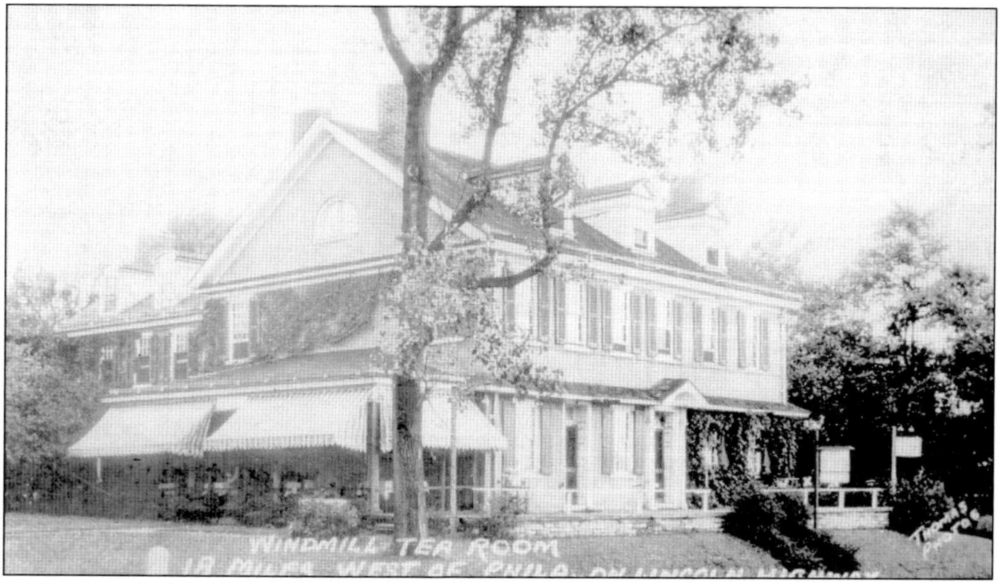

In the years before the family restaurant concept came into existence, tea rooms were rather common sights along highways and in towns. The Windmill Tea Room was one of those establishments, located along the Lincoln Highway in Paoli, 18 miles west of Philadelphia. The typical fare at these restaurants remains much the same today.

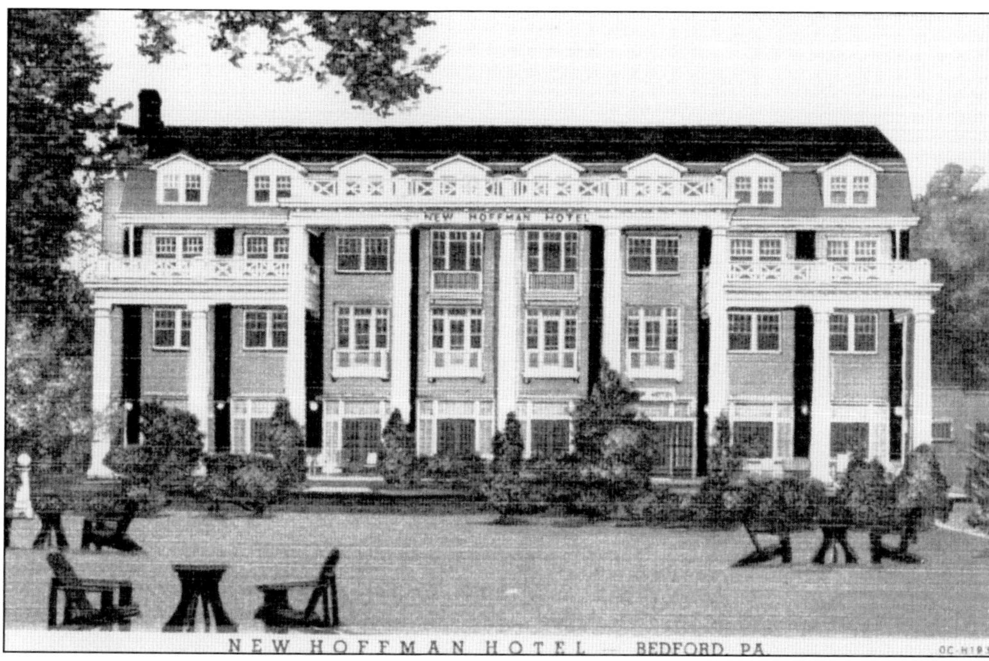

This postcard advertises Bedford's New Hoffman Hotel as "not connected with any other hotel." The establishment, which featured 60 rooms with baths, also provided travelers with a dining room, cocktail lounge, and garage. The business suffered a fire in the 1970s and never reopened.

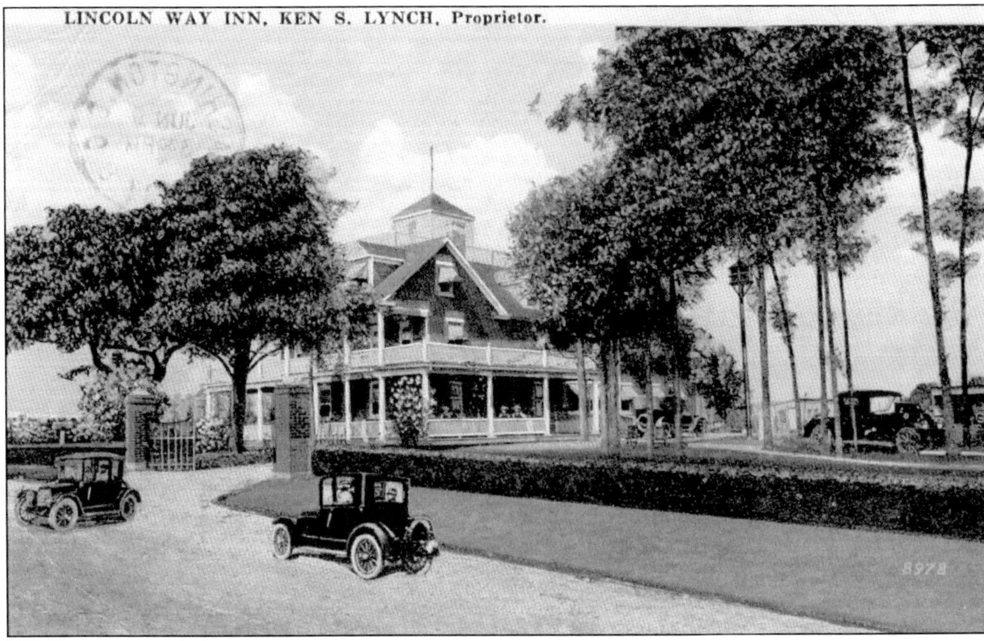

One mile west of Gettysburg, the Lincoln Way Inn no doubt served the needs of travelers and the many tourists visiting the nearby battlefield, the scene of the Civil War's bloodiest confrontation. The establishment was owned by Ken S. Lynch and, like many other restaurants in its day, featured chicken and waffle dinners, a Pennsylvania Dutch dish popular along the Lincoln Highway.

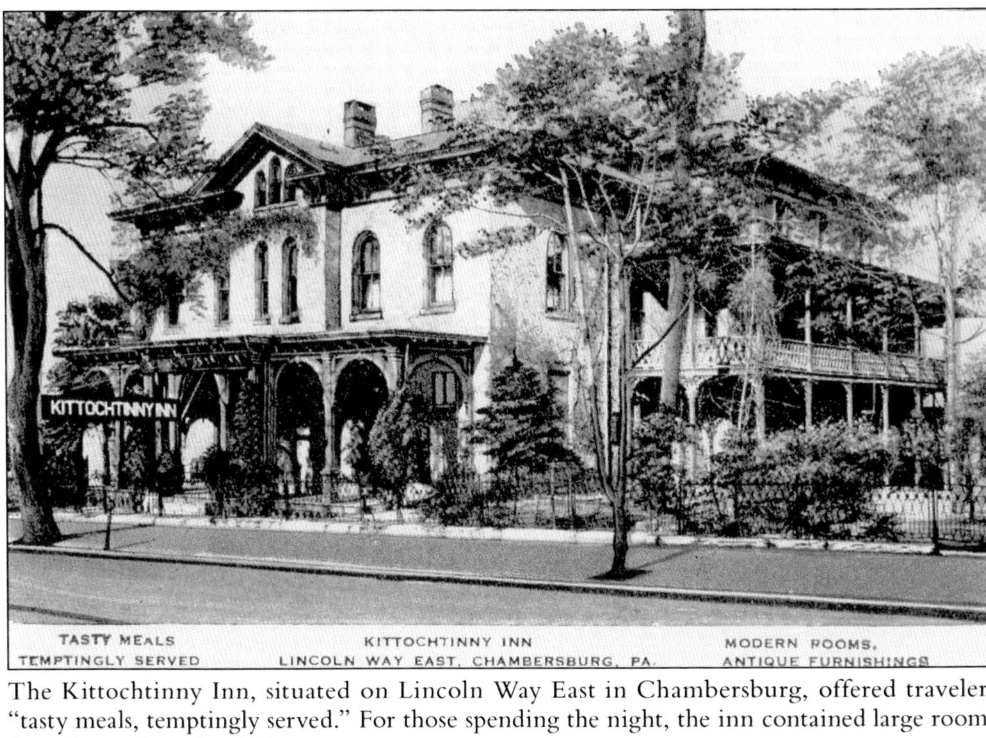

The Kittochtinny Inn, situated on Lincoln Way East in Chambersburg, offered travelers "tasty meals, temptingly served." For those spending the night, the inn contained large rooms featuring antique furnishings.

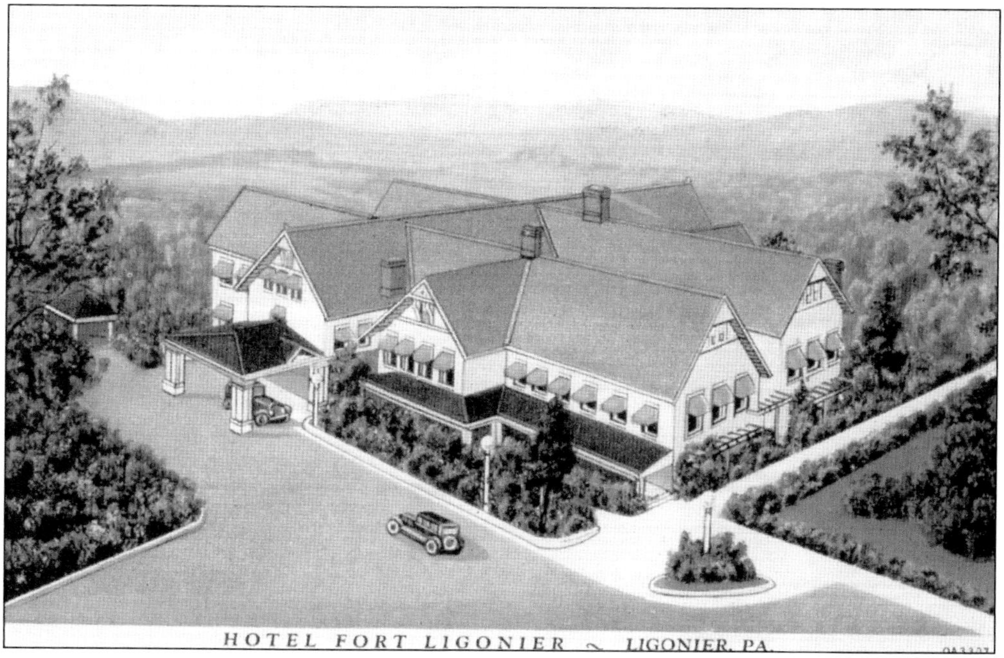

When this card was published, likely in the late 1920s or early 1930s, the Hotel Fort Ligonier offered rooms with baths and two restaurants. The business, 50 miles east of Pittsburgh, drew its name from a nearby historic fort, which was built in 1758. Along with Lincoln Highway travelers, the hotel attracted many who wanted to escape to the mountains as a vacation from the city.

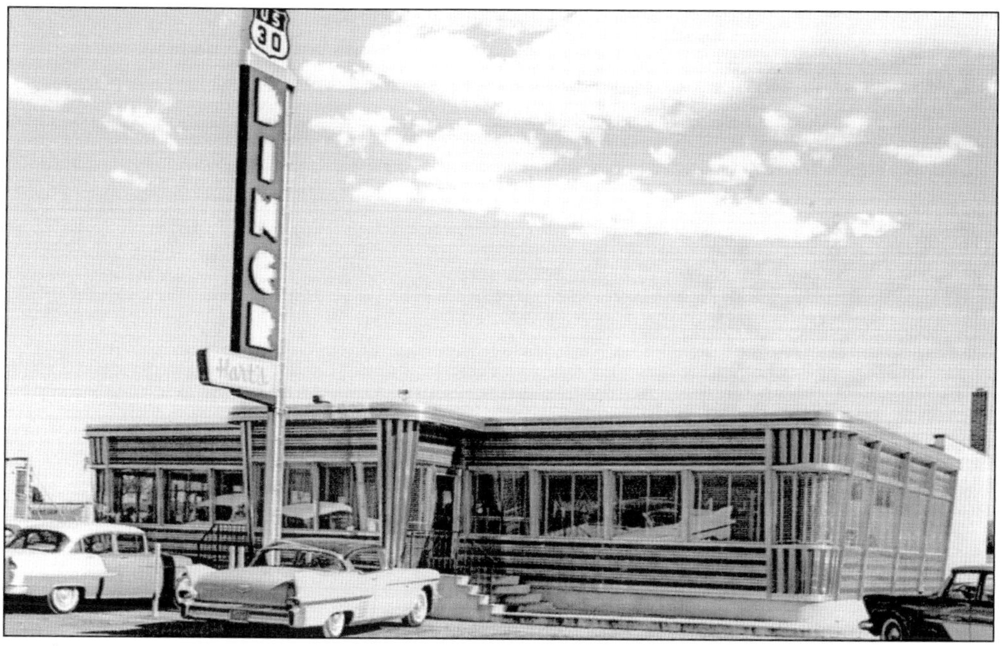

Hart's U.S. Route 30 diner was a roadside dining classic that could be found six miles east of Lancaster, in the center of a very busy tourist area. Advertising "Good Food Made Quickly," the 1957 Kullman-brand diner was moved from the site around 1990. Today the location continues to serve travelers and tourists as a gas station and convenience store.

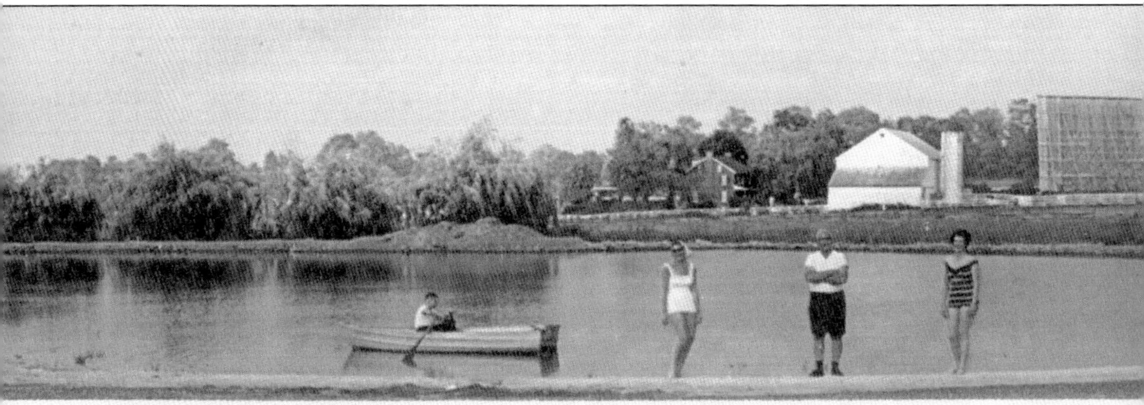

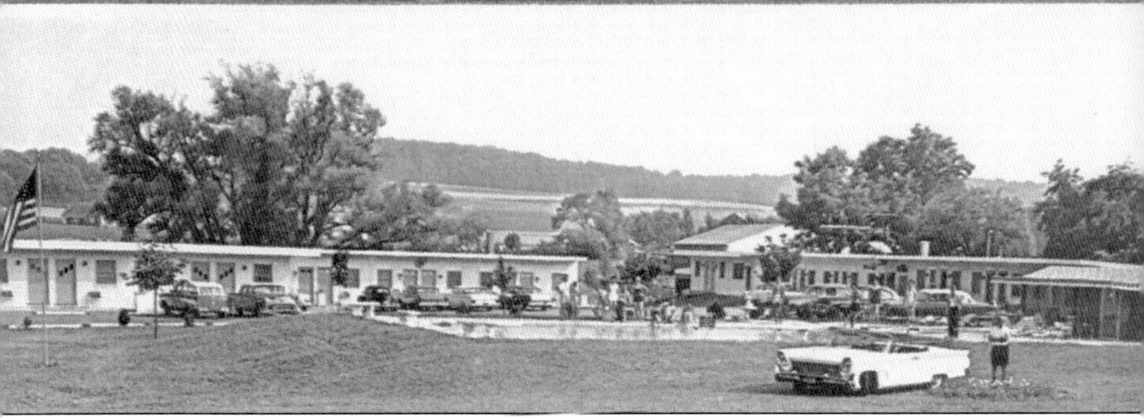

The name of York's Spheel Grund Motel, at 3522 East Market Street, may sound strange but comes from the Pennsylvania Dutch language spoken locally by many, especially older residents. The translation of the name is "play ground," and according to the description on this postcard, guests could *spheel*, *essen*, and *schloffen* "play," "eat," and "sleep." The motel consisted of 70 modern bedrooms, efficiency units, and even a bridal suite. A lake gave opportunities for boating and fishing, while an adjacent Howard Johnson Restaurant provided dining. When this card was published, likely in the 1950s, the motel was owned by Roy H. Grove.

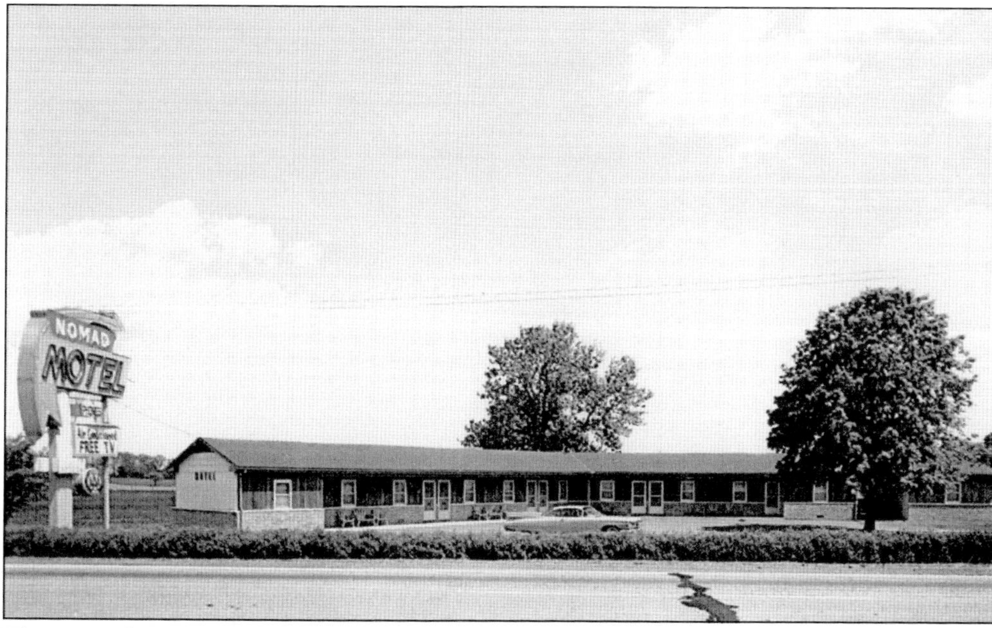

The Nomad Motel, six miles east of Lancaster in the village of Ronks, advertised four television channels for free, along with air-conditioned rooms, when this postcard view was printed in the late 1950s or early 1960s. The classic roadside motel was heavily damaged by fire in the late 1990s, but has since reopened at 2641 Lincoln Highway East.

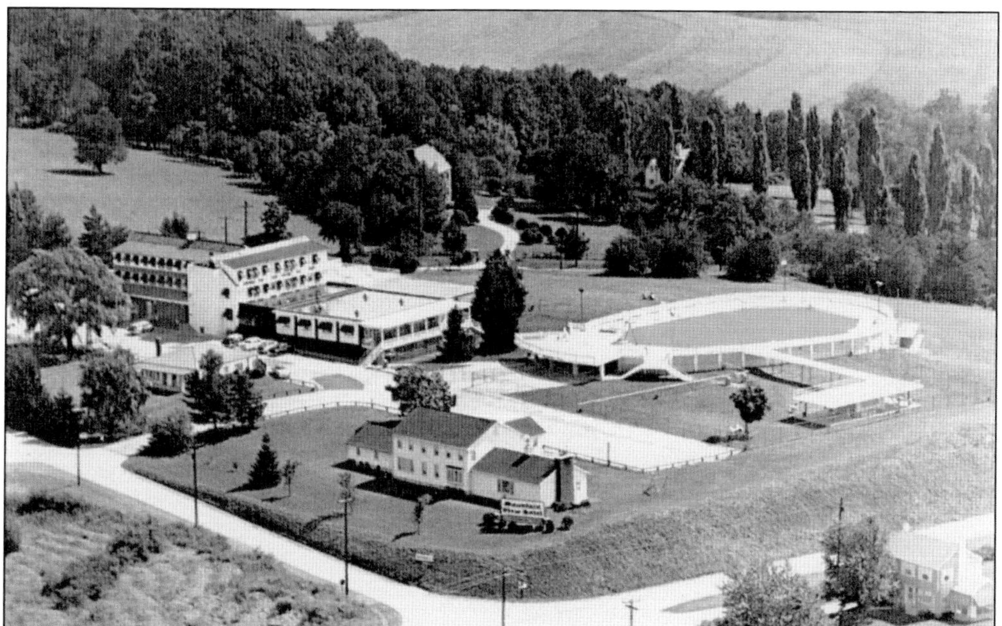

Located four miles east of Greensburg, the Mountain View Inn offered meals, modern rooms, a cocktail bar, and an outdoor swimming pool. Originally known as the Mountain View Hotel, the establishment was owned and managed by the Booher family when this photograph was taken. It eventually grew to a large complex that continues to serve the needs of travelers.

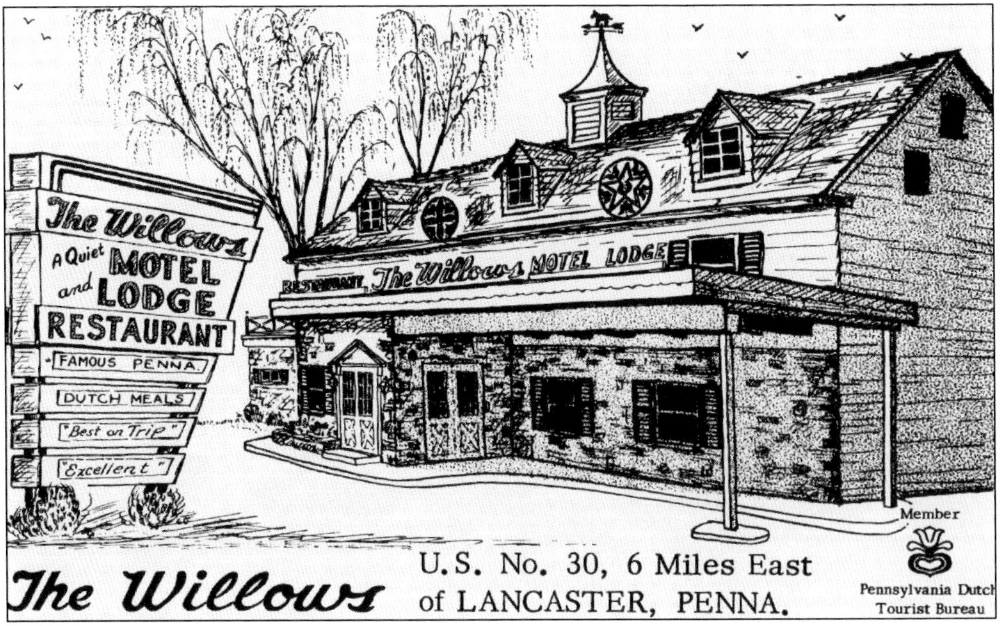

The Willows Motel and Restaurant, established in 1931, offered a Colonial dining room, which, like many other businesses in the Lancaster area, featured Pennsylvania Dutch meals. The well-known roadside destination, situated six miles east of Lancaster, was adjacent to a popular tourist attraction, the Amish Farm and House.

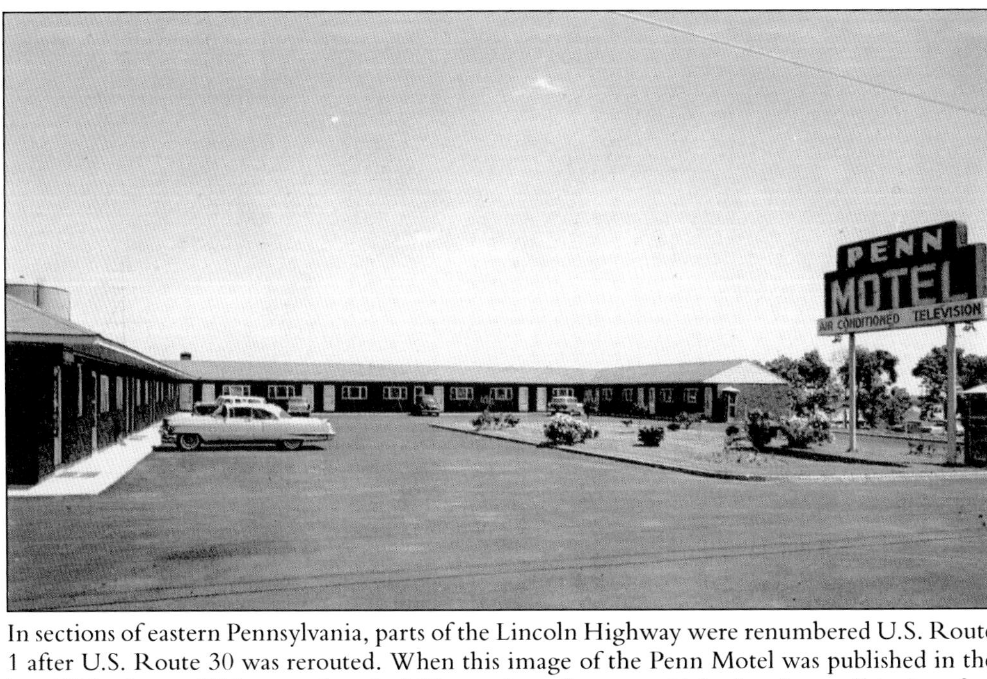

In sections of eastern Pennsylvania, parts of the Lincoln Highway were renumbered U.S. Route 1 after U.S. Route 30 was rerouted. When this image of the Penn Motel was published in the late 1950s, the establishment advertised 98 soundproof rooms with baths, air-conditioning, free television, room-controlled heat, and wall-to-wall carpeting.

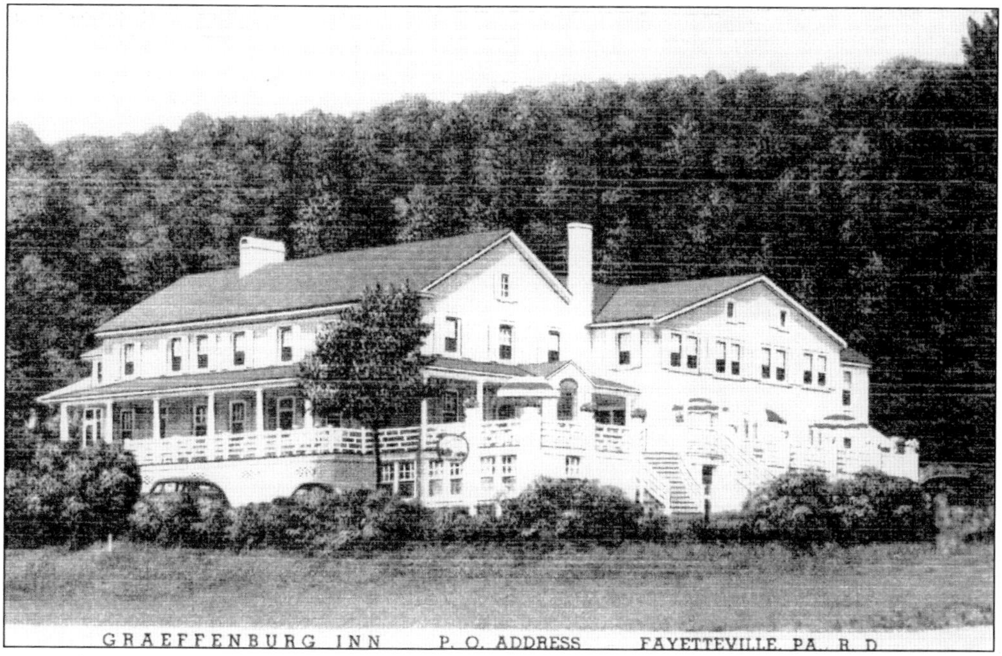

Located 14 miles west of Gettysburg in Fayetteville, the Graeffenburg Inn and Caledonia Golf Club offered meals and rooms in a large structure built in 1841. In later years, the inn was registered with the Historical Sites Commission of Harrisburg.

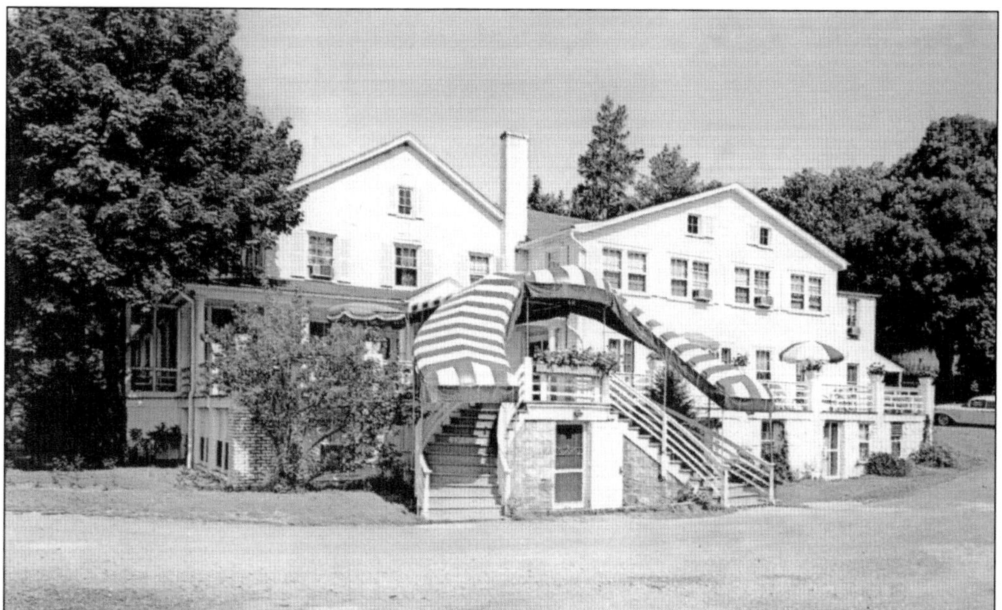

This advertisement for the Graeffenburg Inn, situated between Gettysburg and Chambersburg, was printed late in the business's history and stated the golf course was "Pennsylvania's most beautiful." On March 15, 1980, the historic landmark was destroyed by a fire ruled to be arson.

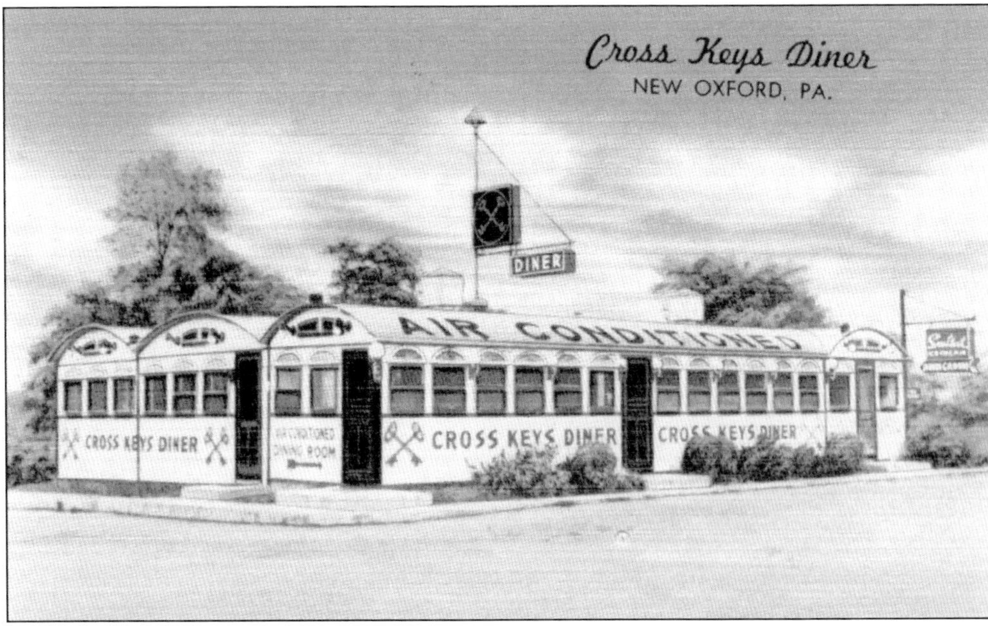

The Cross Keys Diner, 10 miles east of Gettysburg in New Oxford, was anything but a typical roadside eatery. Owner John E. George combined four barrel-roof diners into a single unit with a seating capacity of 70. A hanging sign at the right advertised Sealtest ice cream. Like many other roadside landmarks, the Cross Keys Diner is now merely a part of history.

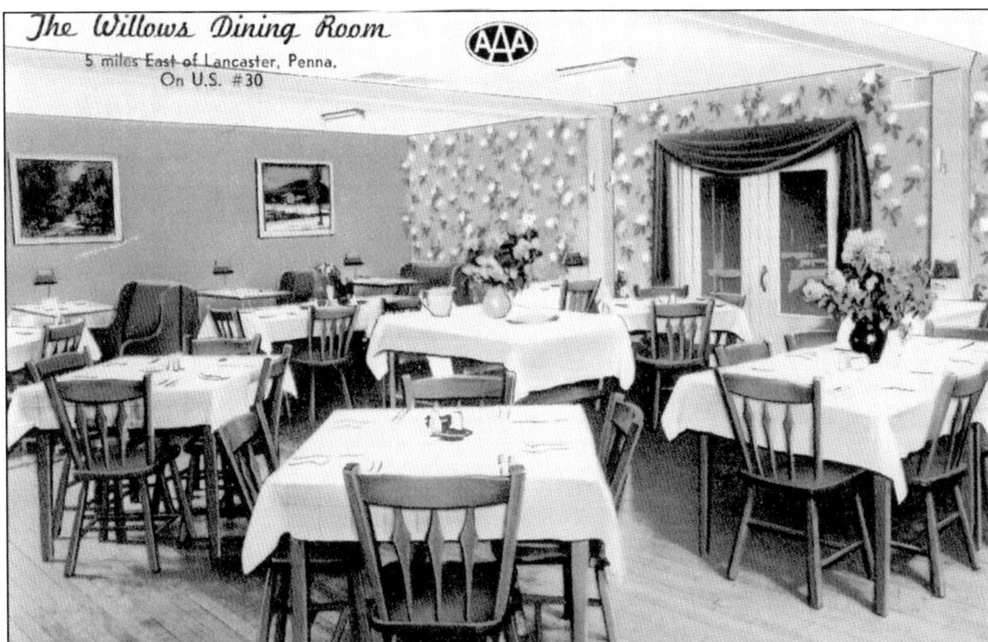

Known far and wide, the Willows Cottages, Hotel, and Restaurant featured a comfortable dining room that attracted many motorists along the Lincoln Highway. Located five miles east of Lancaster, it was approved by the American Automobile Association.

The Greensburger Hotel in Greensburg, Westmoreland County, typical of in-town lodging, featured 100 rooms, a coffee shop, and cocktail lounge. Early establishments such as this often catered to travelers visiting by rail and, unlike cabin courts and motels, were not built exclusively to serve highway travelers. The Lincoln Highway passed through the heart of Greensburg.

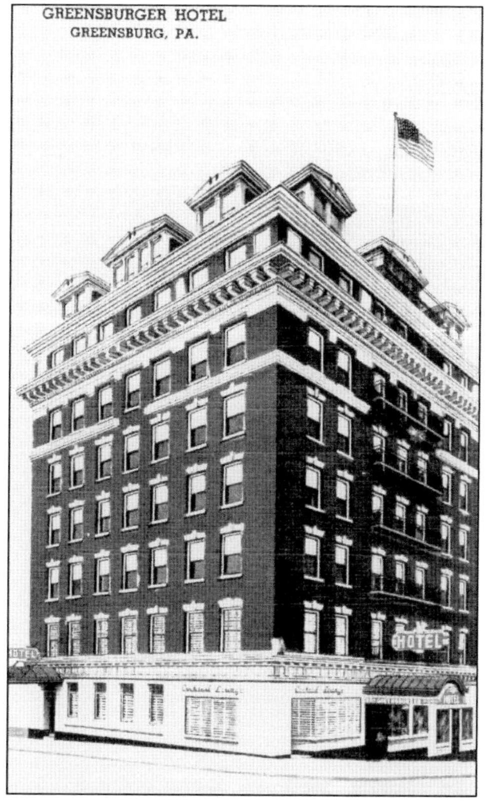

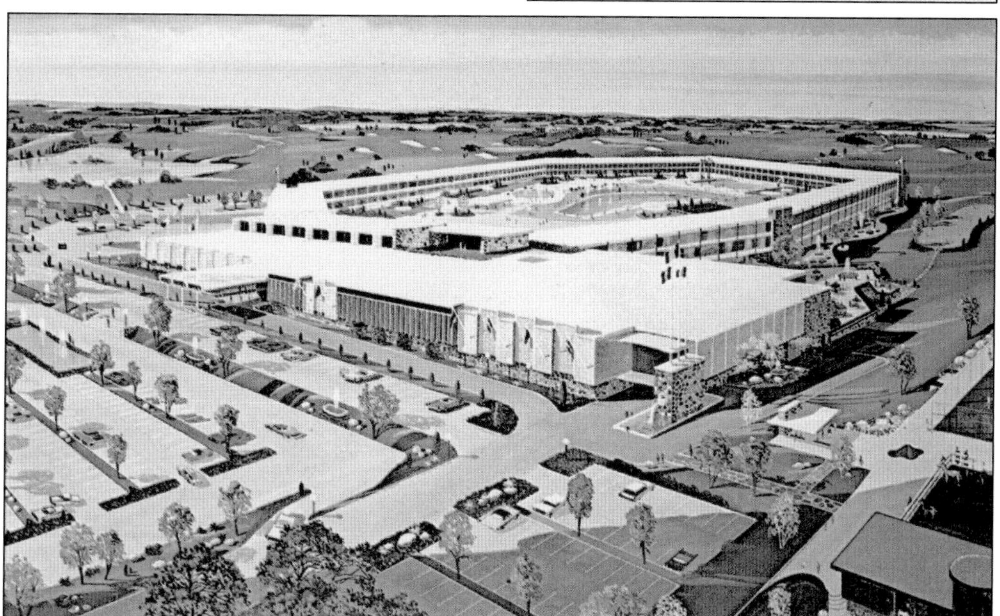

What started as the Host Farm Resort and Motel has grown to become the Lancaster Host Resort and Conference Center. The large facility was already a major destination when this card was published, likely in the early 1960s. At that time, it offered 350 rooms, an 18-hole championship golf course, indoor and outdoor swimming pools, bike paths, and even a model Amish farm.

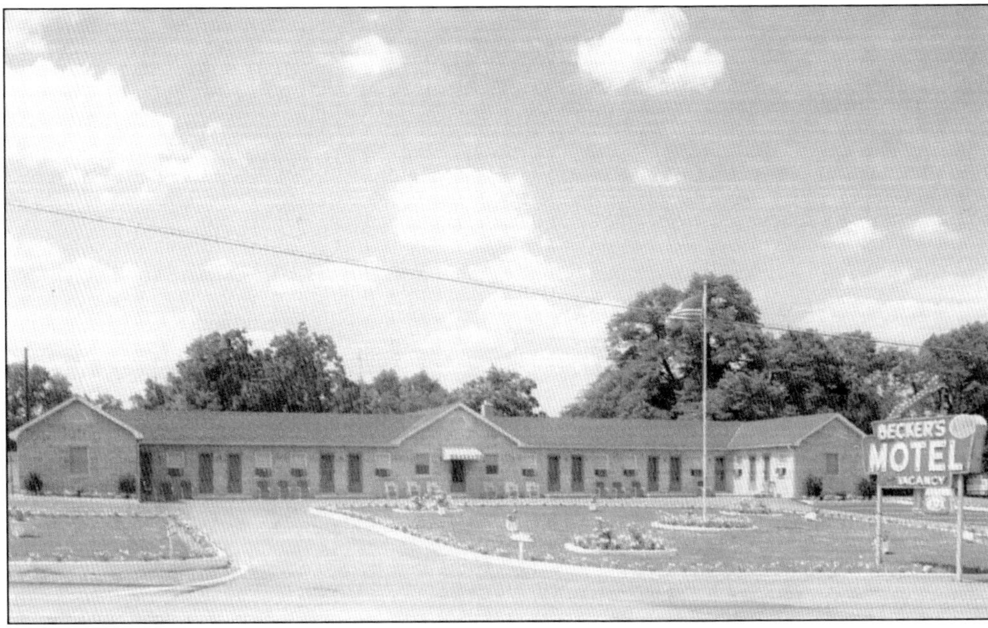

Some nine miles east of York, at 5599 Lincoln Highway in Hallam, Becker's Motel lives on as the Alpine Motel. Like many other similar businesses along the highway, this motel offered free television and radio, along with air-conditioning. The business was operated by Mr. and Mrs. William Becker. Although designated Route 462, this is the original route of the Lincoln Highway, and present-day U.S. Route 30 is to the north.

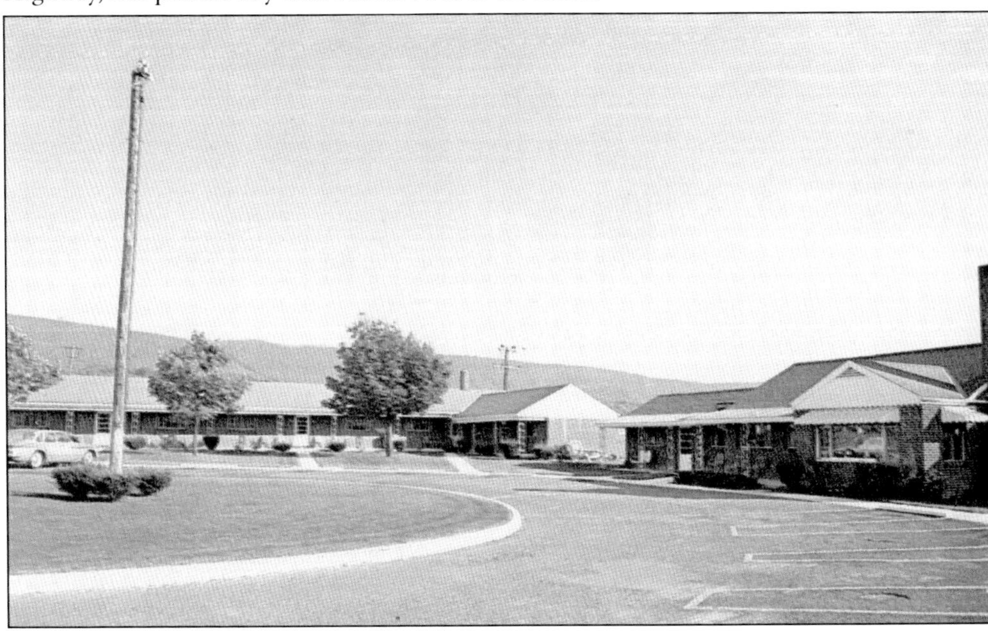

The year-round Johnnie's Motel, at the junction of U.S. Route 30 and state Route 16 in McConnellsburg, featured 16 brick units containing Simmons furniture, rubber foam mattresses, carpeting, and tubs and showers. Heat was provided by a hot-air system and the rooms had cross ventilation. Those staying here could enjoy free radio and television. An adjoining diner served meals.

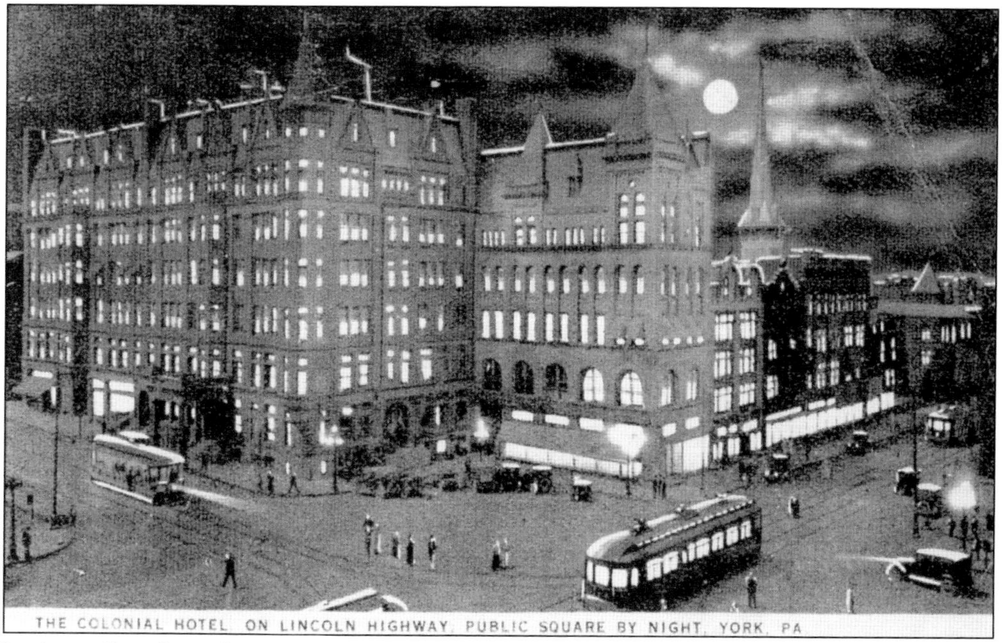

In the earliest days of travel on the Lincoln Highway, motorists had two choices for the night: camping along the road or sleeping at an in-town establishment such as York's Colonial Hotel. These large hotels were usually built before the automobile became the preferred means of travel and generally offered both meals and rooms. As motels and cabin courts came into existence, large city hotels lost their popularity.

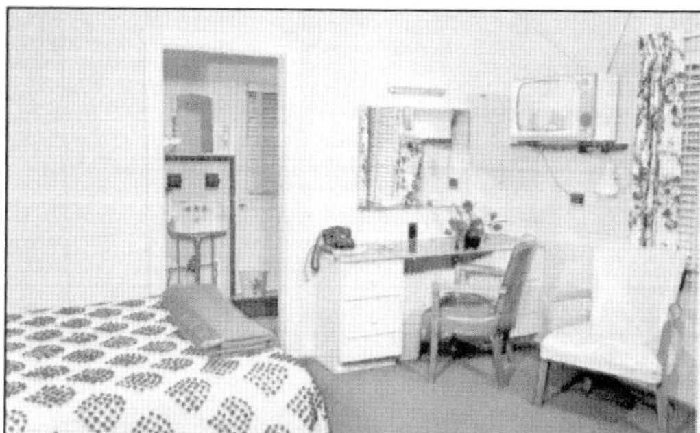

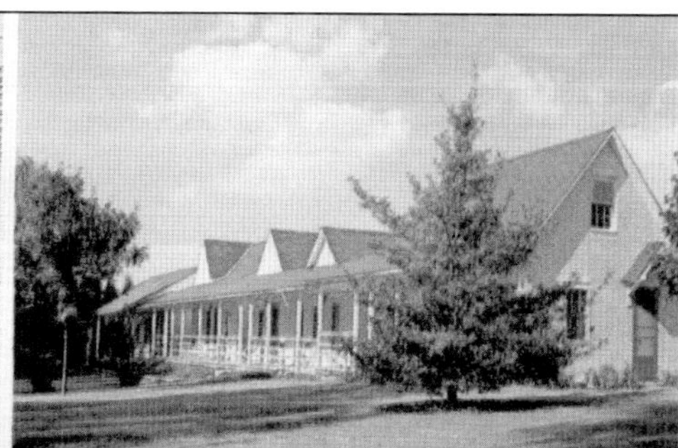

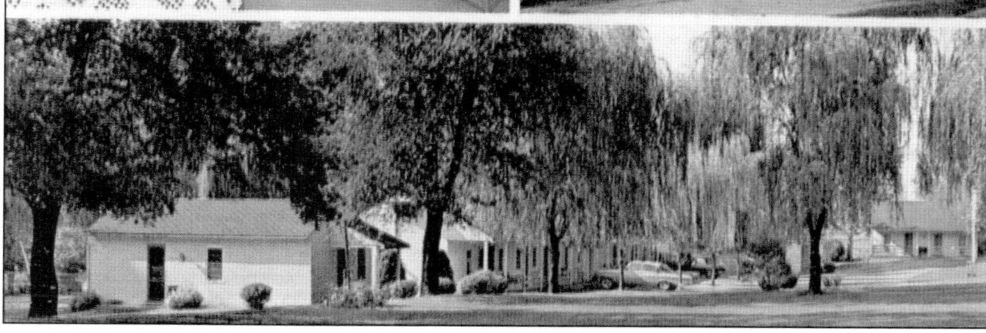

Named for the trees found on its grounds, the Willows Motel, located six miles east of Lancaster, has expanded over the years. This *c.* 1962 postcard view promotes a quiet setting and spacious lawns. The motel offered rooms by the day, week, or month. In recent years, the Willows and its restaurant were demolished and replaced with a large entertainment complex.

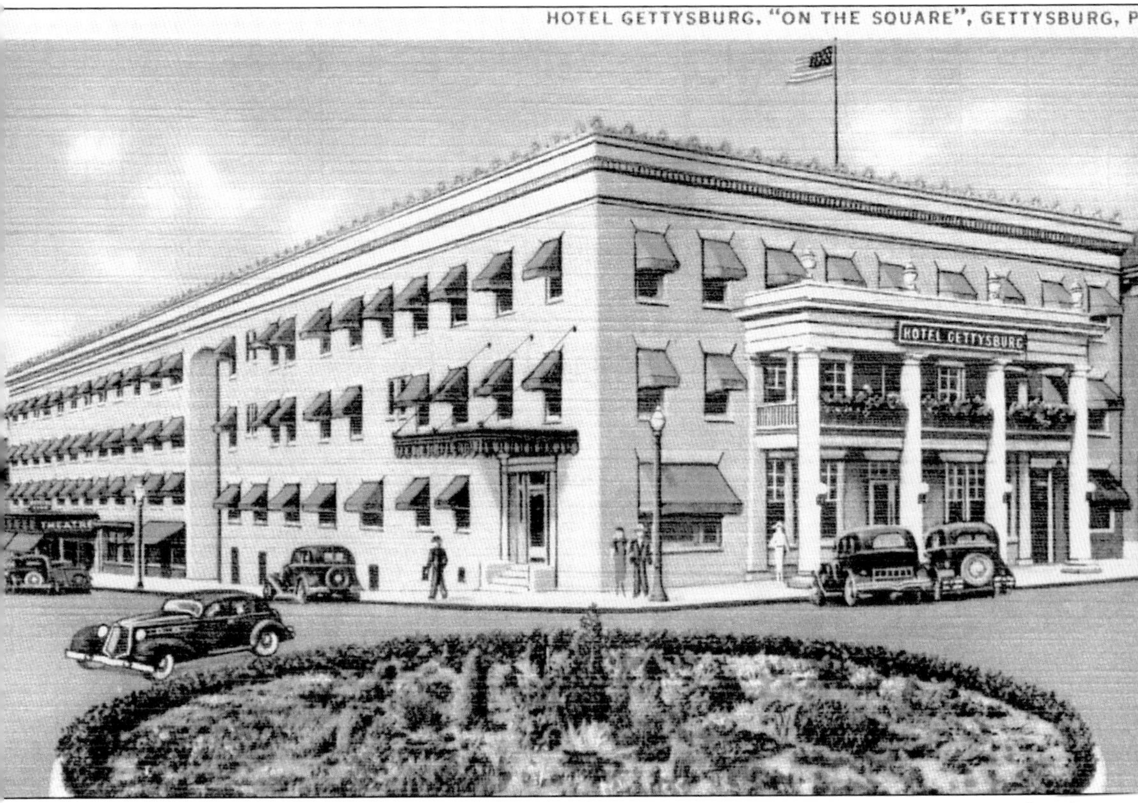

At over 200 years old, the Hotel Gettysburg is today the Best Western Gettysburg Hotel and is located in the town's famous square. Through the years, the facility has hosted guests such as Pres. Dwight D. and Mamie Eisenhower, Carl Sandburg, Daniel Webster, and even Gen. Ulysses S. Grant. When this *c.* 1937 card was published, the hotel hosted thousands of visitors each year, most coming to see the historic battlefield and its many monuments.

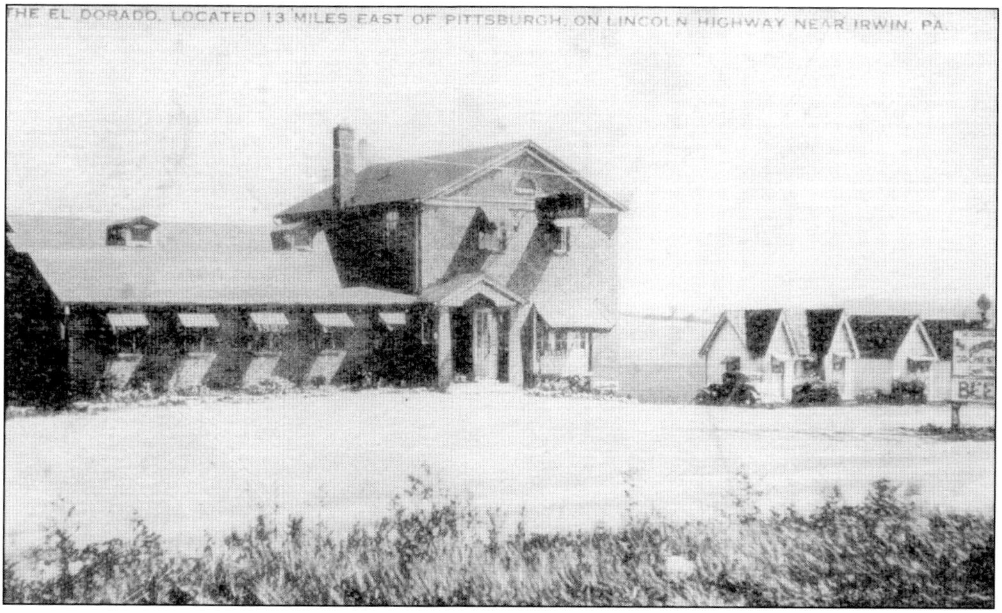

The El Dorado was situated 13 miles west of Pittsburgh near Irwin. Typical of many roadside establishments, it offered meals and cabins to early Lincoln Highway travelers. Judging by this *c.* 1935 postcard view, the business had ample parking, which would have undoubtedly made it a popular stop with truck drivers.

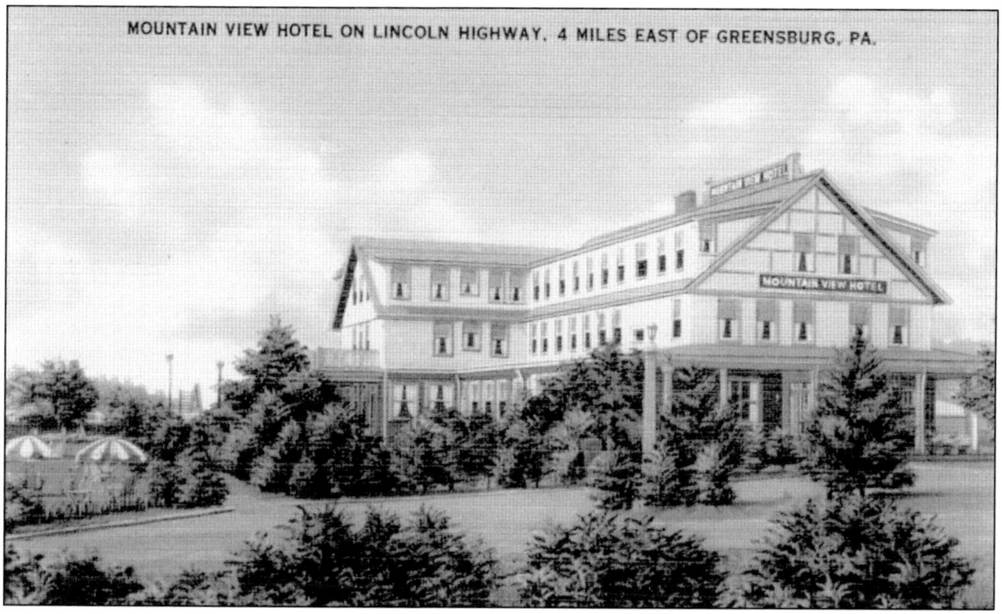

This postcard of the Mountain View Hotel, four miles east of Greensburg, reveals that the building had been expanded since its construction in 1924. The original hotel was housed in the section with the signs, to the right. According to this 1940s view, the business offered "excellent food, comfortable rooms and reasonable rates."

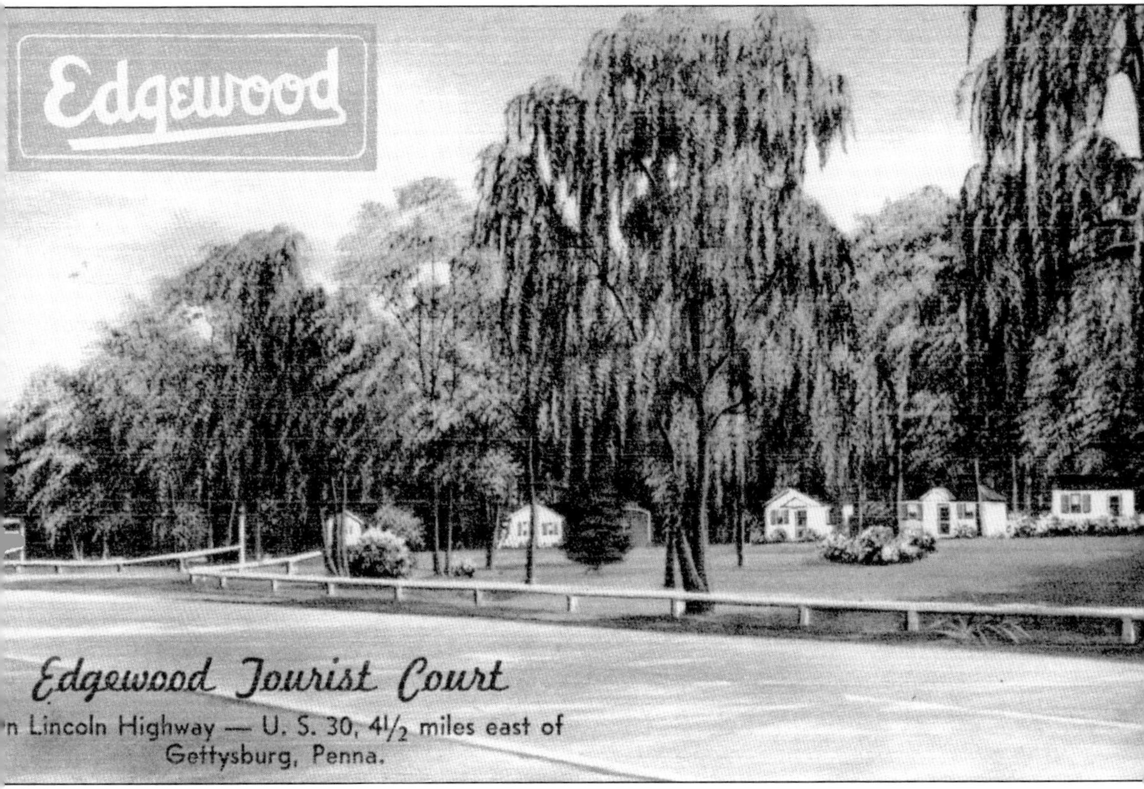

The Edgewood Tourist Court, four and one-half miles east of Gettysburg and its historic Civil War battlefield, was advertised in the 1940s as "quiet and homelike." This classic roadside tourist court offered cottages and cabins at the edge of a wooded area. The cabins were equipped with automatic electric heat and private showers. At the time of this postcard, the business was owned by Carl and Irene Schutt.

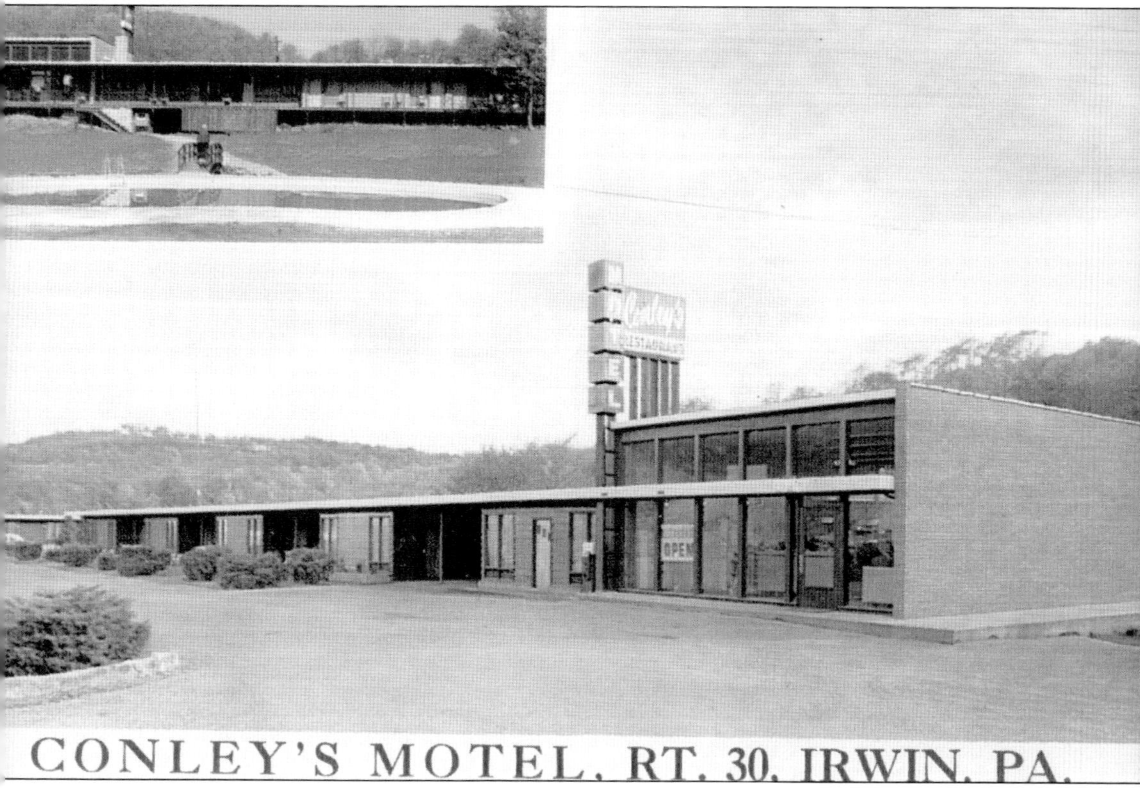

Conley's Motel, one mile west of the Pennsylvania Turnpike's Irwin interchange, was promoted as an "ultra-modern, first class" motel having 30 units. Among the amenities provided to travelers were free television, radiant heat, a children's playground, swimming pool, wall-to-wall carpeting, and carports. After the turnpike's completion, it was common for motels and other businesses catering to the traveling public to locate near the interchanges.

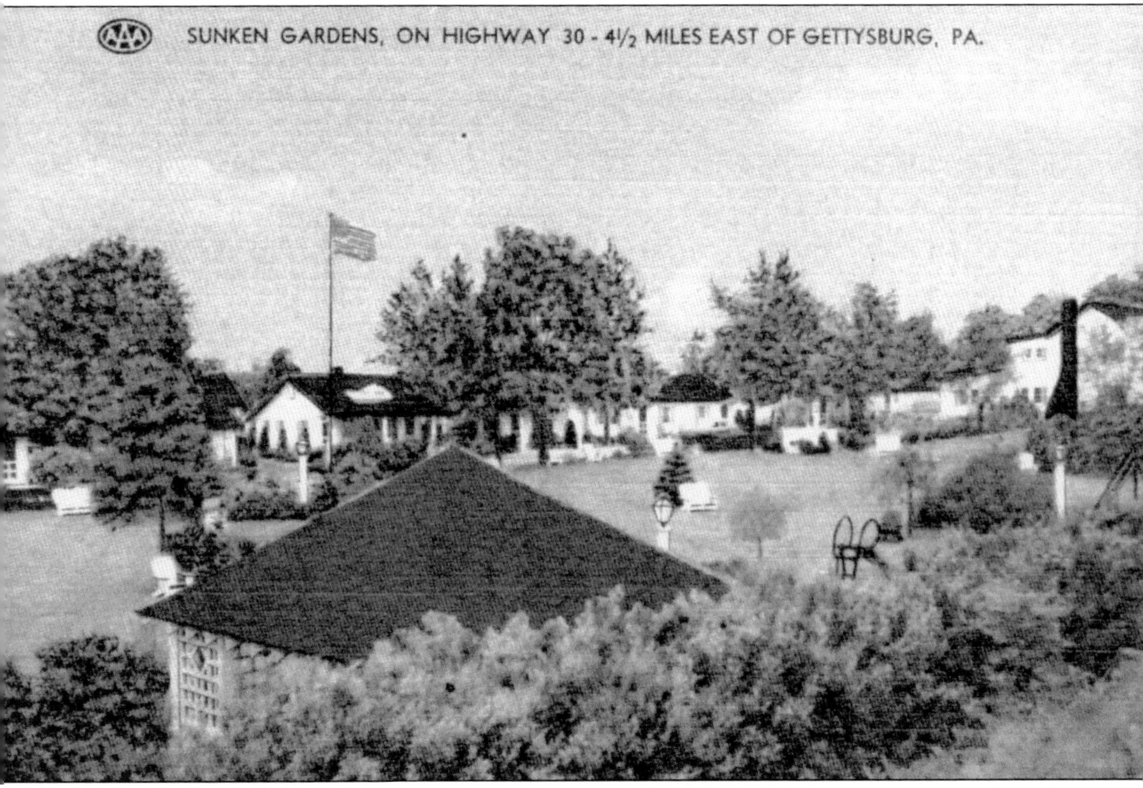

Gettysburg is the location of the Civil War's most famous battle, and owing to that, the Adams County community has for many years been a popular tourist destination. East of town was Sunken Gardens, advertised as being one of Pennsylvania's "most attractive tourist courts." This view, likely from the late 1930s or early 1940s, shows some of the establishment's 19 modern cabins. The year-round complex also included a landscaped park, playgrounds, shuffleboard, horseshoe, and croquet courts. Due to the proximity to Gettysburg, a number of other tourist courts and restaurants operated in the vicinity.

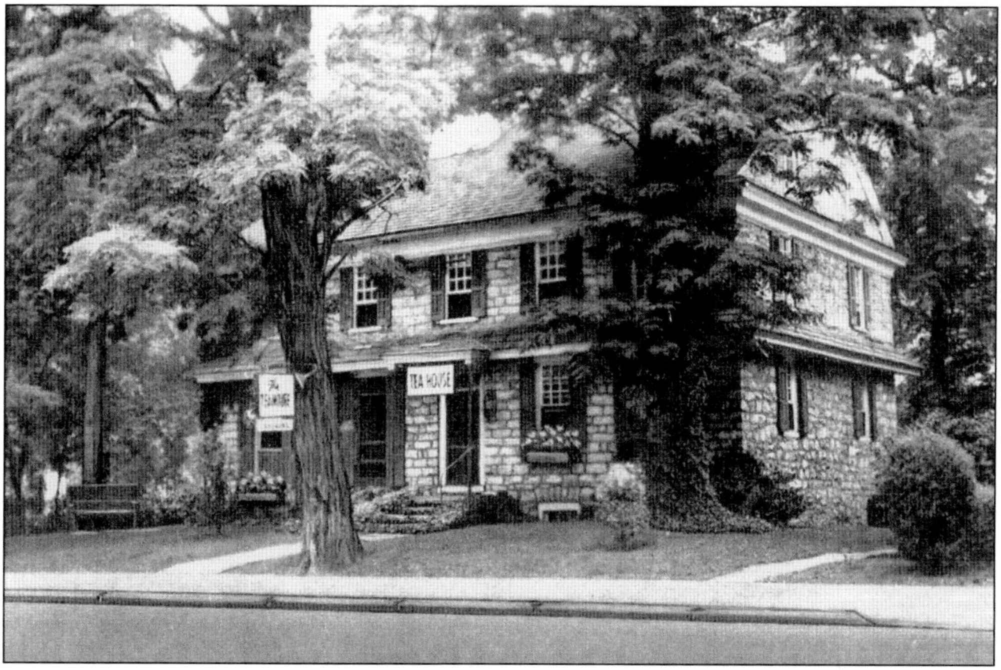

The Tea House, at 343 Lincoln Highway East in Downingtown, was typical of the 1940s and earlier eating establishments along the route. Owned by Donald McIlvaine, the restaurant featured luncheons, afternoon tea, and dinners. This 1946 card advertising the business's 32nd season recommended that reservations be made.

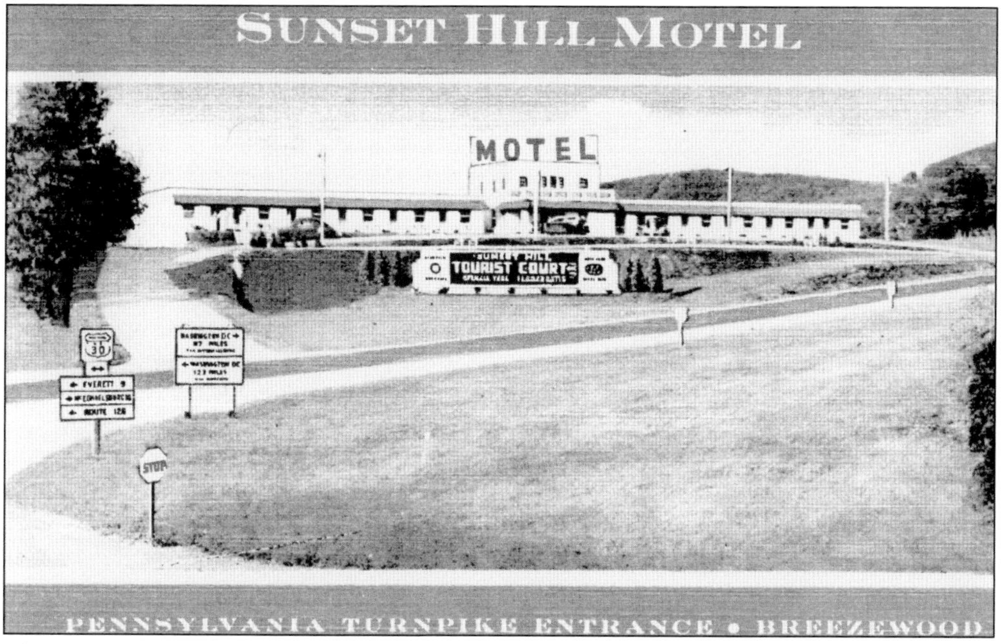

The opening of the Pennsylvania Turnpike was responsible for many restaurants, motels, and service stations locating at the interchanges. The Sunset Hill Tourist Court in Breezewood, Bedford County, was one such establishment. Road signs in front of the motel told travelers the mileage and directions to places along the Lincoln Highway.

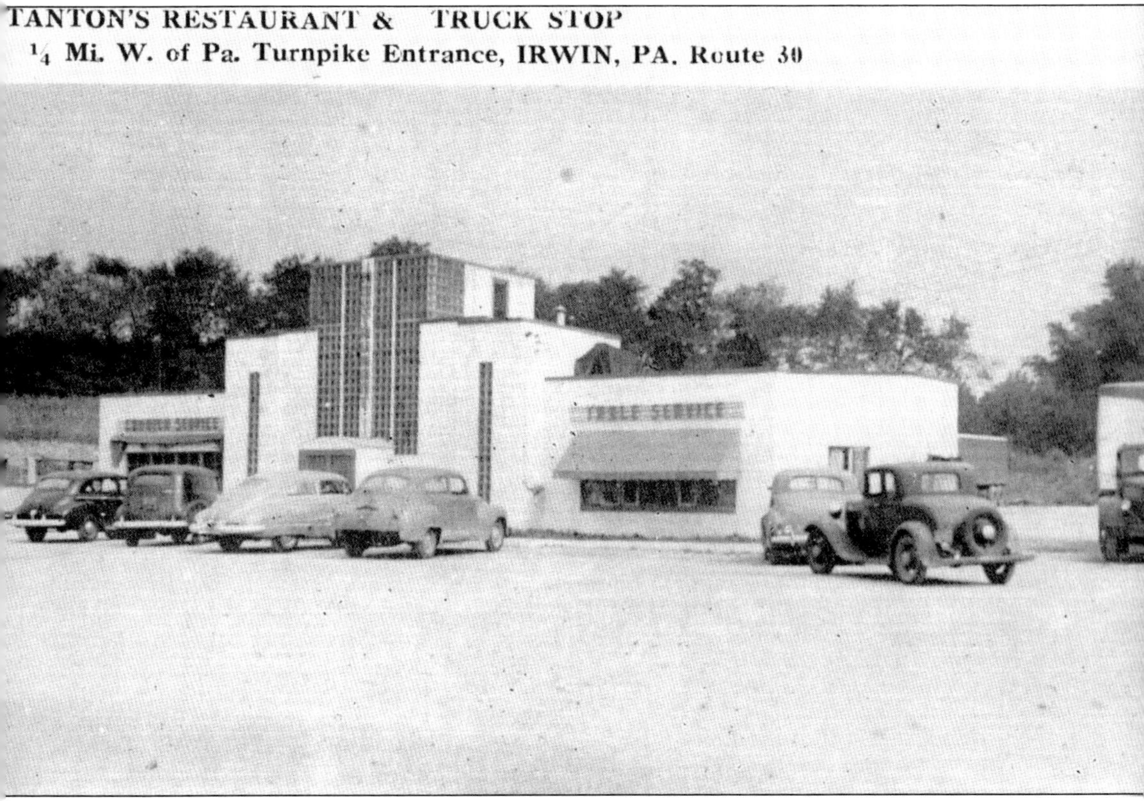

Stanton's Restaurant and Truck Stop, situated along U.S. Route 30, just west of the Pennsylvania Turnpike entrance, advertised "table" and "express" service in its large, art deco building. Many structures in the area were large and eye-catching in an effort to attract motorists. Along with food, this business provided fuel and oil.

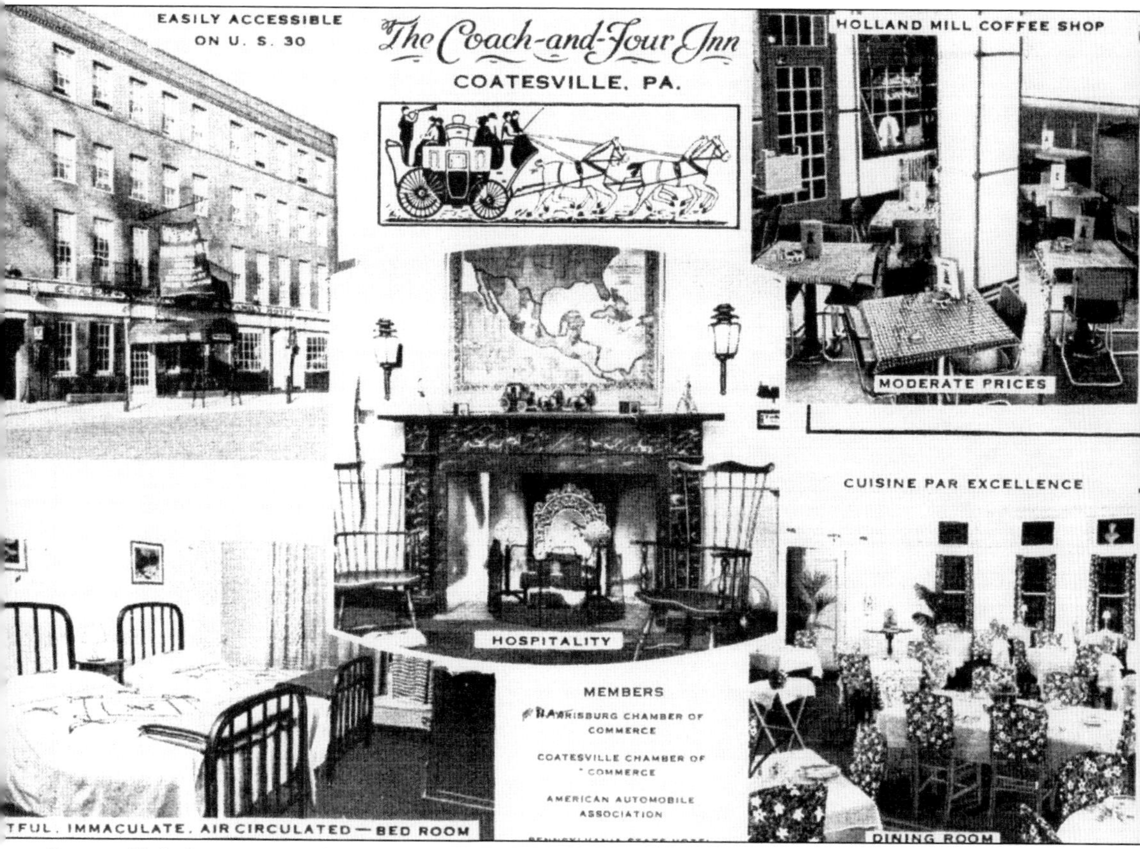

Coatesville's famous Coach-and-Four Inn fell to an urban renewal project, but in its heyday was a popular place along the route. Under the direction of general manager J. Van Kleef, the hotel was advertised as having an "atmosphere of early coaching days" and containing 56 rooms, elevator service, and free parking. The management considered details to be important to customer service.

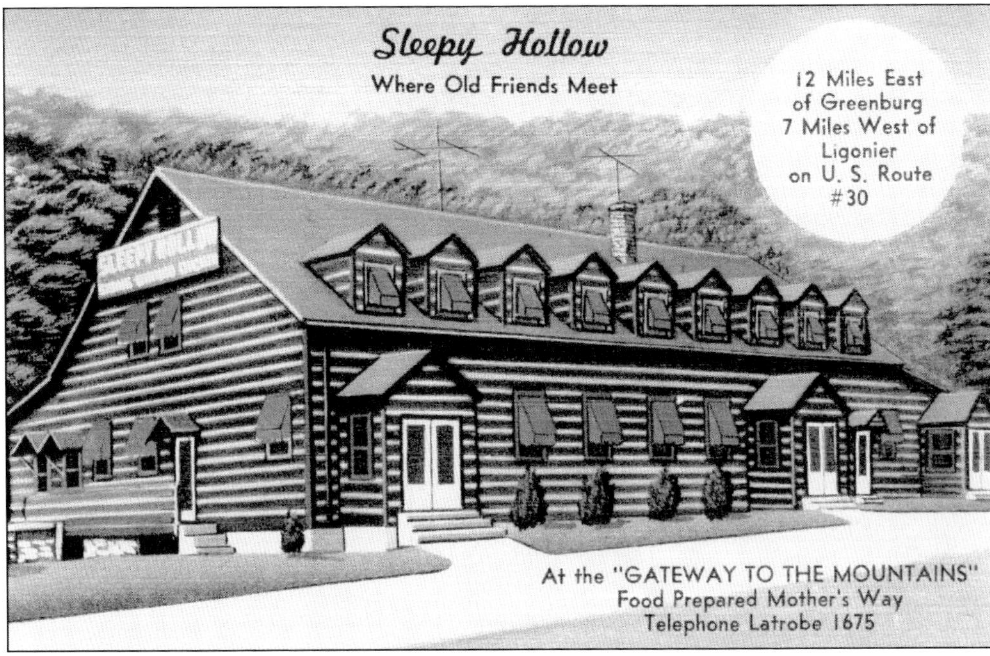

Some 12 miles east of Greensburg and 7 miles west of Ligonier, Sleepy Hollow was a rustic roadside eatery known for its steak, seafood, and chicken prepared "mother's way." The reverse of this 1940s card states that patrons could "eat midst rustic style and luxurious surroundings."

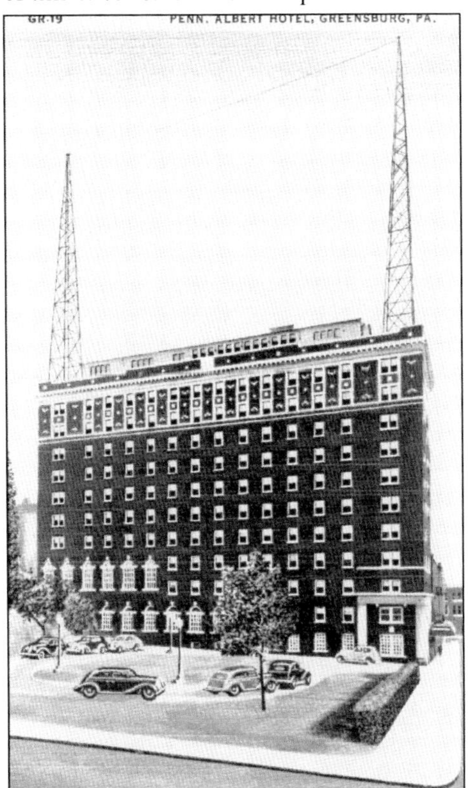

Greensburg's Penn Albert Hotel, built in 1923, was a popular stop with travelers along the route. Like many large hotels of the era, this building is now being used as an apartment complex: the Penn Towers Apartments.

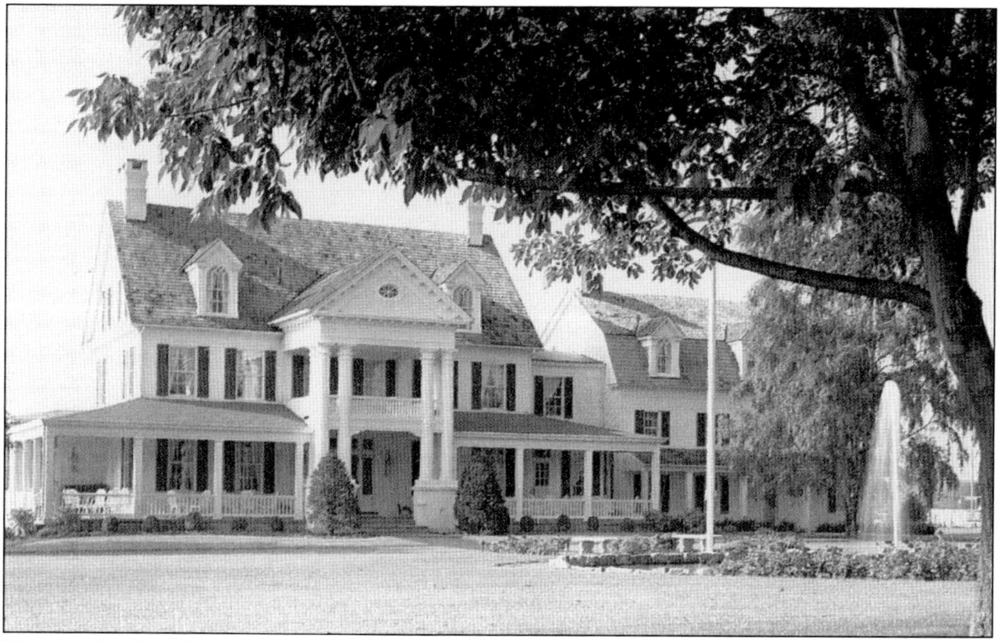

The Meadowbrook in York County provided diners with a "taste of elegance" in a historic Georgian Revival mansion. East of the city of York, the structure has stood for over 200 years.

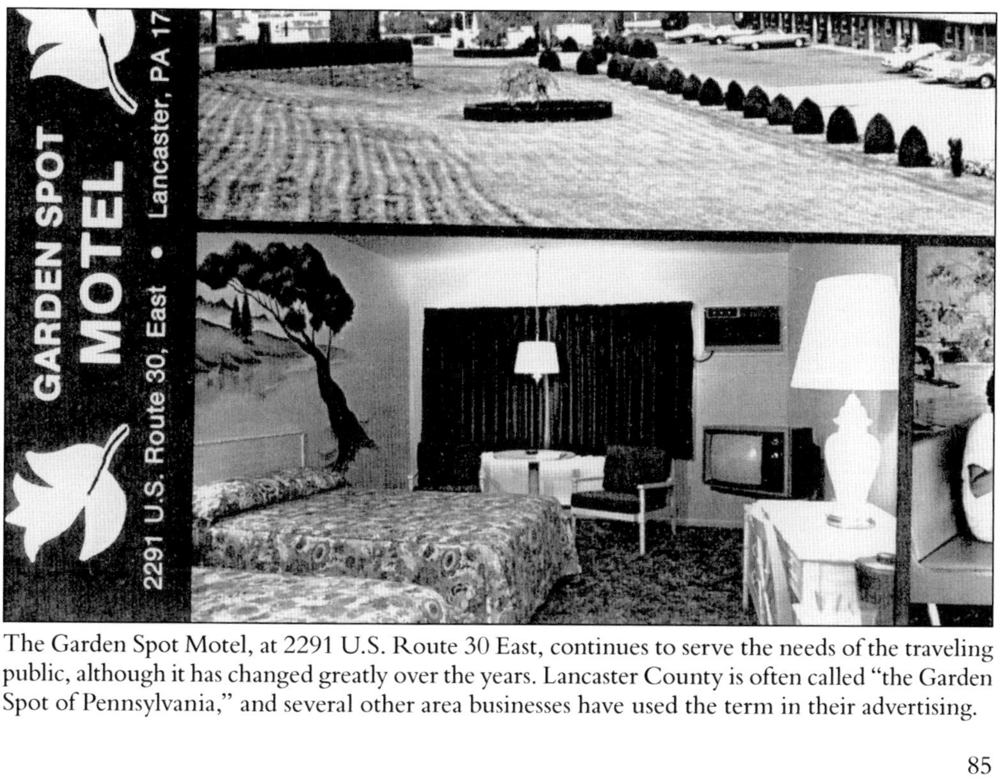

The Garden Spot Motel, at 2291 U.S. Route 30 East, continues to serve the needs of the traveling public, although it has changed greatly over the years. Lancaster County is often called "the Garden Spot of Pennsylvania," and several other area businesses have used the term in their advertising.

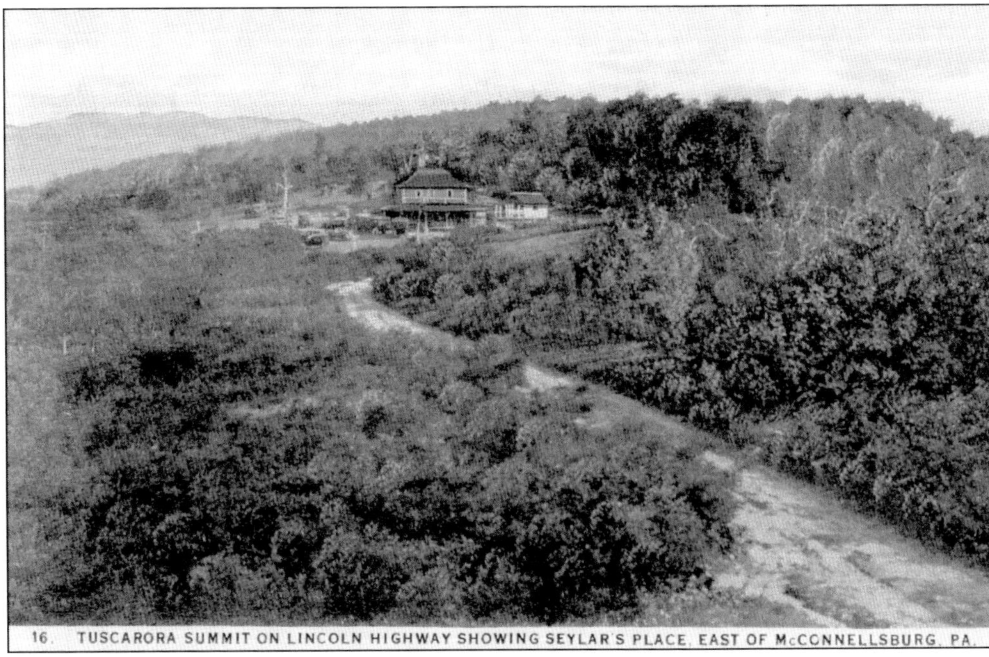

Like a host of other entrepreneurs, Leslie "Doc" Seylar saw there was money to be made along the Lincoln Highway and set up his place at Tuscarora Summit. Seylar's offered the usual roadside amenities like food, gas, souvenirs, water for overheated engines, and cabins where travelers could spend the night.

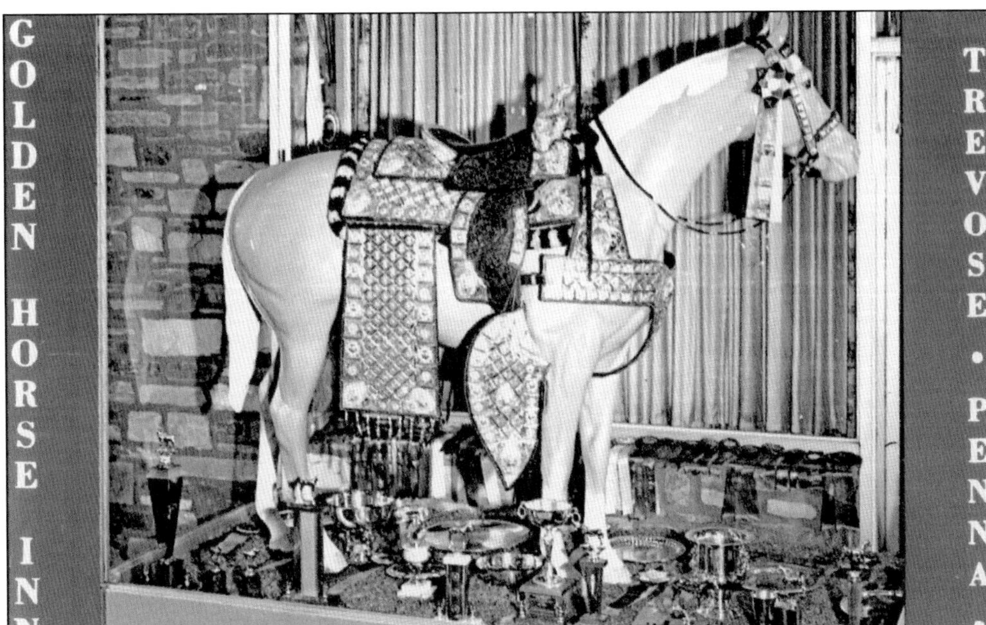

The Golden Horse Inn in Trevose, Bucks County, was a popular place known for its prime rib. The inn's name is derived from the nationally known champion golden Palomino horses, which the owners bred on their nearby farm.

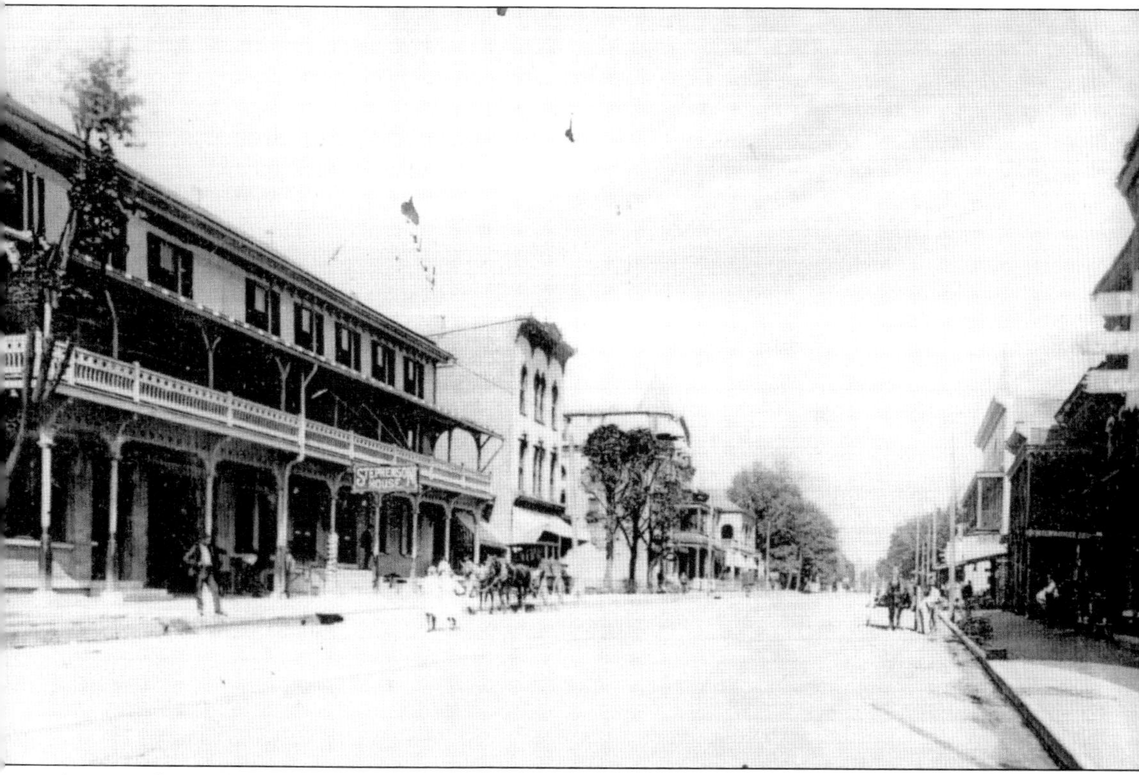

The Lincoln Highway's route through Coatesville in Chester County passed the Stephenson House, shown here at left. This large structure later became the Grand Hotel. Coatesville is probably best known for the Lukens Steel Corporation, once the county's largest employer.

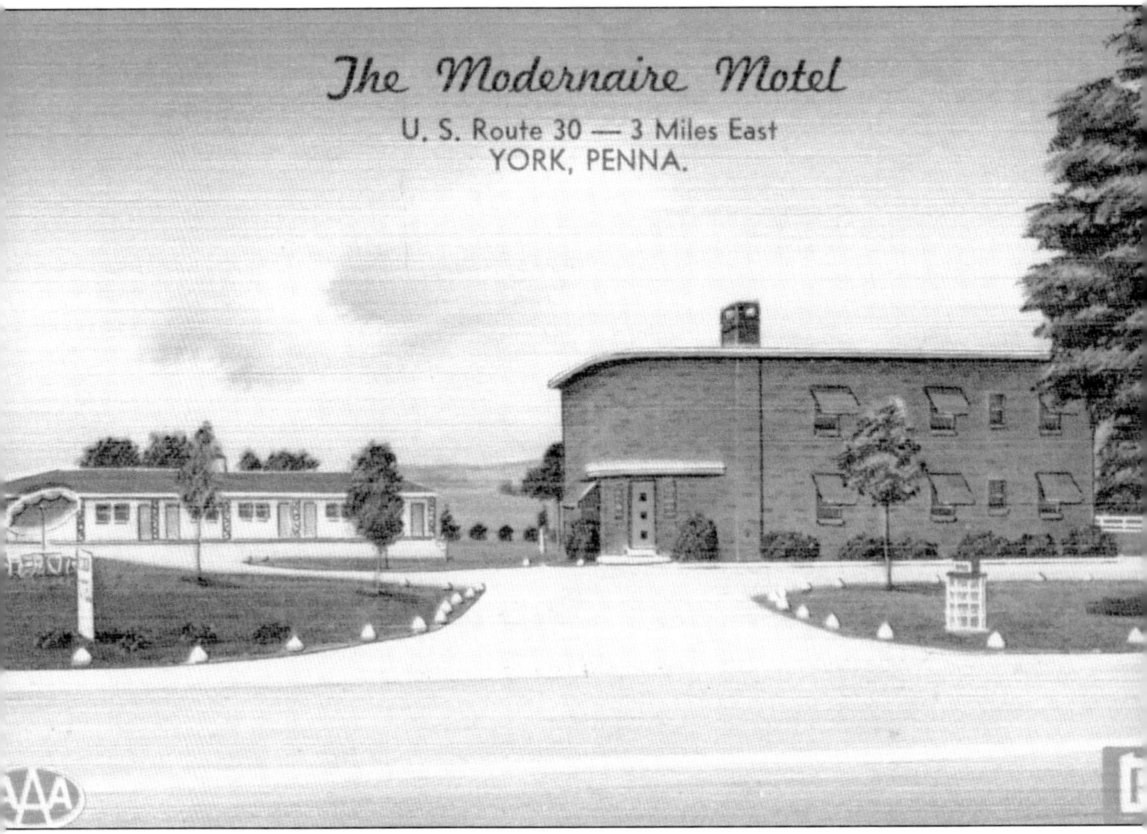

The Modernaire Motel, at 3311 East Market Street in York, obviously took its name to advertise its optional air-conditioning. It offered the usual amenities such as television or radio and modern rooms with private baths. Unlike many establishments from the highway's golden era, the Modernaire Motel continues to serve the traveling public.

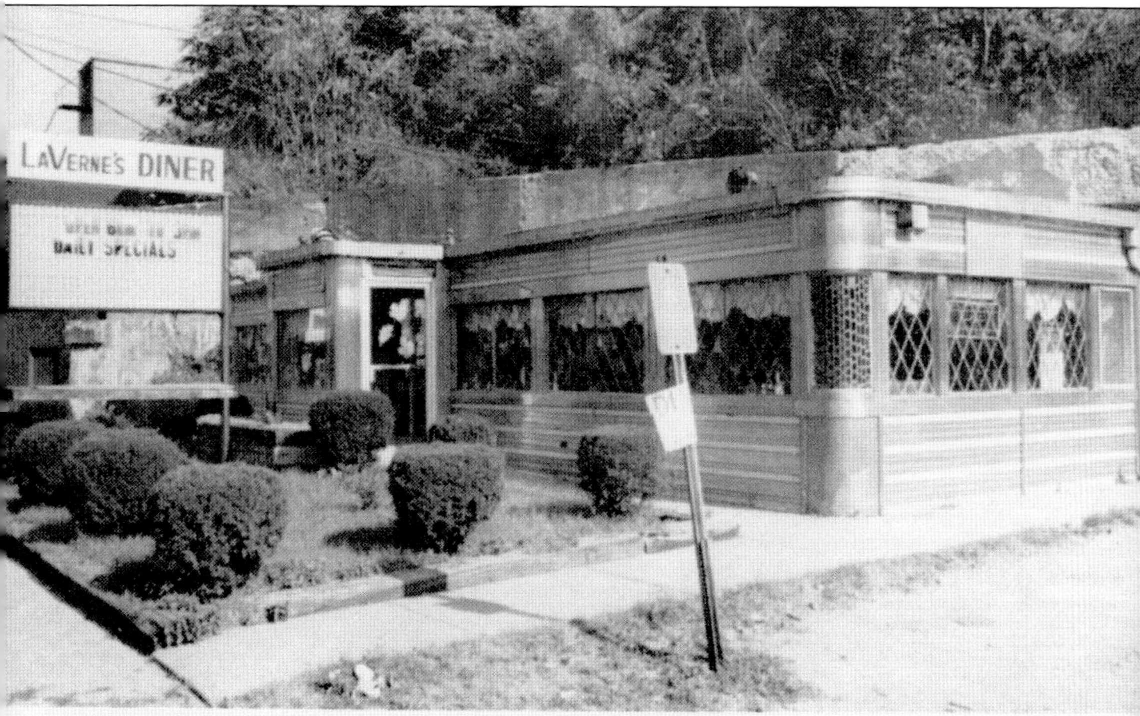

LAVERNE'S (BLUE DELL) DINER: WEST END: PITTSBURGH, PA

Laverne's Blue Dell Diner, a 1959 Silk City brand, stood along U.S. Route 30 at the west end of Pittsburgh. The diner had been moved to this site from another location along the Lincoln Highway.

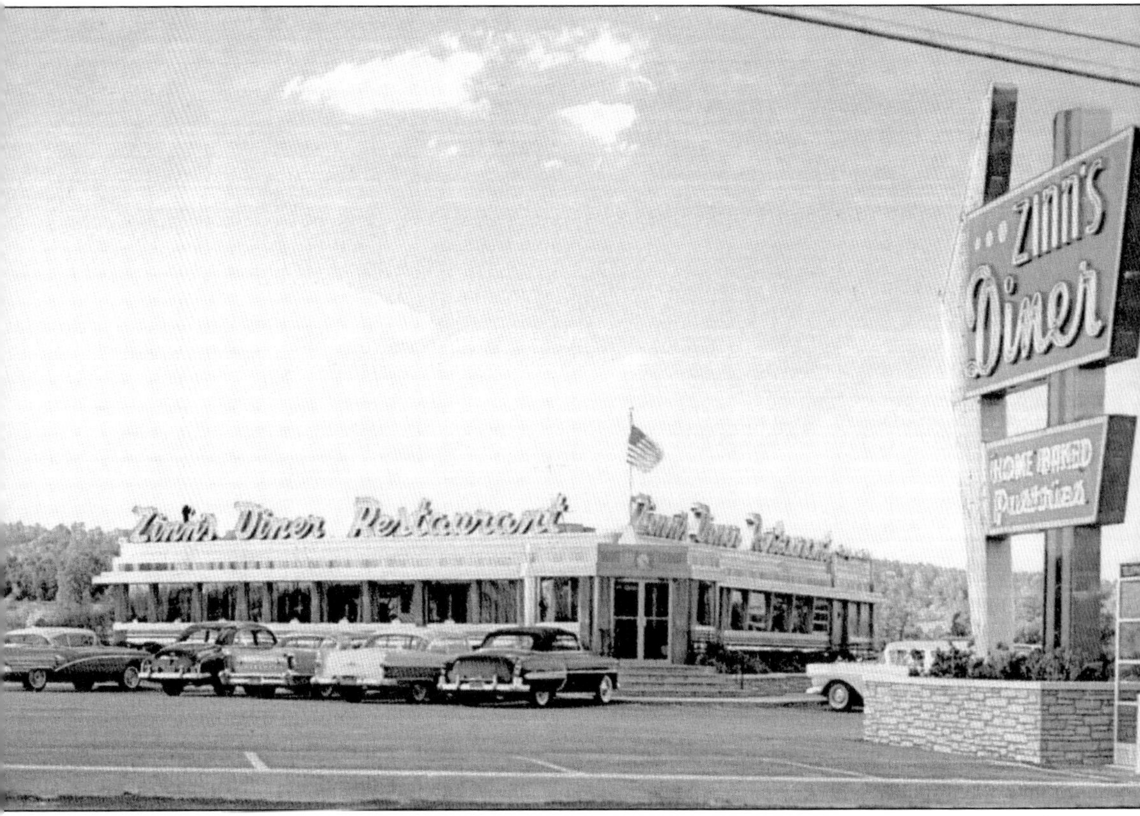

A 1956 Fodero brand, Zinn's Diner was located in Thorndale and had a seating capacity of 120. In addition, the facility included two dining rooms that could hold up to 150 people and was famous for serving "fine foods in immaculate cleanliness." In 1966, the L-shaped diner was sold and renamed the Ingleside, which contained a banquet hall known as the Zinn Room. The diner continued to operate until late 2001. This roadside classic was sold and, on January 27, 2003, was dismantled and trucked to a temporary storage site near Lancaster. Today a WaWa convenience store occupies the spot once held by the diner.

Three

Grand View Point and the Ship Hotel

For many people familiar with roadside landmarks, October 26, 2001, was a sad day, for it was then that the Lincoln Highway's—and probably the country's—best-known attraction burned to the ground in what may have been an arson fire. The SS Grand View Point Ship Hotel, located 17 miles west of Bedford, was completely consumed by the fast-moving blaze, and firefighters could do little more than spray water on the flaming building.

From a humble beginning as a roadside stand, the hotel and restaurant was built by owner Herbert Paulson, a lover of the sea, on the steep side of Mount Ararat. Apparently the commonwealth of Pennsylvania opposed this site, as officials told Paulson they feared the building would set sail down the mountainside. Paulson would not be dissuaded, however, and told the critics that if they refused to permit construction, they could buy the land from him. He built his first lodging on the site and, a year later, expanded the business into a four-story hotel with a castle theme.

With the popularity of the highway increasing, Paulson decided to enlarge his business again, and the famous Ship Hotel was born. One of the reasons he decided on a ship was that fog in the valley below at times looked like the ocean. It was not long before the ship became not only a popular stop along the highway, but a destination. Many have fond memories of dinners and other events that were held there.

As the years progressed, the landmark's days became numbered. The ship was sold in 1978. The new owners tried to bring the business back to life, but it was to no avail, and the vacant building fell prey to the elements. At one point, vagrants were reportedly living in the structure. According to Clara Gardner, Bedford resident and Paulson's granddaughter, the large telescope on the ship's bow had been removed and thrown down the mountain. Gardner has the distinction of being the only person born in the ship.

At one point, the Lincoln Highway Heritage Corridor attempted to purchase the building, but the owners were not interested in the $40,000 offered, as their asking price was $900,000. It was reportedly uninsured when the fire broke out.

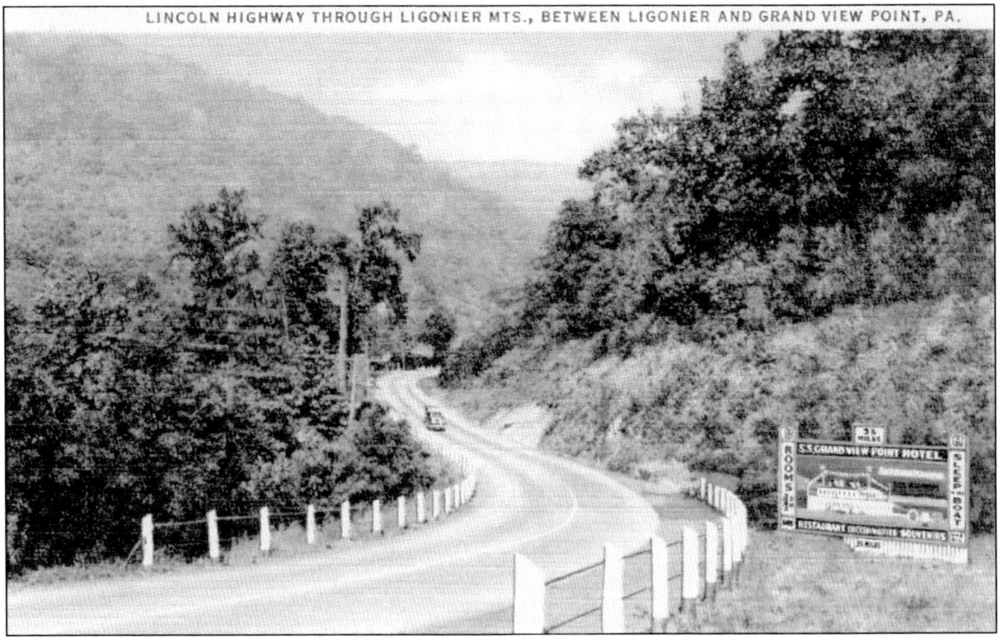

The large billboard in the lower right of this 1940s view advertises the SS Grand View Point Ship Hotel as being 35 miles from this location, between Ligonier and Grand View Point. According to the sign, the establishment offered rooms at $1 and up, along with chicken and waffle dinners in the ship's restaurant.

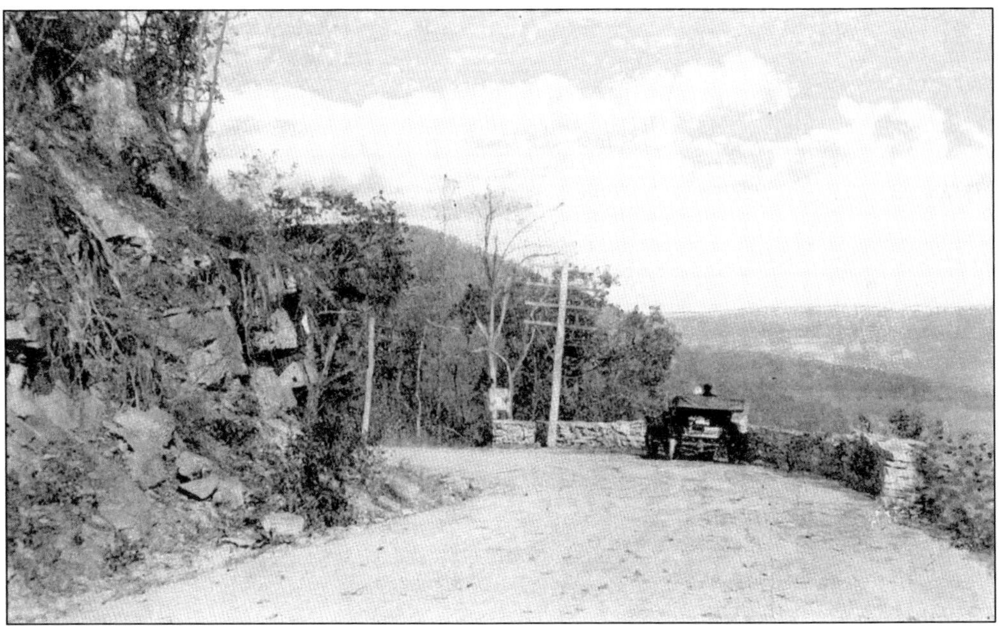

The spectacular view of three states and seven counties inspired Herbert Paulson to build the Grand View Point Hotel, and later the SS Grand View Point Ship Hotel. Before construction, the site was already well known by travelers and quickly became a popular stop along the Lincoln Highway.

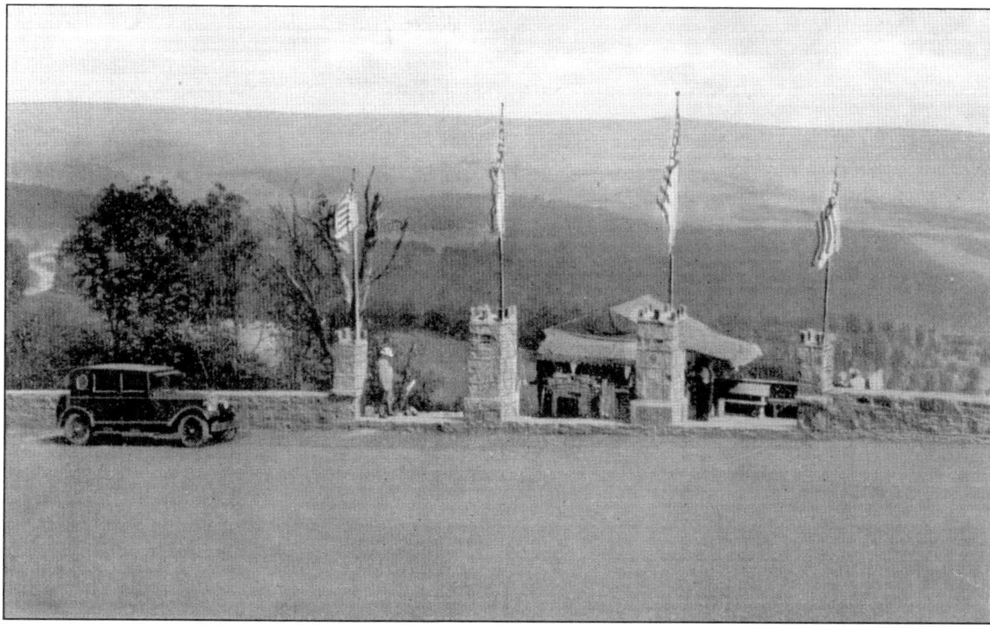

Growing from a small wayside stand, Grand View Point, 17 miles west of Bedford, became one of the country's premier roadside tourist attractions. Location is everything, and with the point offering an incredible view, it was a natural site to start a business.

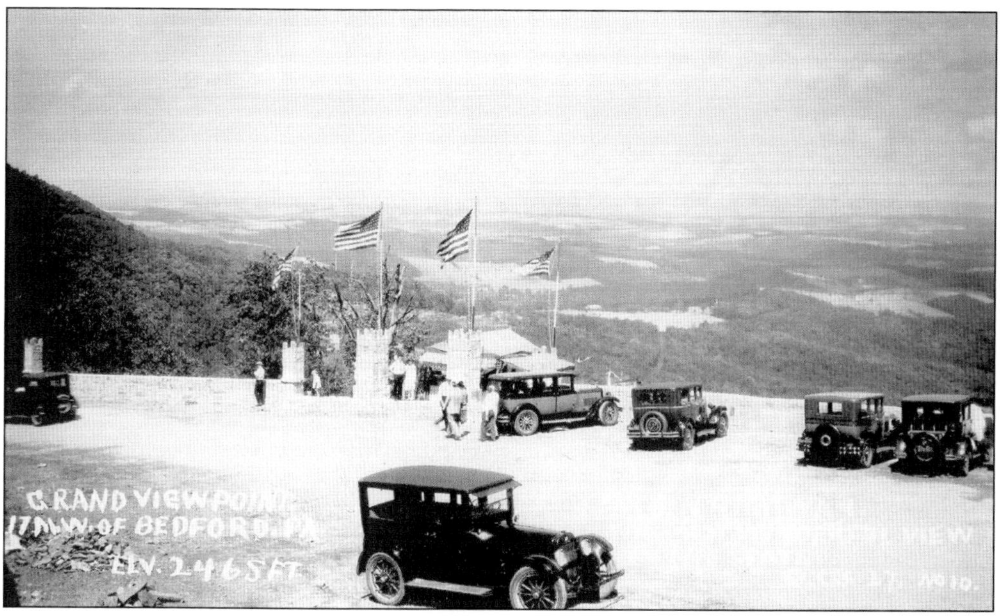

According to the description on this real-photo postcard, Grand View Point offered travelers the "most wonderful view in the state" from its elevation of 2,465 feet above sea level. Several years later, the small stand in the foreground would be replaced by the Grand View Point Hotel and later still, the famous "Steamship of the Allegheny Mountains."

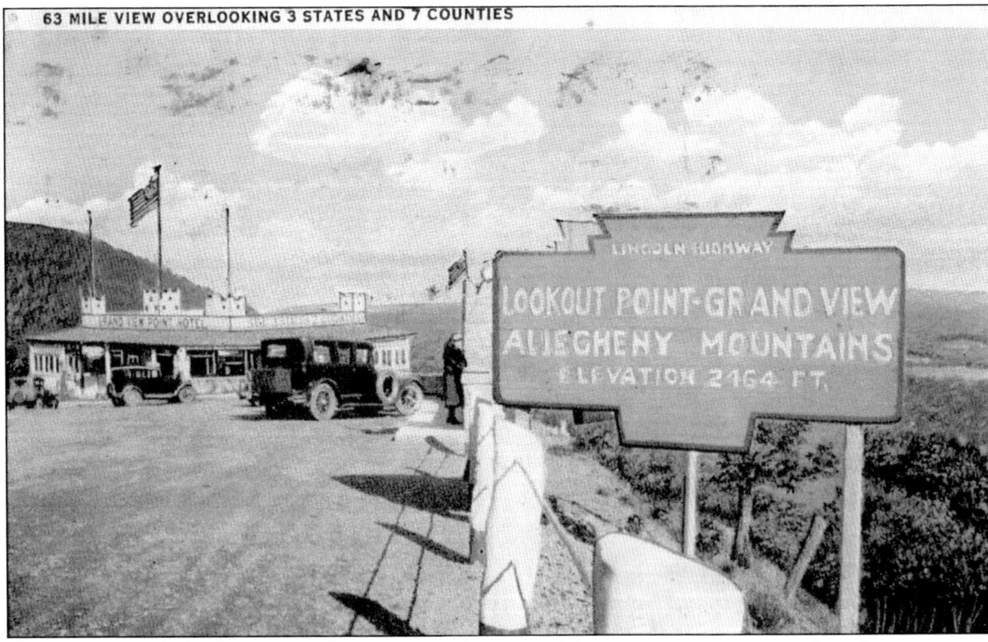

This postcard view of the Grand View Point Hotel was mailed in 1933, after the SS Grand View Point Ship Hotel was built. The description states that the location offered a 63-mile view overlooking three states and seven counties.

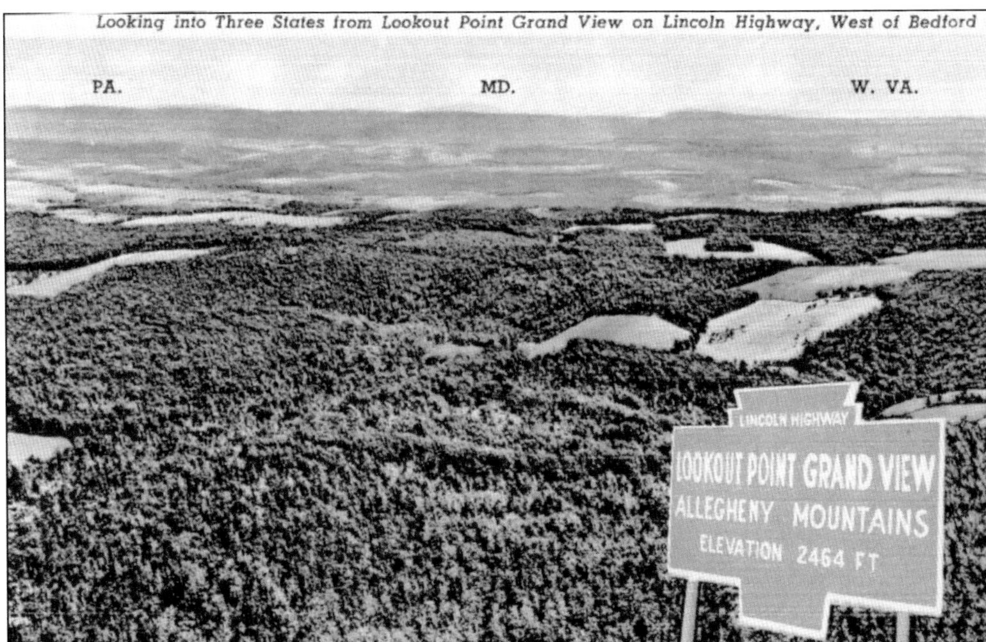

The famous view from Lookout Point shows portions of Pennsylvania, Maryland, and West Virginia. Herbert Paulson knew that this would be the ideal place for a roadside stop, and judging by the popularity of his business, he was right.

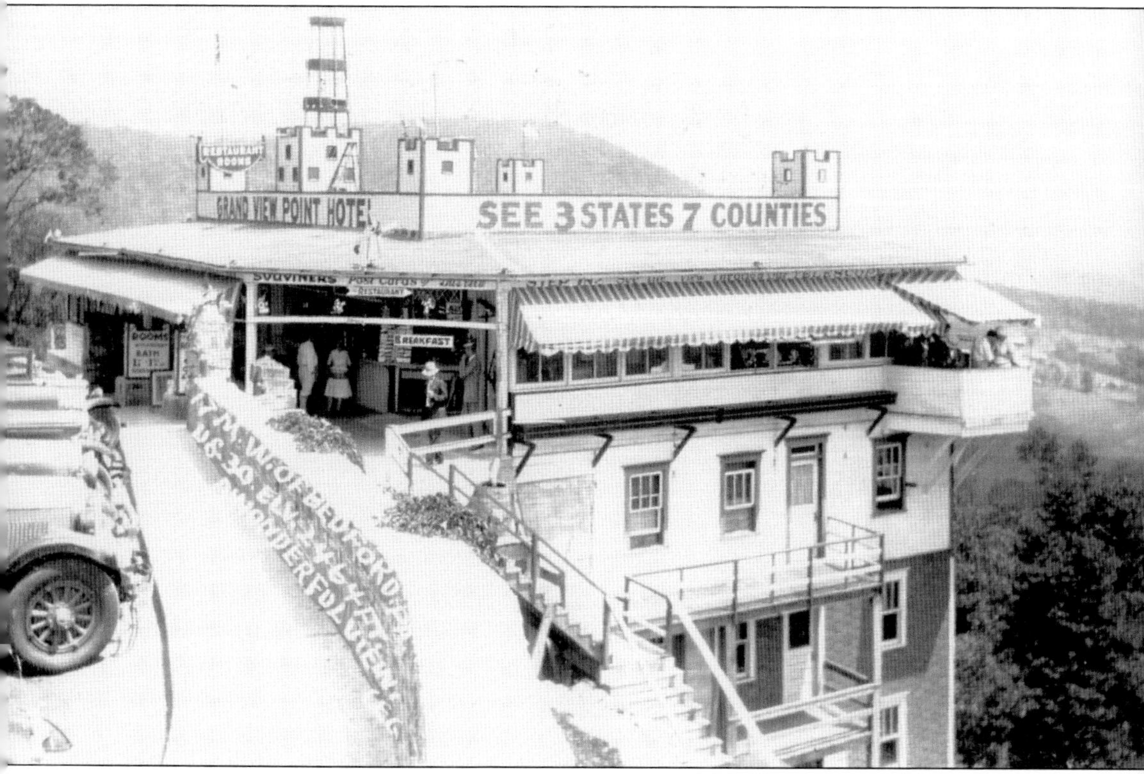

What grew to become the SS Grand View Point Ship Hotel was constructed around the Grand View Point Hotel, which had a castle theme. Already a popular stop along the Lincoln Highway, the building offered a "grand view" from a balcony on its west side. Some of the signs at the entrance advertised souvenirs and postcards. Along the eave of the building were the words "Step in. See the View Through Our Telescope."

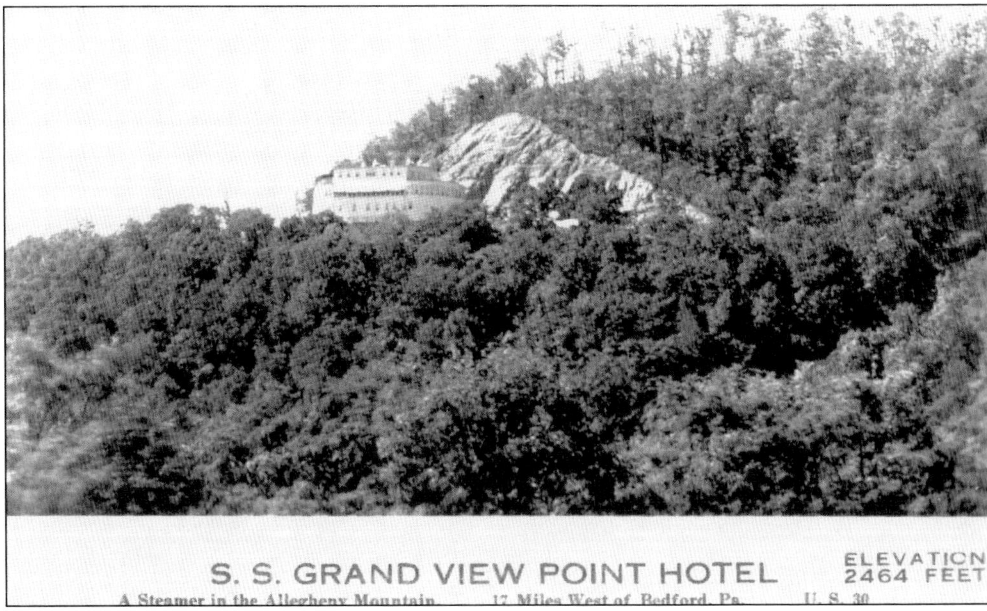

The SS Grand View Point Hotel clings to the side of Mount Ararat, 17 miles west of Bedford. More than 63 tons of steel were used for the base of the building, which cost $125,000 when constructed in 1932.

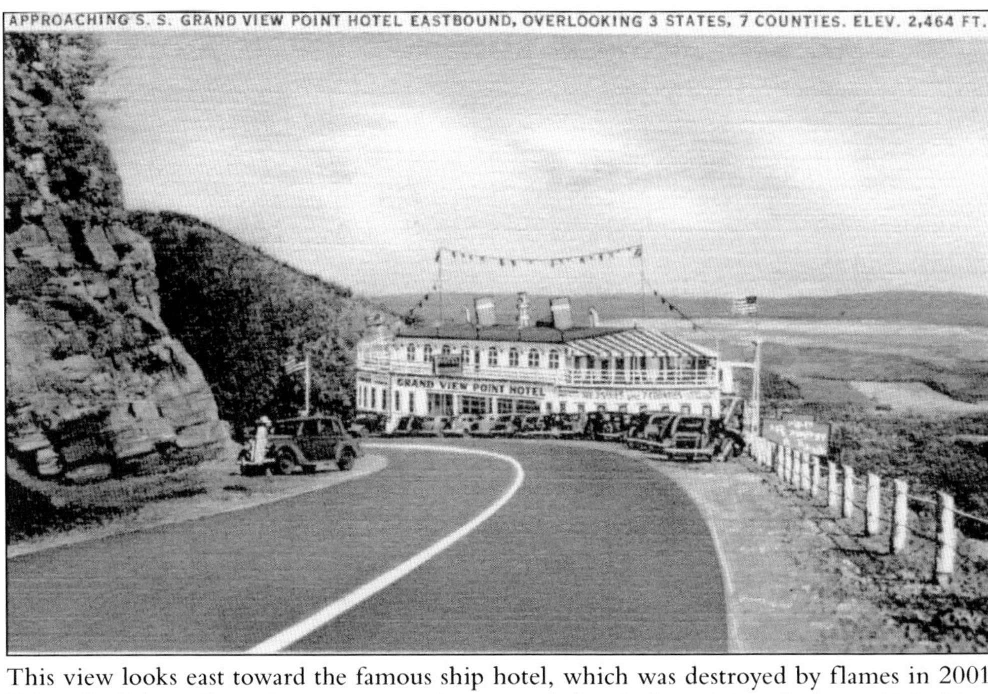

This view looks east toward the famous ship hotel, which was destroyed by flames in 2001. When firefighters from nine area companies responded to the late night call, they said the blaze was so bright that it looked like the sun was coming up.

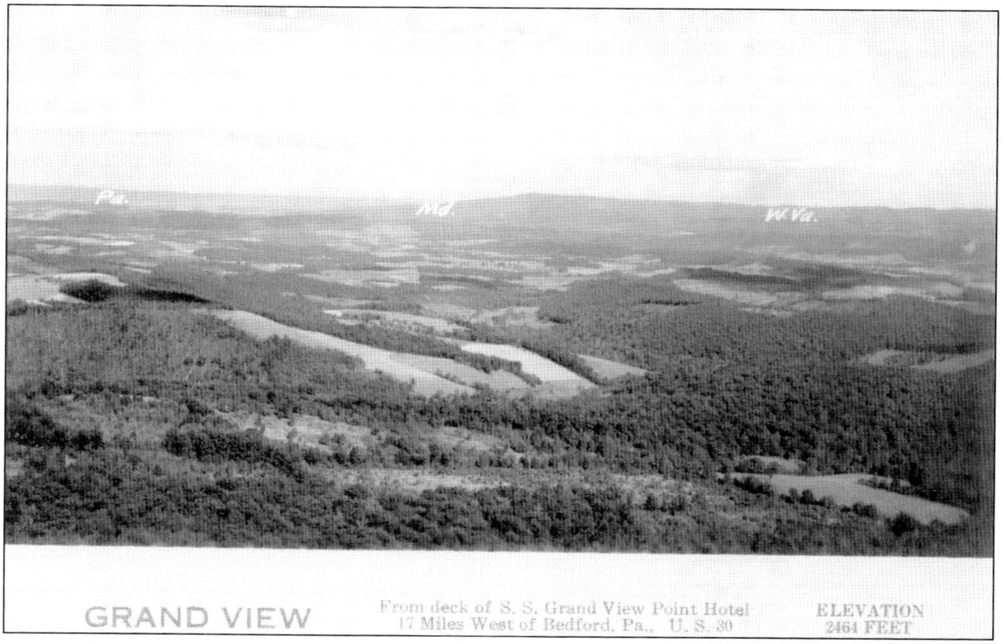

This real-photo postcard shows the view from the deck of the SS Grand View Point Hotel, likely the Lincoln Highway's most loved attraction. Although some people said it would not be practical to build on the site, Herbert Paulson moved forward to create the landmark.

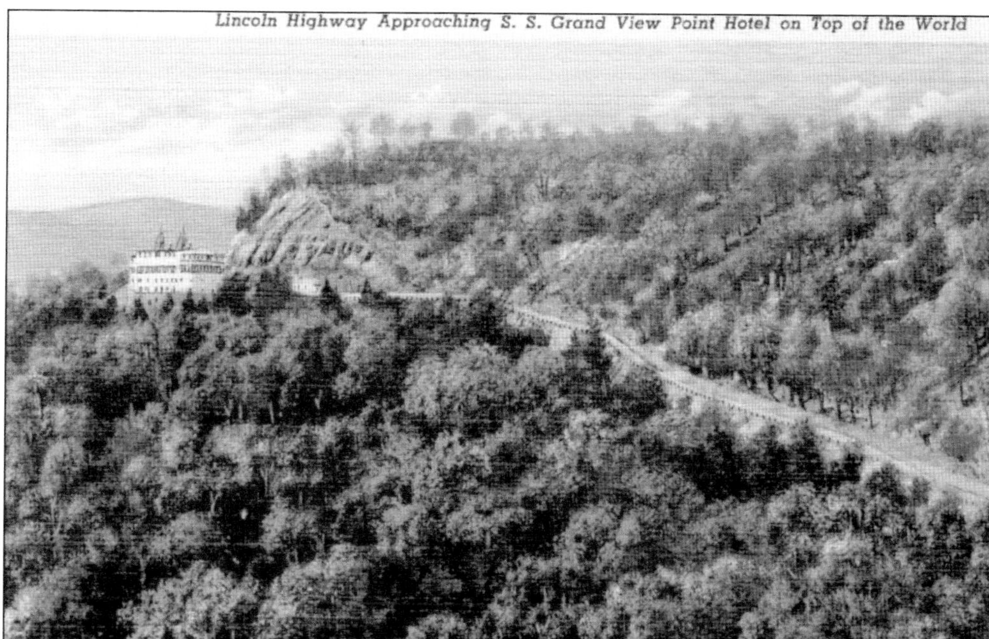

Sailing on the crest of the Allegheny Mountains, the SS Grand View Point Hotel was unmistakable as it was approached from the east. The hotel quickly became one of the highway's most popular attractions and drew tourists and travelers from all over the world.

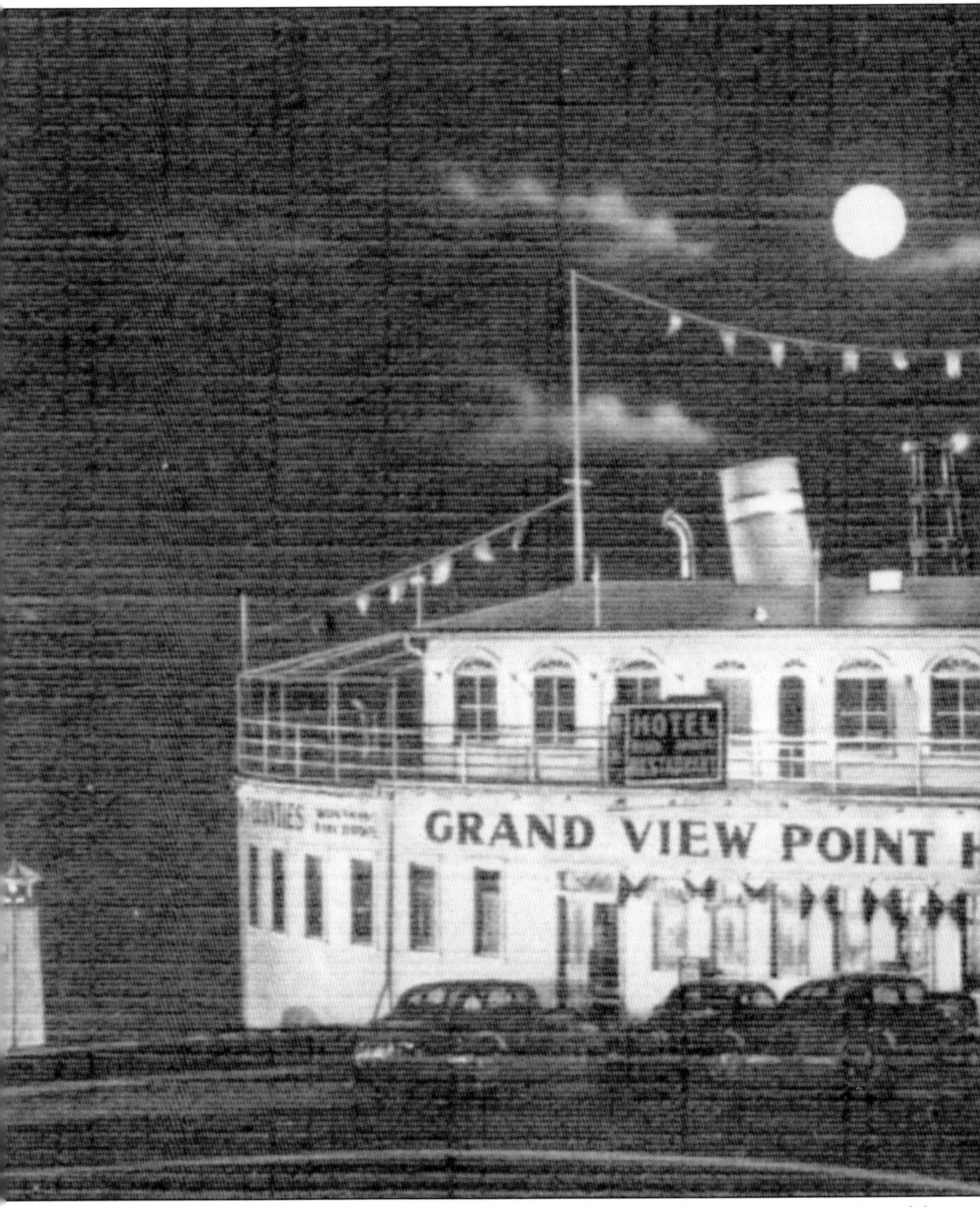

A full moon rises over the SS Grand View Point Ship Hotel, often called the Steamship of the Alleghenies. During an interview several years before it was destroyed by fire, Bedford resident Clara Gardner, who was born in the ship, said several large I-beams that anchored the structure to the mountainside had started to deteriorate. In the ship's glory days, it offered lodging for 49 in first class, second class, and steerage rooms. Although it remained a popular attraction after

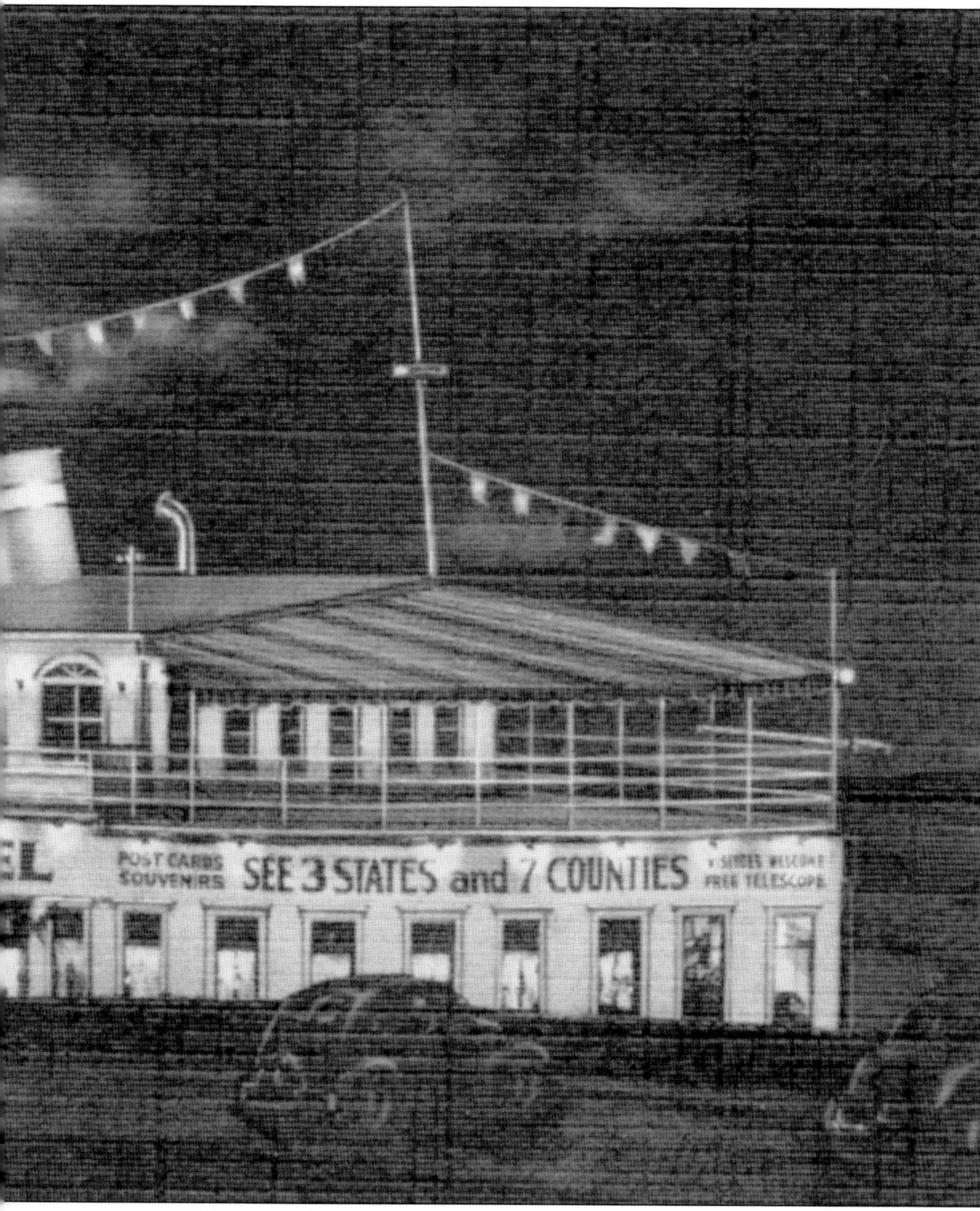

the completion of the Pennsylvania Turnpike, business fell off and following the 1973 death of owner Herbert Paulson, the establishment was sold. The new owner covered the exterior with wood and renamed the place Noah's Ark. Ironically this point on the mountain is called Ararat. Later the Lincoln Highway Heritage Corridor, based in nearby Ligonier, unsuccessfully attempted to purchase and preserve the historic roadside building.

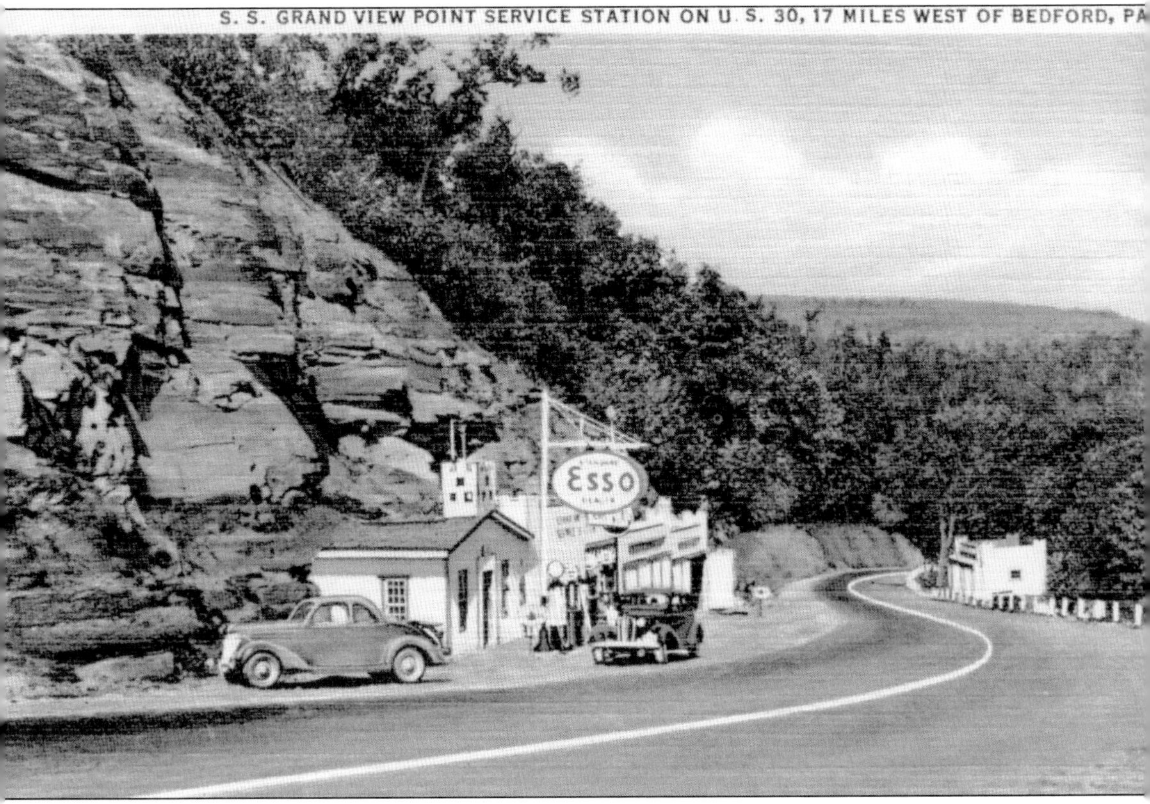

Just east of the ship hotel, and on the opposite side of the road, was the Grand View Point Service Station, which offers Esso gas in this late-1930s view. In later years, the former service station became a petting zoo, but the business failed.

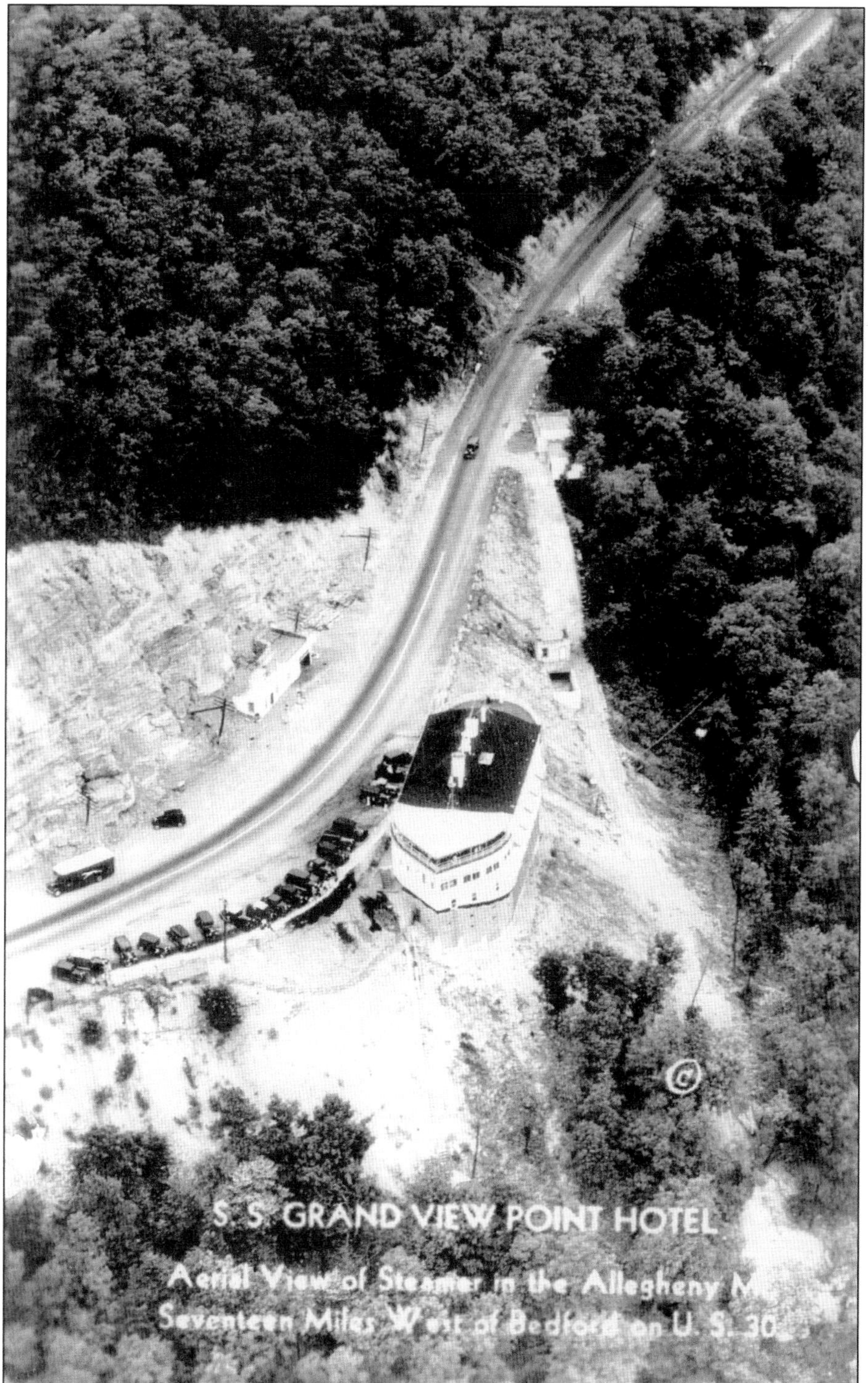

This aerial view of the ship hotel also shows the Grand View Point Service Station in the left foreground. Members of the nonprofit Lincoln Highway Heritage Corridor plan to erect a replica of the ship, which burned to the ground in 2001.

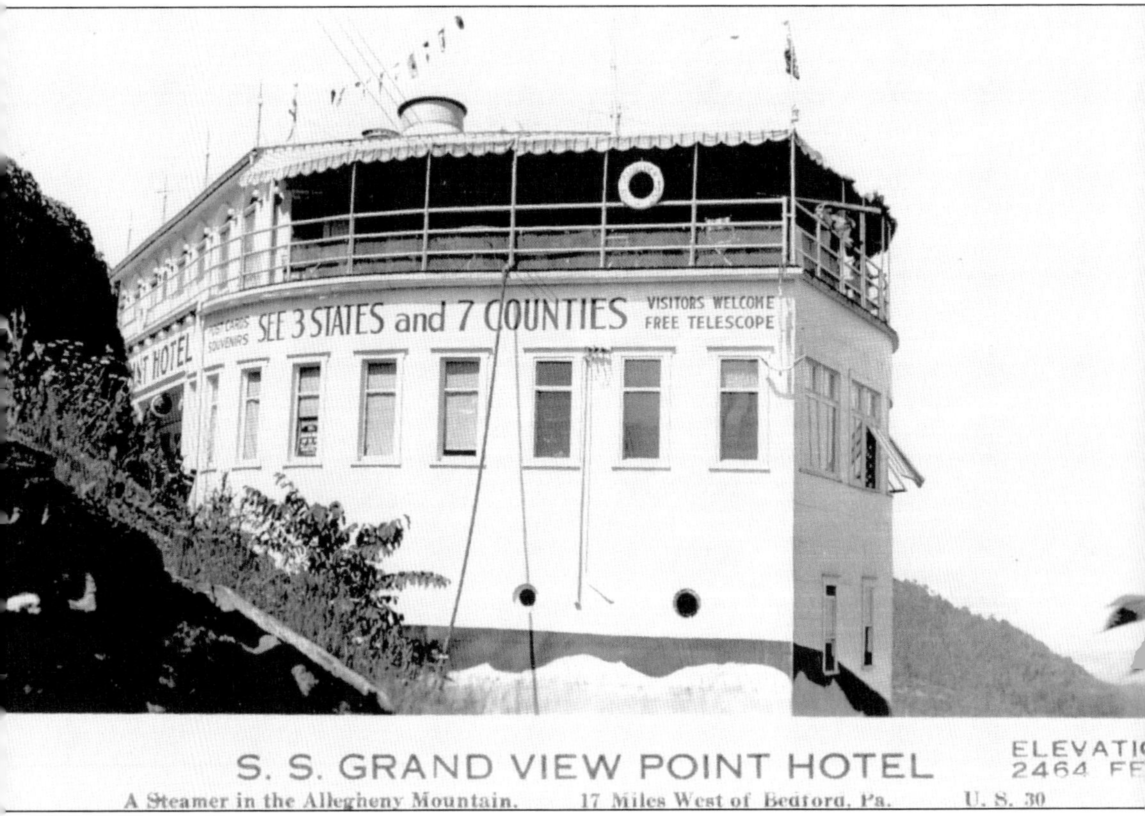

One of the best-known landmarks on any highway in the country, the SS Grand View Point Hotel attracted tourists from near and far. The establishment kept log books, which contained names of celebrities such as Greta Garbo, Tom Mix, and Henry Ford who stopped to visit the Steamship of the Alleghenies.

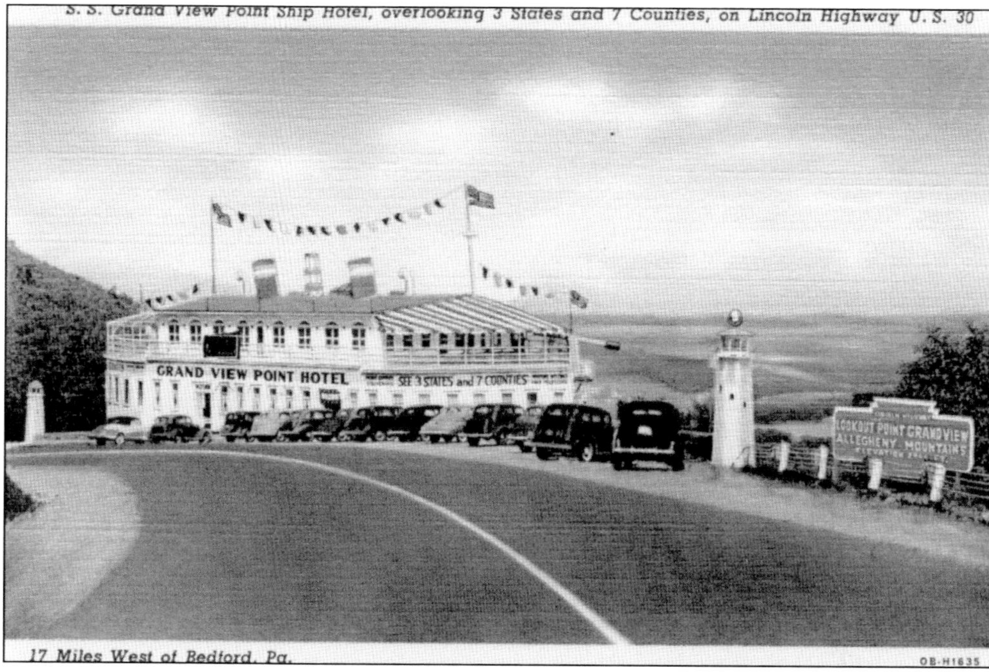

Herbert Paulson, owner of the SS Grand View Point Ship Hotel, carried the nautical theme by installing wooden lighthouses at each end of his establishment. On busy days, cars would line the Lincoln Highway on either side of the road, and often for a considerable distance east and west.

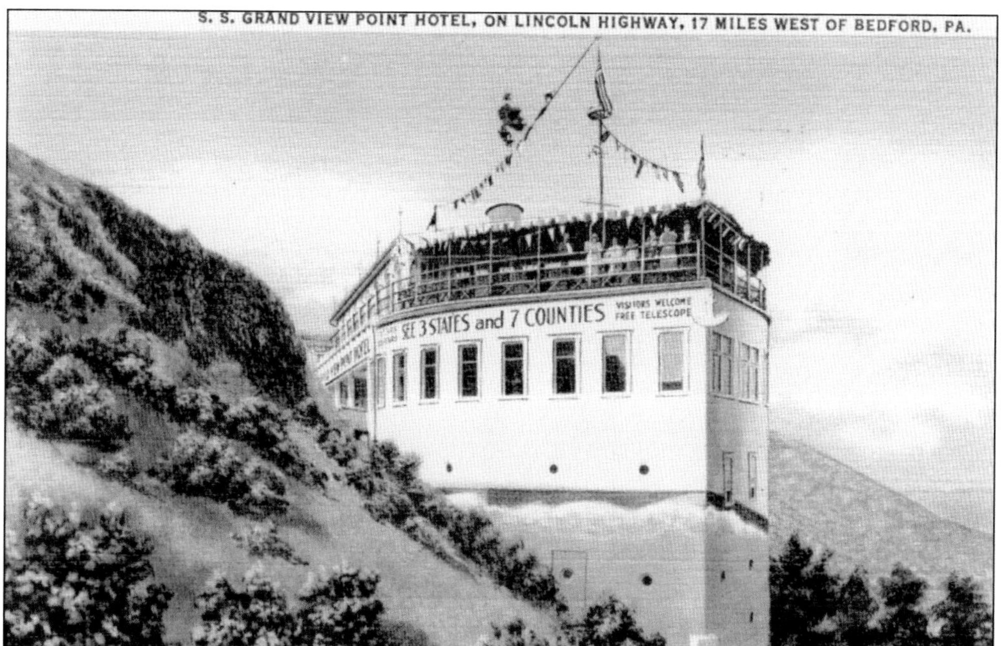

It was common for visitors to line the bow observation deck of the famous landmark, as shown in this 1940s view. Although it is now gone, many people still stop to admire the majestic vista from Grand View Point.

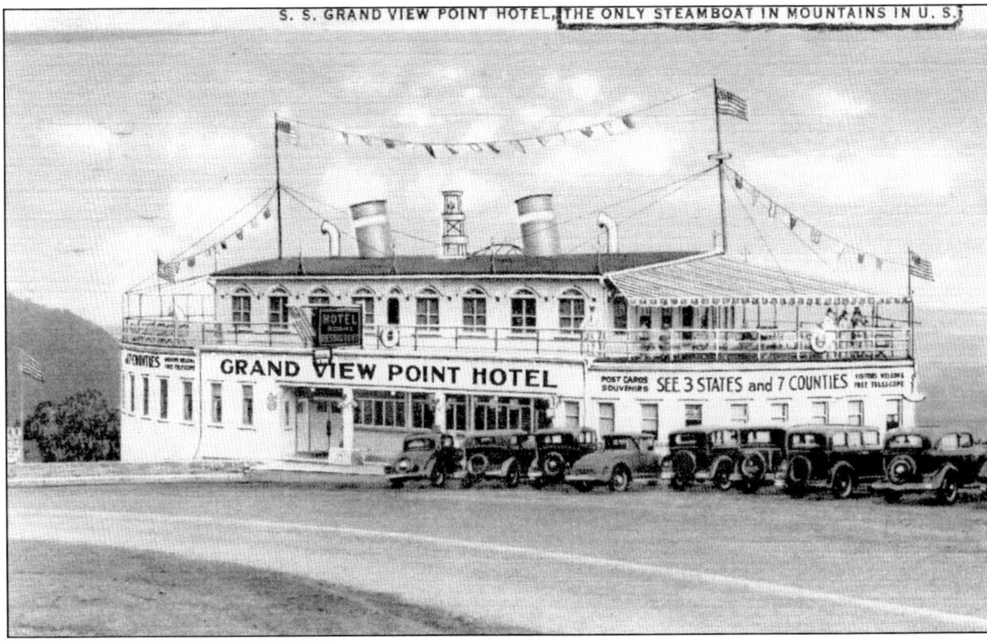

When "Captain" Herbert Paulson decided to enlarge the Grand View Point Hotel in 1931, he felt that a ship theme would be good because of his love of the sea. This earlier view shows the hotel before the front entrance was closed off.

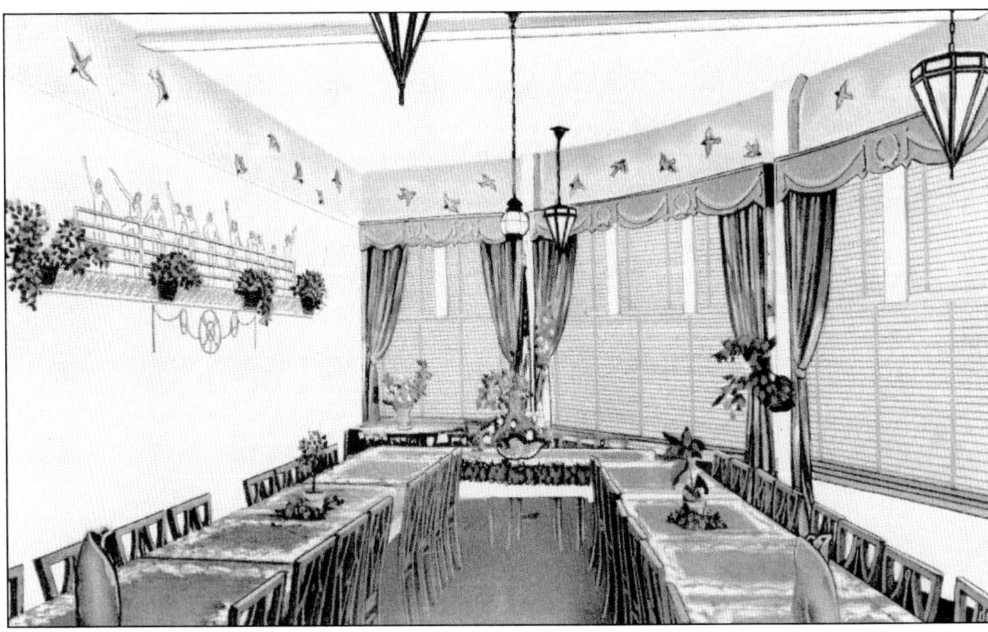

The ship hotel's elegant banquet room attracted a wide range of diners. Along with the many celebrities who visited the establishment, log books show that visitors arrived there from 72 foreign countries. The hotel was also a popular place for high school proms.

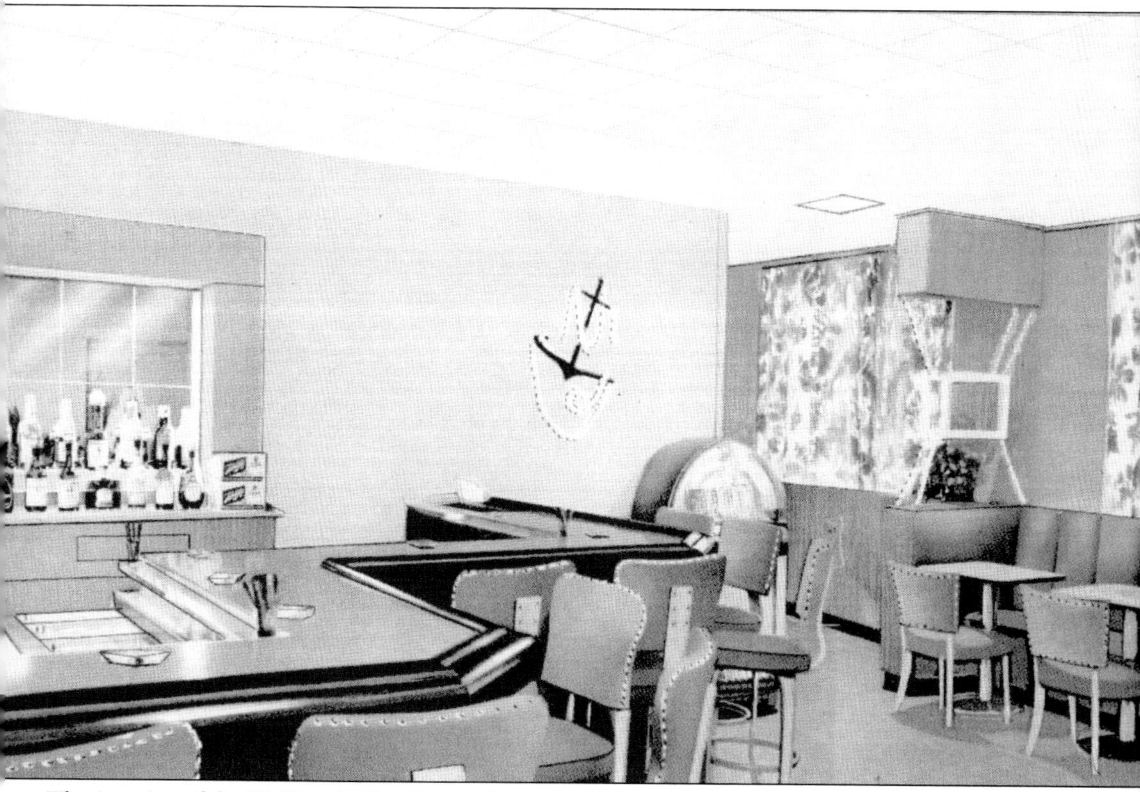

The interior of the SS Grand View Point Ship Hotel carried on the nautical theme in the Coral Room. Over the years, the ship was visited by a long list of celebrities, including Clara Bow, Joan Crawford, and Thomas Edison.

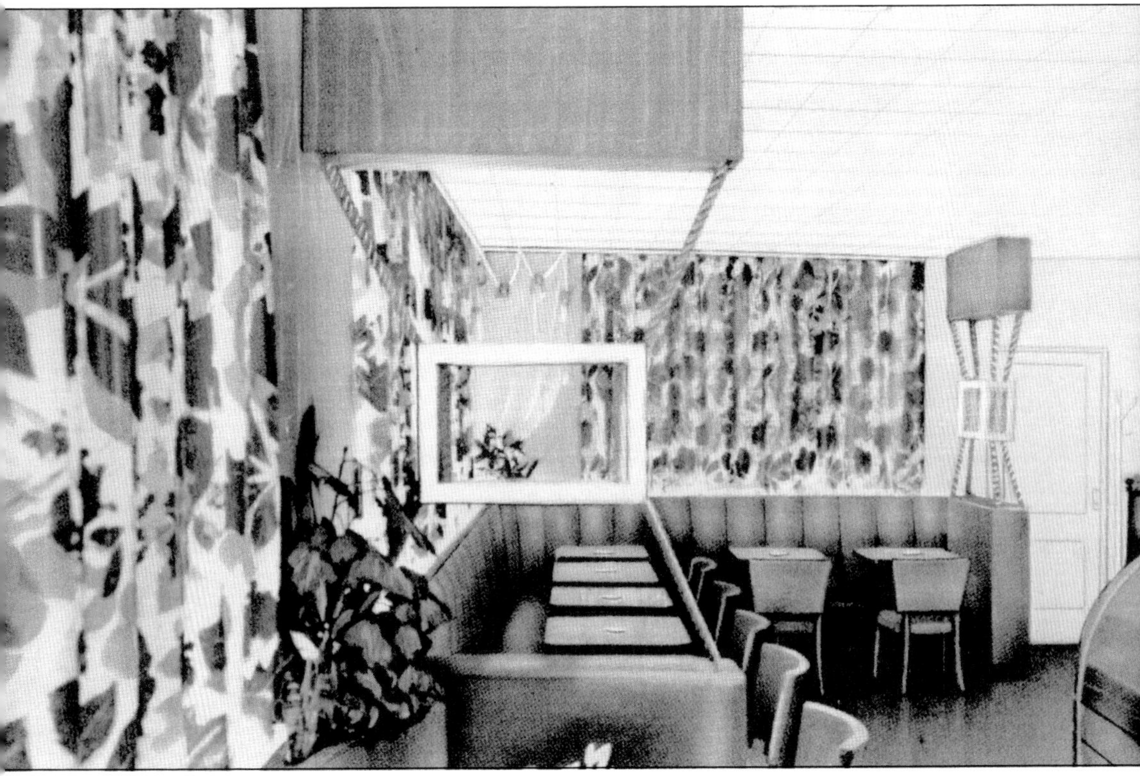

The entrance to the ship's Coral Room Cocktail Lounge reveals comfortable furnishings. After the business closed, the seating and other interior objects from the lounge and banquet room were reportedly sold.

Four

Along the Highway

When one thinks of travel by today's standards, interstate highways, turnpikes, and limited-access roads immediately come to mind. Even finding directions has become a simple task, and many travelers no longer need to rely on maps but trust the Internet to provide the shortest route between two points. But this was not always the case. There was a time when the journey was half the fun. Unlike the modern interstate system, the Lincoln Highway presented an ever-changing scene of roadside businesses, historic sites, and an endless list of places known as "tourist traps."

Locating a business along the highway almost guaranteed success, and in the earliest days, many communities lobbied for the route to pass through their town, which would ensure growth. Prosperity, however, did not last forever. While some of these businesses remain, many have been relegated to history and live on only in memory and an occasional postcard. It was travel that created them and, ironically, also caused their demise.

After the Pennsylvania Turnpike—"America's Super Highway"—was completed, more and more motorists started making use of the famous limited-access highway, leaving many Lincoln Highway businesses with half of their former traffic. Some, like the ship hotel, held on for a considerable length of time, while others closed their doors almost immediately.

The route was also home to a number of historic sites, which continue to attract visitors today. Ligonier's Lincoln Highway Heritage Corridor is doing its part to preserve the route's past.

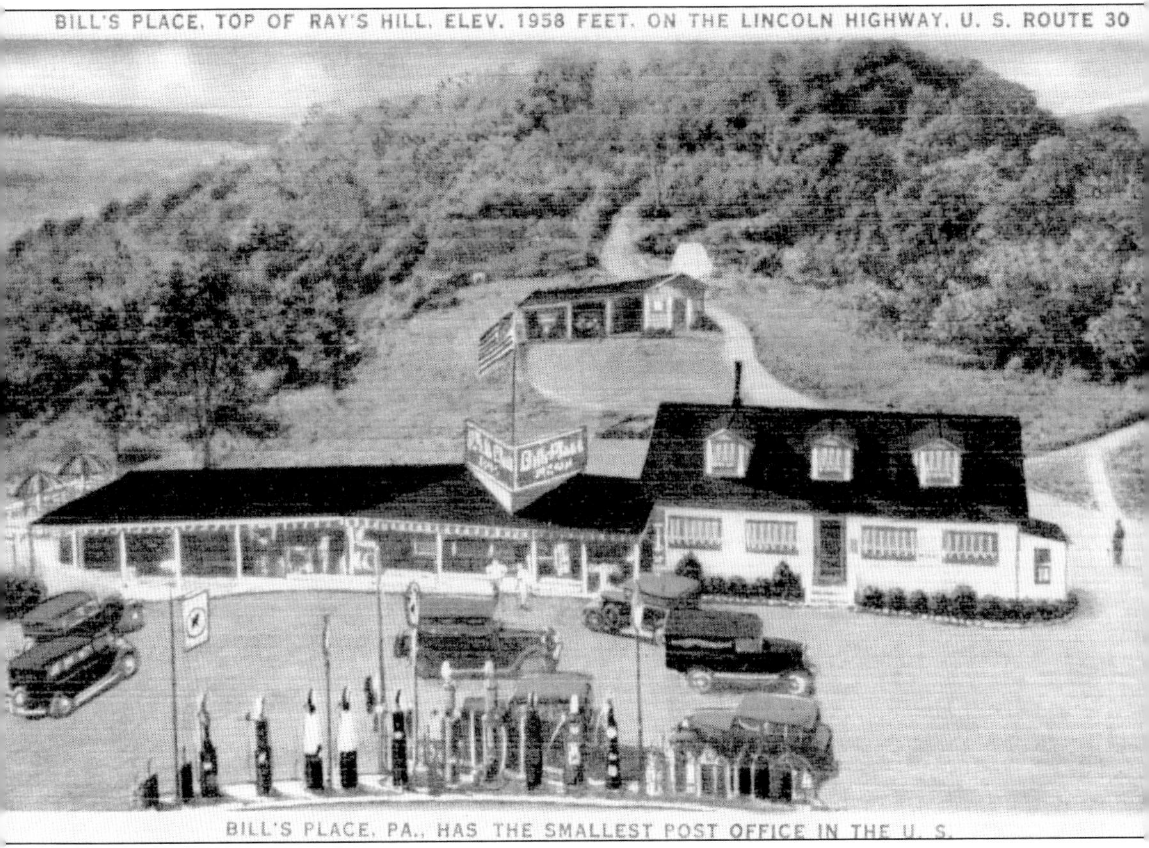

At least 10 gas pumps are visible in this *c.* 1952 view of Bill's Place atop Ray's Hill, 11 miles east of Everett. Opened as a small stand by William Wakefield on June 10, 1923, the roadside stop grew to become an attraction in its own right. Wakefield reportedly sold a variety of items, ranging from lunch to souvenirs and, of course, gas and oil. The establishment was sold in the early 1960s and razed in 1968, when the nearby Pennsylvania Turnpike made a huge cut to bypass Ray's Hill Tunnel.

Bill's Place in Fulton County boasted a population of only six and the smallest post office in the country. The inside dimensions of the building were four feet and one-half inches by seven feet three inches. Although it was a popular attraction, the facility, which opened on May 2, 1935, was discontinued by the United States Postal Service on November 30, 1953.

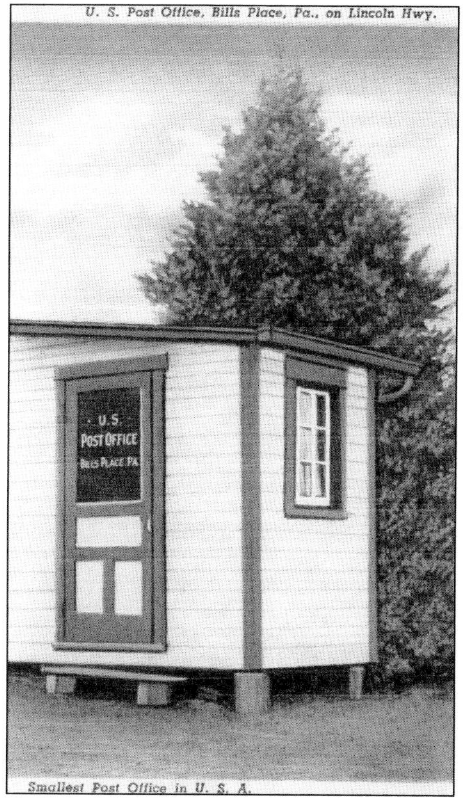

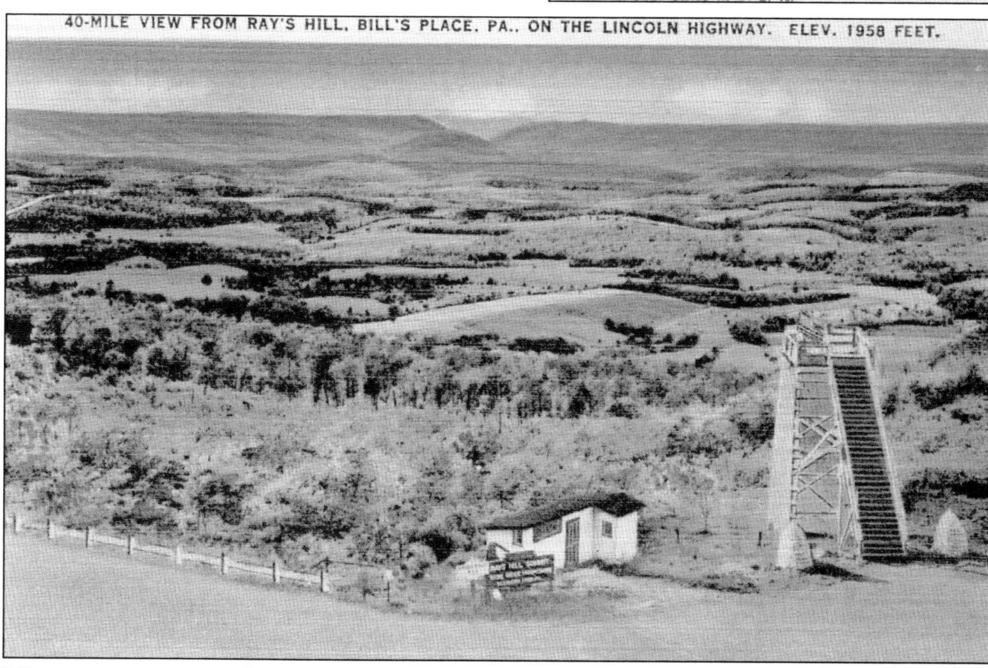

Like many operators of mountaintop roadside stands, William Wakefield built an observation tower to attract business to Bill's Place. This postcard states that visitors could enjoy a 40-mile view from the tower's 1,958-foot elevation.

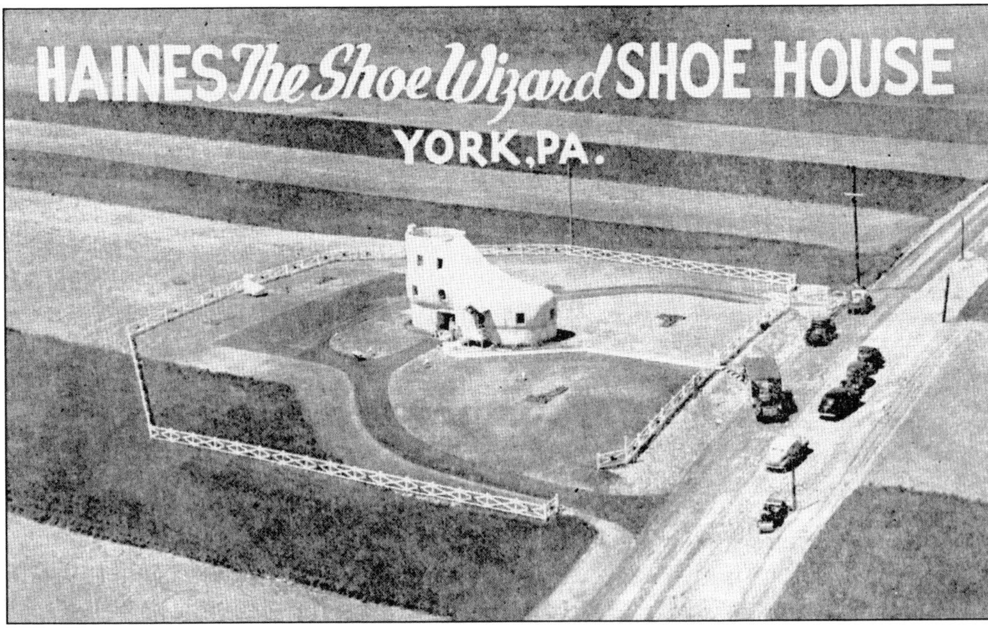

Roadside buildings came in all shapes and sizes, as evidenced by the famous Haines Shoe House, four miles east of York. The building contained a living room, three bedrooms, two baths, a kitchen, and a garage. It was built in 1948 by Mahlon "Colonel" Haines, who was also known as "the Shoe Wizard."

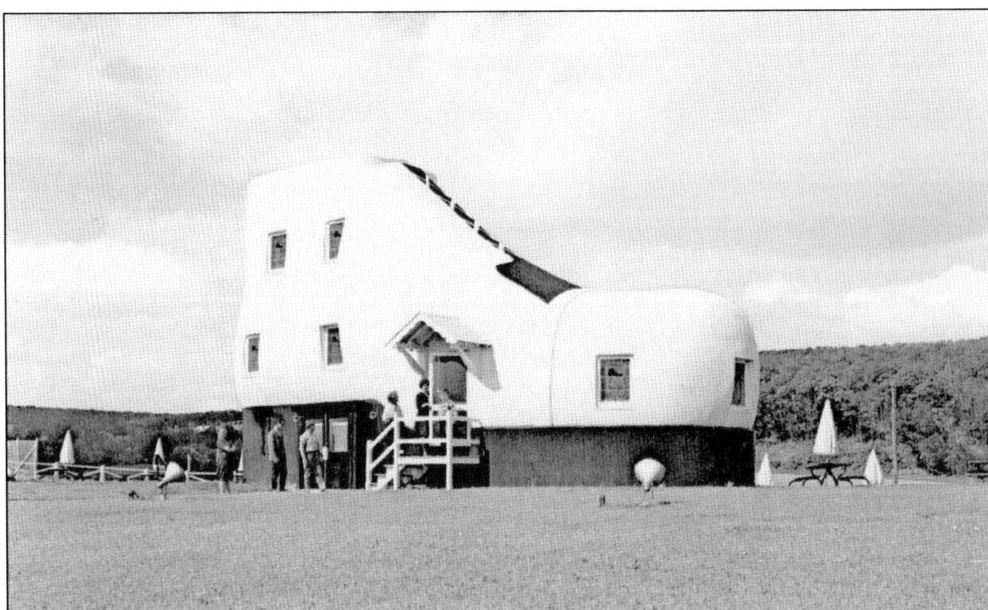

The Haines Shoe House appears during the time it functioned as an ice cream shop, smorgasbord, and gift shop. According to the advertisement on the reverse of this card, customers could create their own ice-cream sundaes. Unlike many other roadside landmarks, this unique building remains standing.

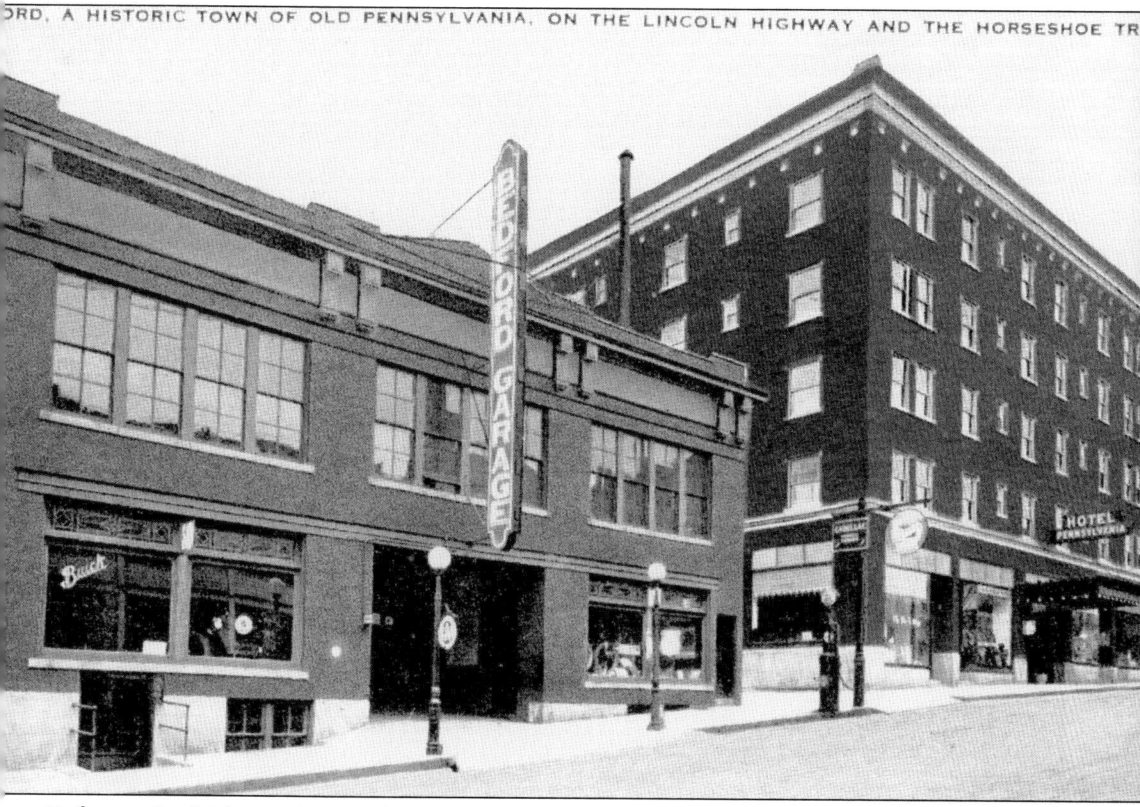

Before major highways bypassed towns, it was common for facilities to locate right along the main street, usually in the business district. This *c.* 1926 postcard shows how businesses could often complement each other. To the right is the Hotel Pennsylvania, while the Bedford Garage, advertised to be "known from coast to coast," is at the left. Another garage, Kings, was located across the street and was reportedly fireproof. In the window at the lower left of the Bedford Garage is a Buick advertisement. In the early days of the Lincoln Highway, towns often competed for the route, as it was excellent for local business.

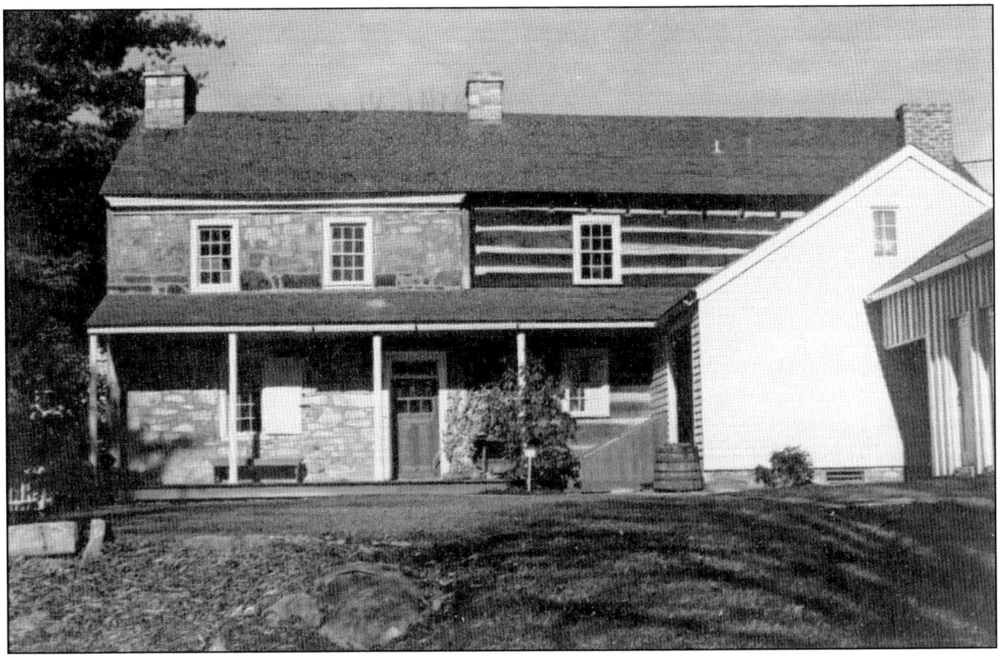

Laughlintown's Compass Inn, along the Lincoln Highway three miles east of Ligonier, is a landmark listed on the National Register of Historic Places. Dating to 1799, the former stagecoach stop now houses the Ligonier Valley Historical Society Museum, which restored the building to its original condition.

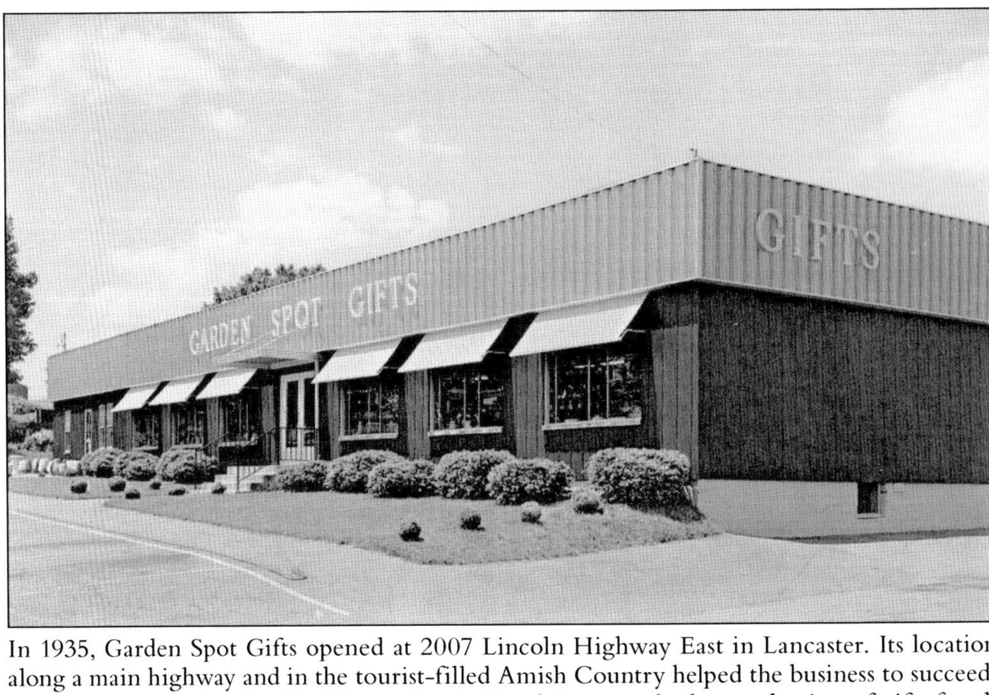

In 1935, Garden Spot Gifts opened at 2007 Lincoln Highway East in Lancaster. Its location along a main highway and in the tourist-filled Amish Country helped the business to succeed. It offered a "complete line" of Pennsylvania Dutch items and a large selection of gifts for all occasions. Once also known as the Garden Spot China Company, it has since closed.

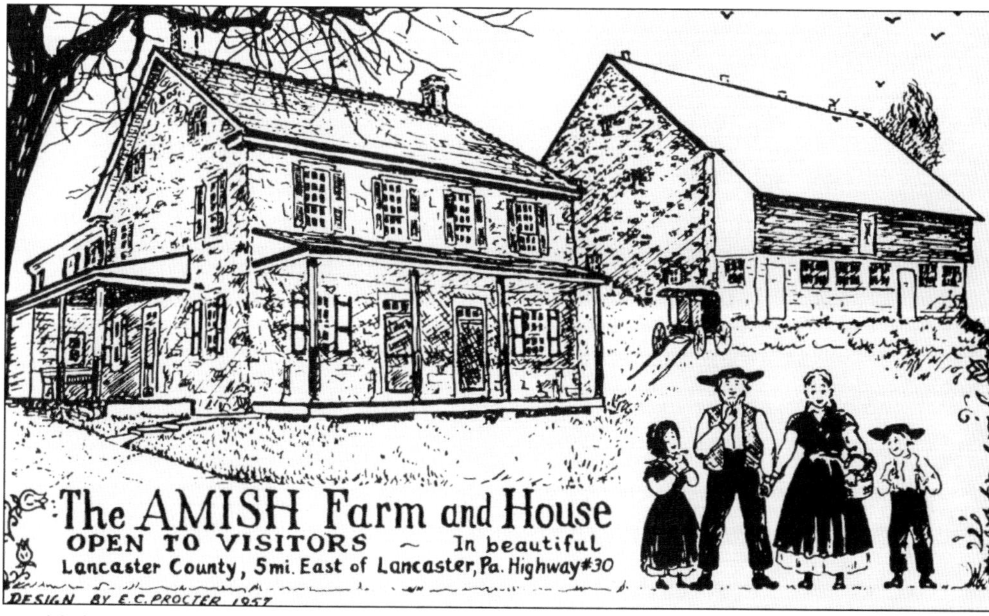

Established in 1955, the Amish Farm and House was one of the earlier Dutch Country tourist attractions. The business offered, and continues to provide, a glimpse into the lives of the Old Order Amish who populate the area, along with locally produced items.

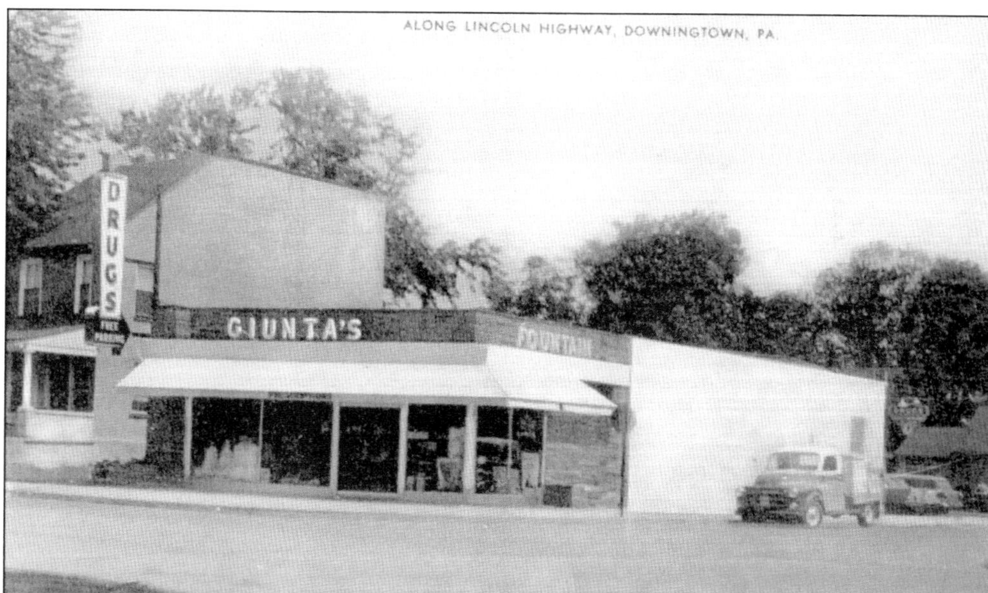

In many locations along the Lincoln Highway, business names have lived on into the days of the U.S. Route 30 era, as this 1940s view of Giunta's Drugs shows. Common of drugstores of its day, Giunta's offered fountain service and free parking to the rear. The Guinta name continues to live on in Downingtown, at Giunta's Family Market.

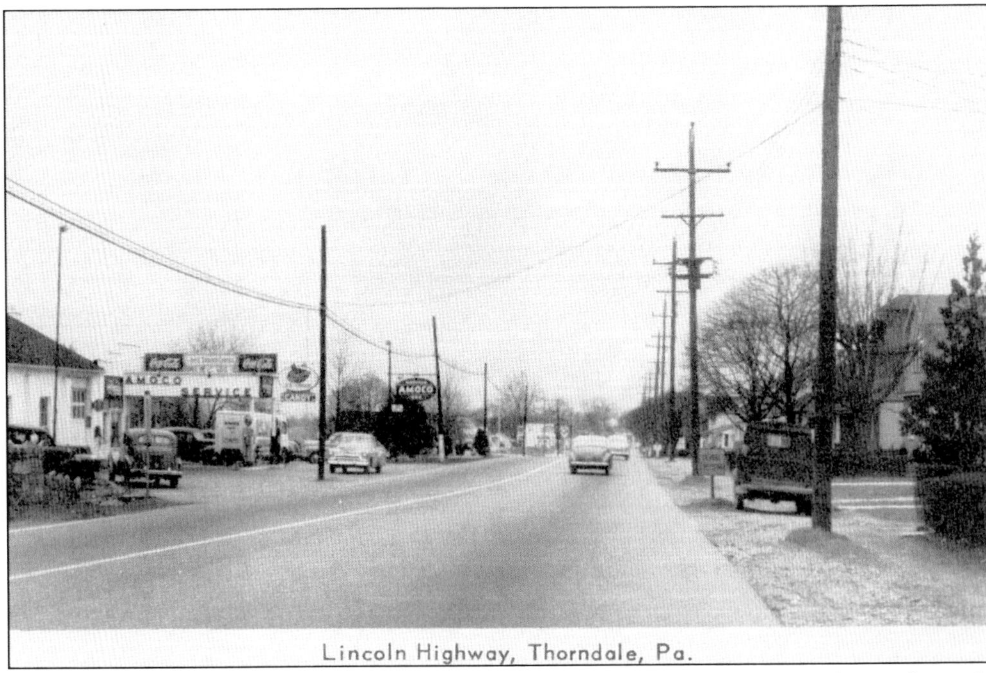

Typical of service stations of its day, Jon's Service Center, along the Lincoln Highway in Thorndale, Chester County, provided many needs to the motoring public. Along with selling Amoco fuel, the center had a repair garage and offered snacks, ice cream, Coca-Cola, and other travel necessities. Over the years, most businesses such as this have given way to self-service gas stations and convenience stores.

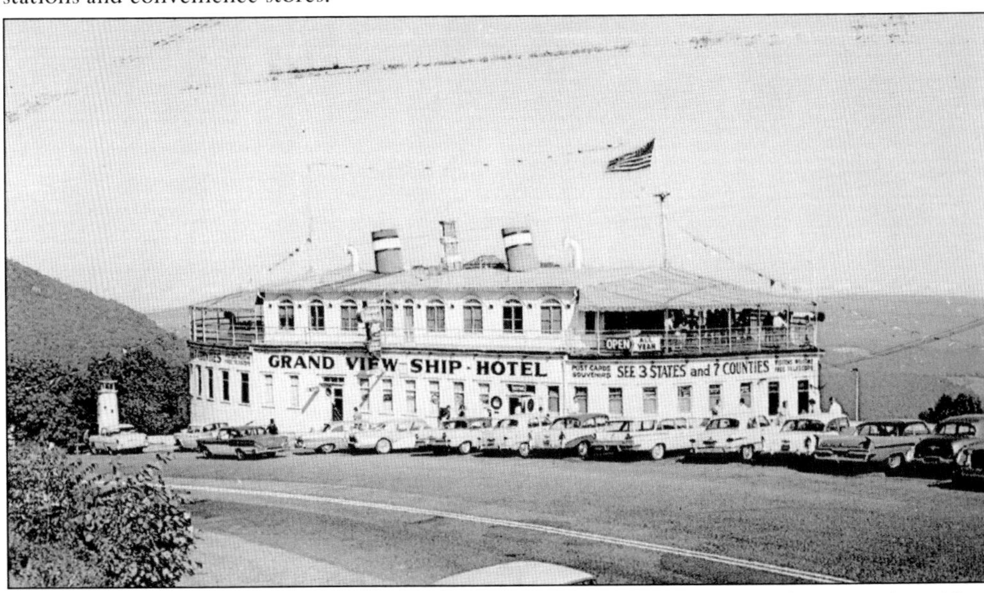

The Grand View Point Ship Hotel was still going strong when this postcard was purchased by a visitor in July 1966. At an elevation of 2,464 feet above sea level, the ship was promoted as "the only steamboat in the mountains." Eight years after this card was purchased, owner Herbert Paulson died and the business was sold. Although this view dates to well before the purchase date, it shows a parking lot filled with cars, while others are parked along the Lincoln Highway.

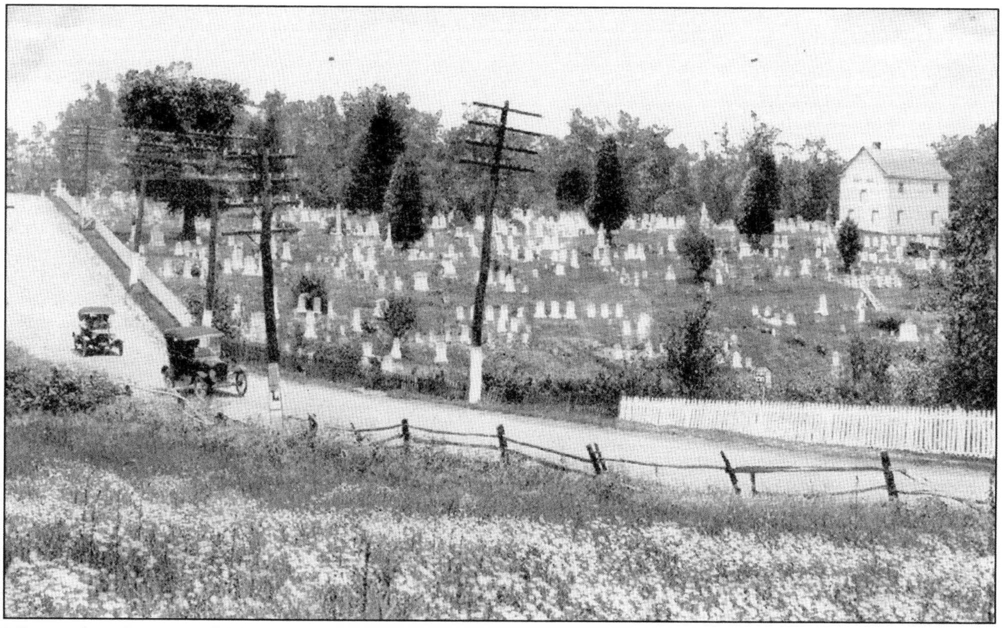

The red, white, and blue Lincoln Highway logo is visible on the pole in the left foreground, where the route skirts the Schellsburg and Chestnut Ridge Union Cemetery and church. This view of the highway and historic edifice likely dates to around 1920.

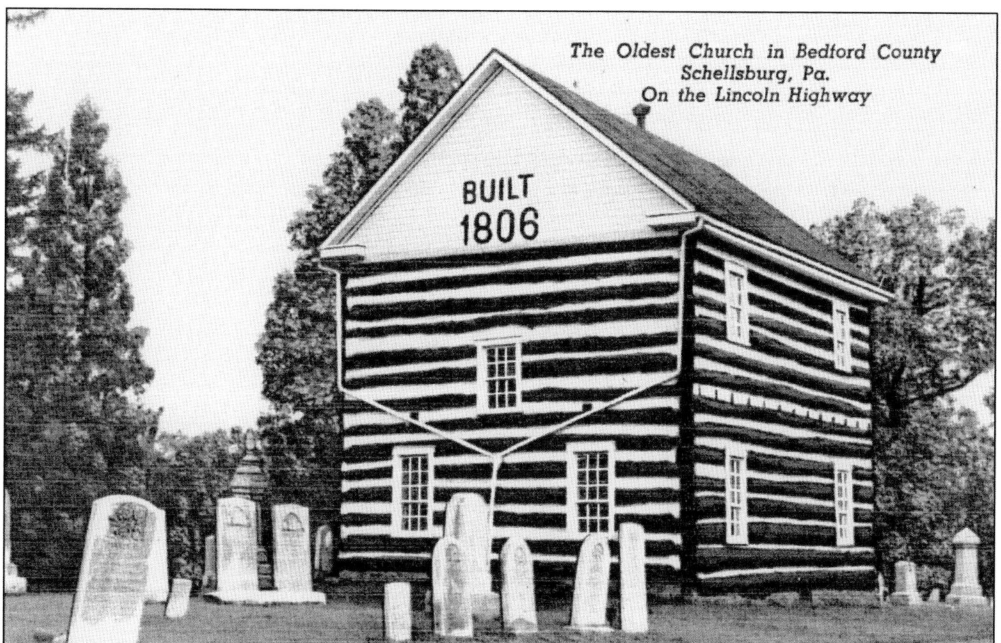

Built in 1806, Bedford County's oldest church, near Schellsburg, is also a Lincoln Highway landmark. The original route of the highway ran through the cemetery of the old church but was later rerouted. Today the church and cemetery are owned by the Chestnut Ridge Cemetery Association.

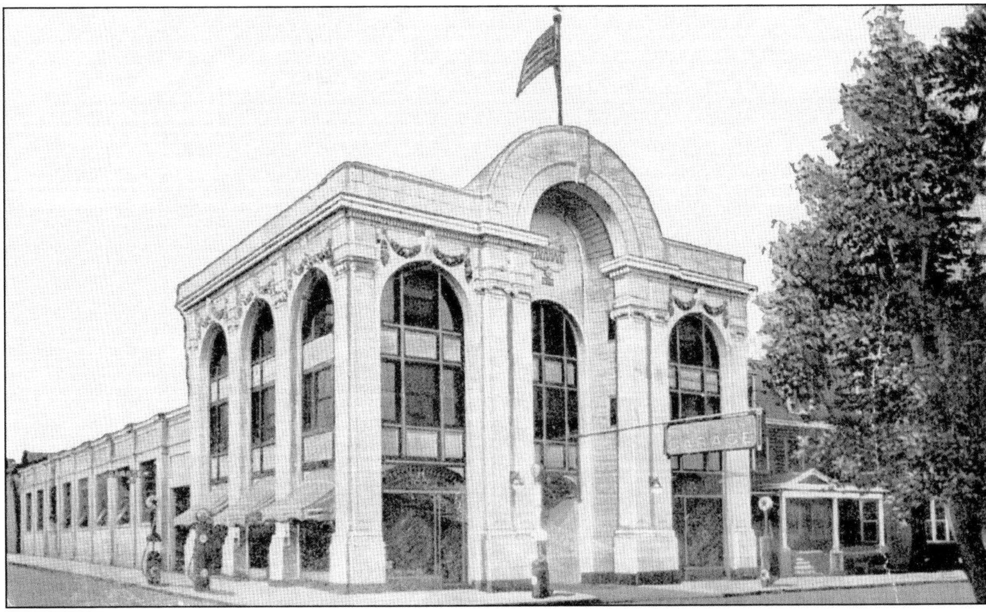

Although it was built to house a movie theater and never did, the Eberhart Garage in Gettysburg was undoubtedly the most elegant service station on the Lincoln Highway's coast-to-coast route. Under the ownership of C. W. Epley, the business stood opposite the Eagle Hotel and was advertised as being the "finest garage in southern Pennsylvania." It offered restrooms on the first floor, mechanics on duty, day and night service, storage, supplies, and repairs in the "absolutely fireproof" building.

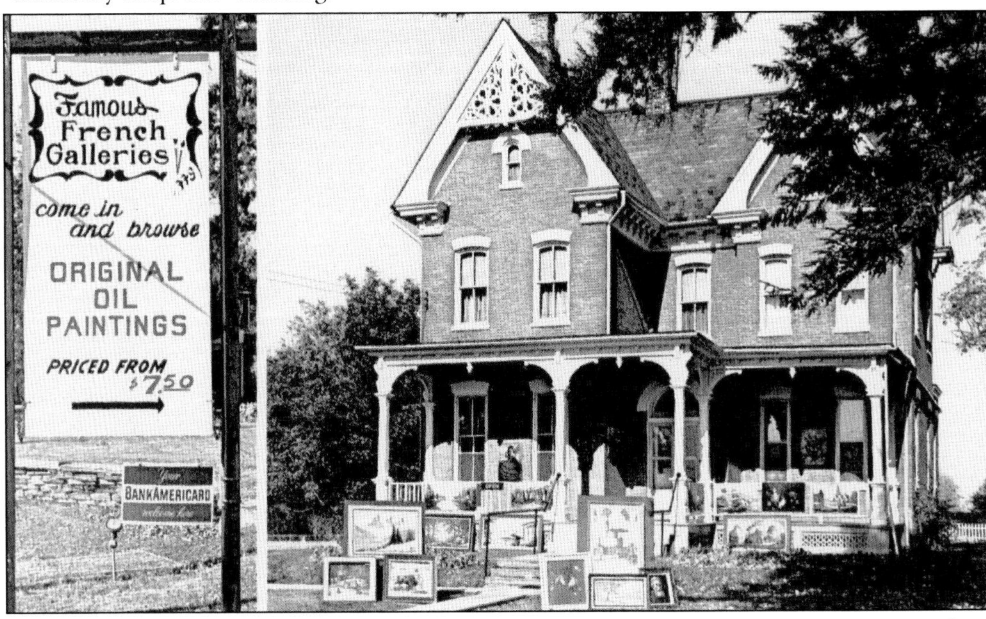

Tourism and business go hand in hand, a statement especially true in Lancaster County, where U.S. Route 30 cuts through a significant part of Amish Country. Famous French Galleries, also called "the Old Mansion in Paradise," featured hundreds of original oil paintings, priced as low as $7.50 each. The business also offered framing and would send purchases to customers via Greyhound bus.

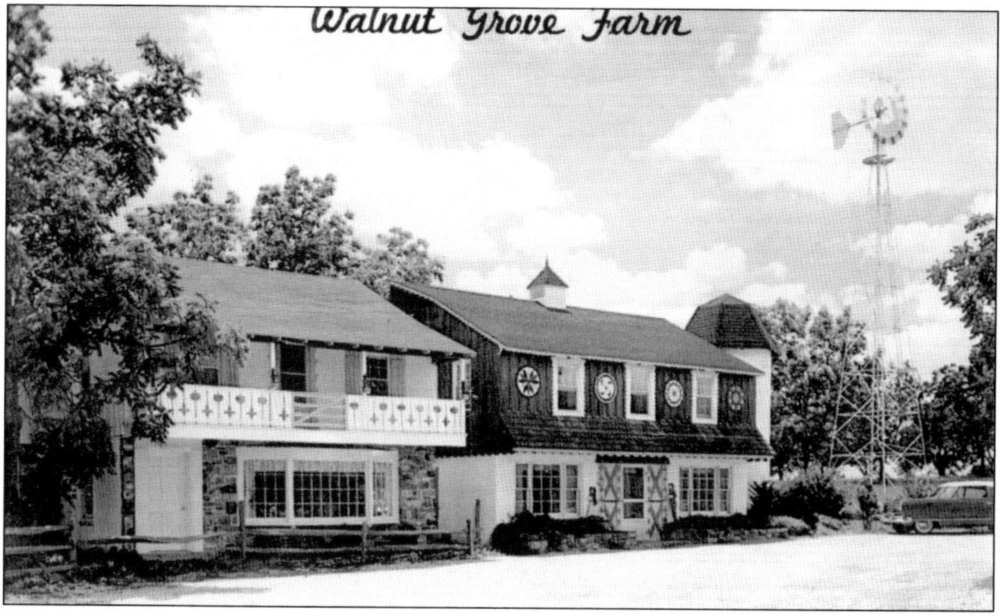

Walnut Grove Farm was located close to the eastern edge of Lancaster County's tourist area. The concern, promoted as being in the "heart" of the Pennsylvania Dutch Country, sold candies and Amish souvenirs. Although the business closed, the building lives on as professional offices.

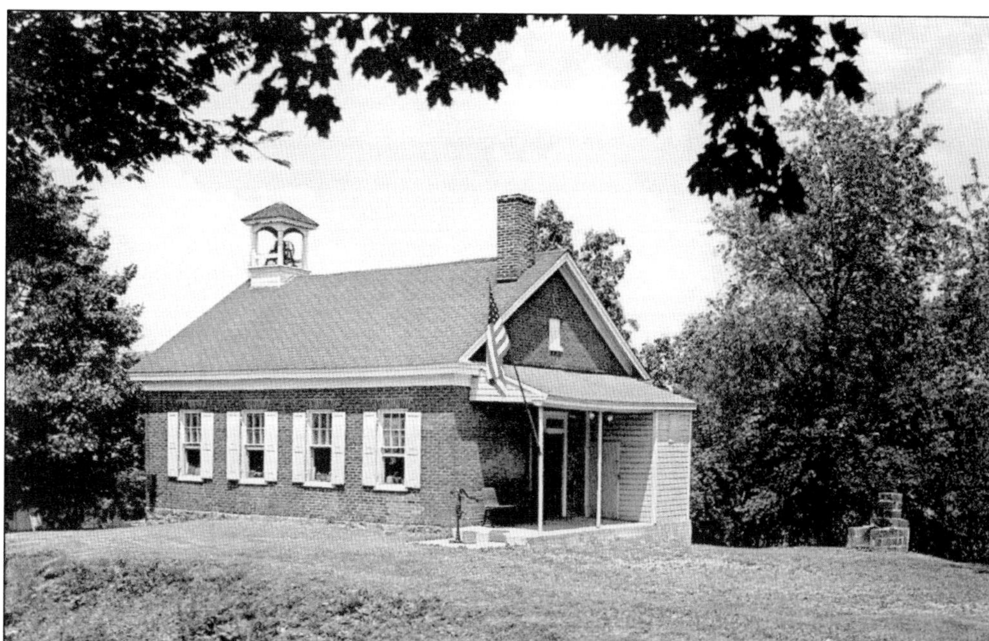

Lincoln Highway travelers who wanted to take their time and enjoy the ride had many places of historic interest to stop along the route. One of these is the Little Red School House Museum, 12 miles west of York. The 100-year-old authentically restored building housed a potbellied stove and life-sized mannequins of children and their teacher dressed in period clothes.

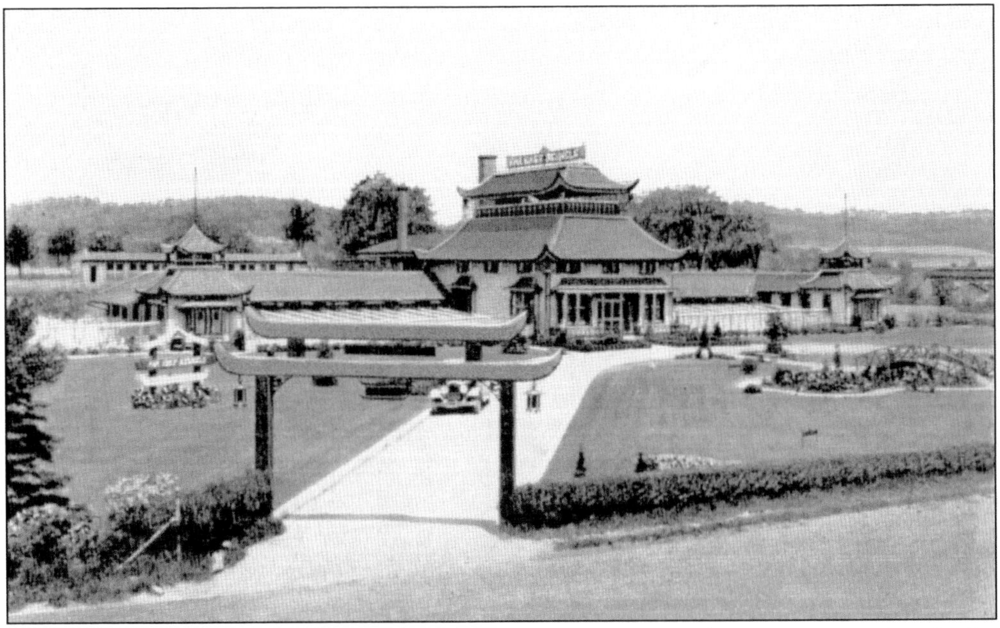

Not every business located along the Lincoln Highway was geared to service travelers. In the case of Far East Kennels, just east of Columbia, chow puppies were the specialty, with prices starting at $50. Like many other buildings along the roadside, this ornate landmark was razed to make room for industry.

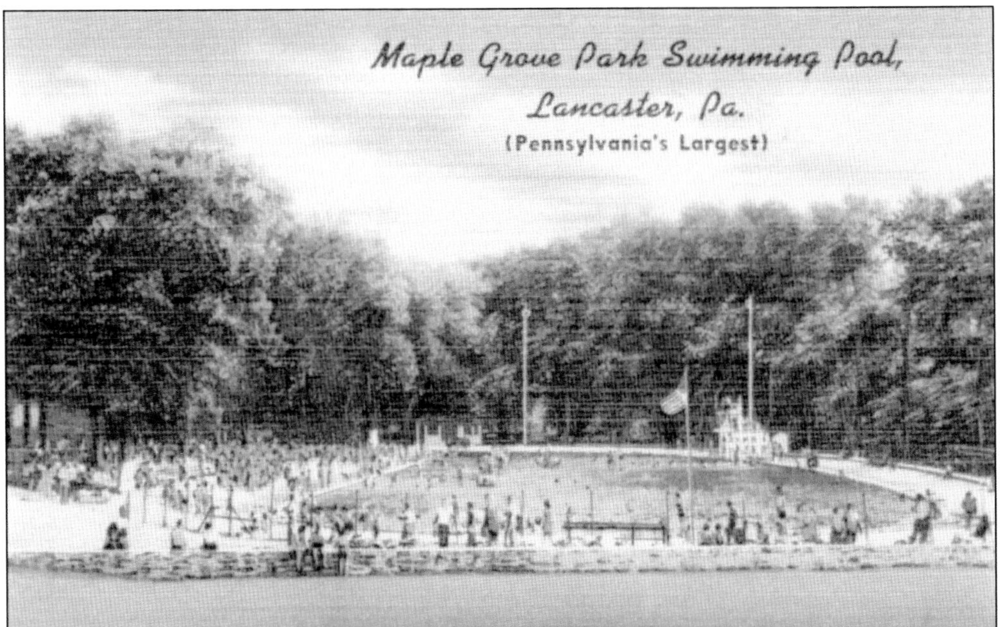

Lancaster's Maple Grove Park swimming pool, shown here in the 1940s, was billed as one of the state's largest. On the Lincoln Highway, one mile west of Lancaster, the huge swimming facility had a capacity of one and a half million gallons of water. Operated by Don Templeton, Maple Grove Park also had a large roller coaster and skating arena. An adjoining stand provided refreshments.

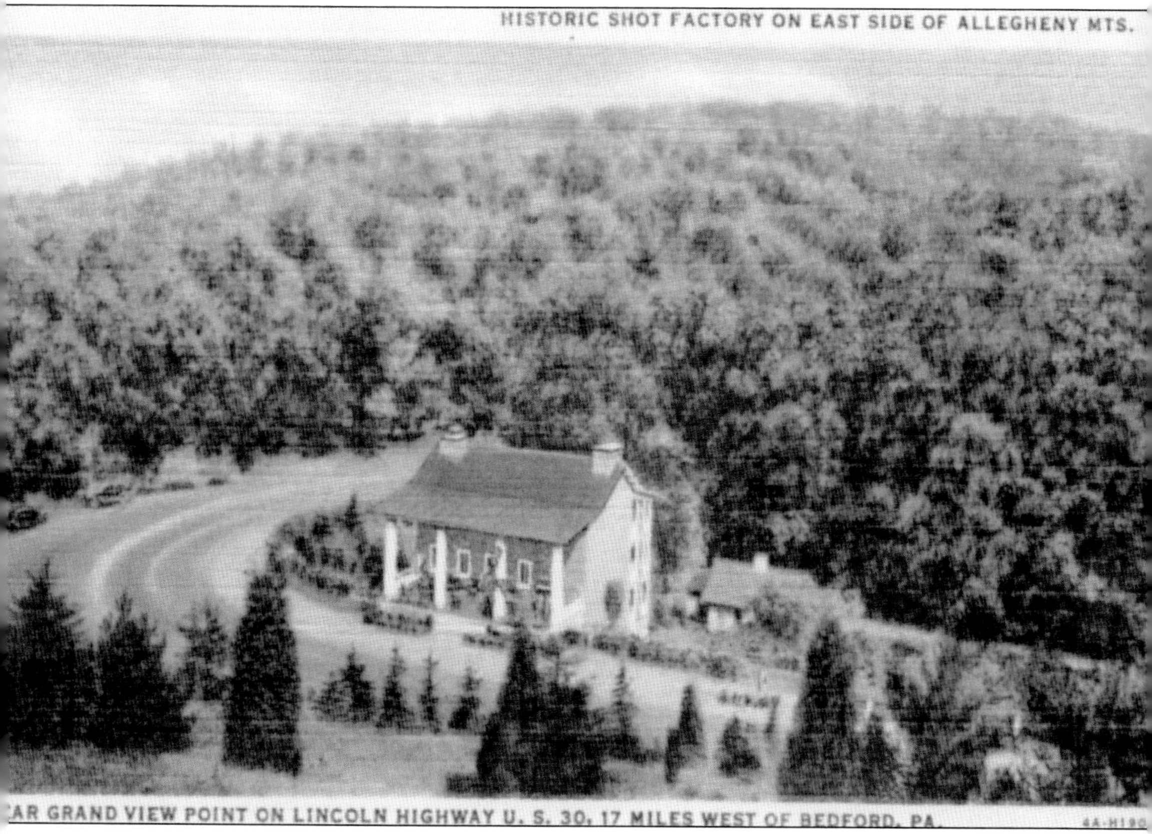

This building, approximately 17 miles west of Bedford, has for years been known as the Historic Shot Factory. At a hard curve on the Lincoln Highway just east of the site of the former Grand View Point Ship Hotel, munitions were reportedly made during the Civil War. Molten lead was dropped from the second floor to create shot, a common practice in an earlier era. Some sources state that cannon shot was also manufactured there during the Revolutionary War.

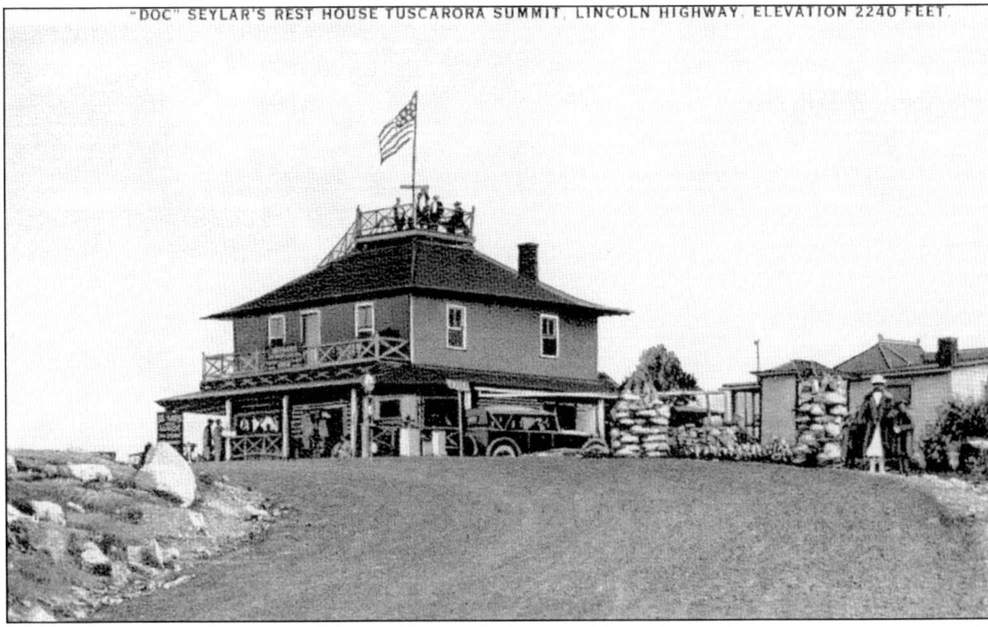

Leslie "Doc" Seylar's place was a well-known stop along the Lincoln Highway at Tuscarora Summit, where he opened the Tuscarora Summit Inn. In the early days of travel, mountaintops were especially attractive places to set up business, as cars would often overheat on climbs. Seylar offered most roadside necessities, including meals, cold drinks, and ice cream at Seylar's Quick Lunch.

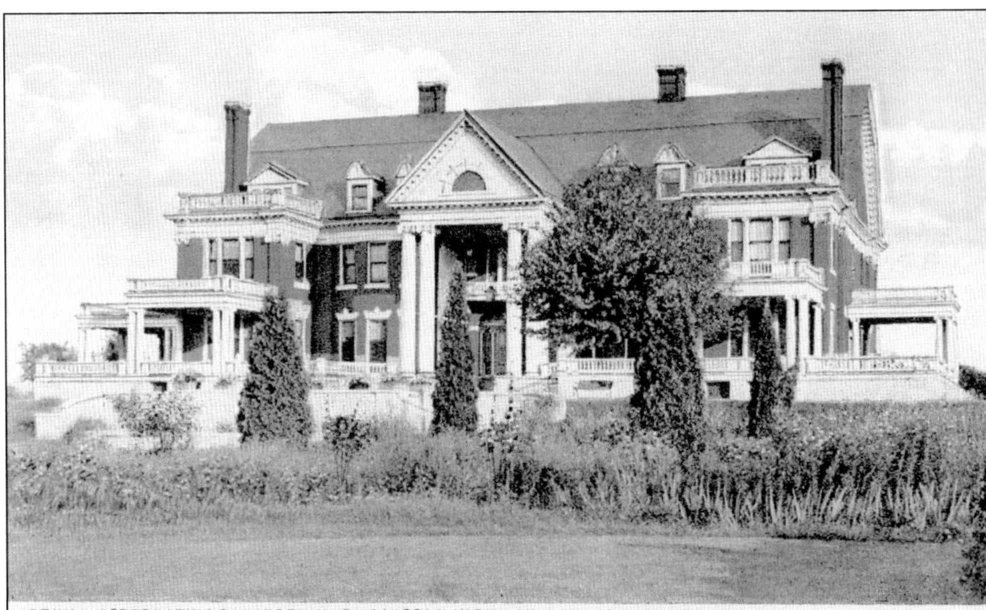

The Pennsylvania Osteopathic Sanatorium stood on the Lincoln Highway five miles east of York. This stately building, also known as Dr. Crandall's Health School, reportedly burned in 1949.

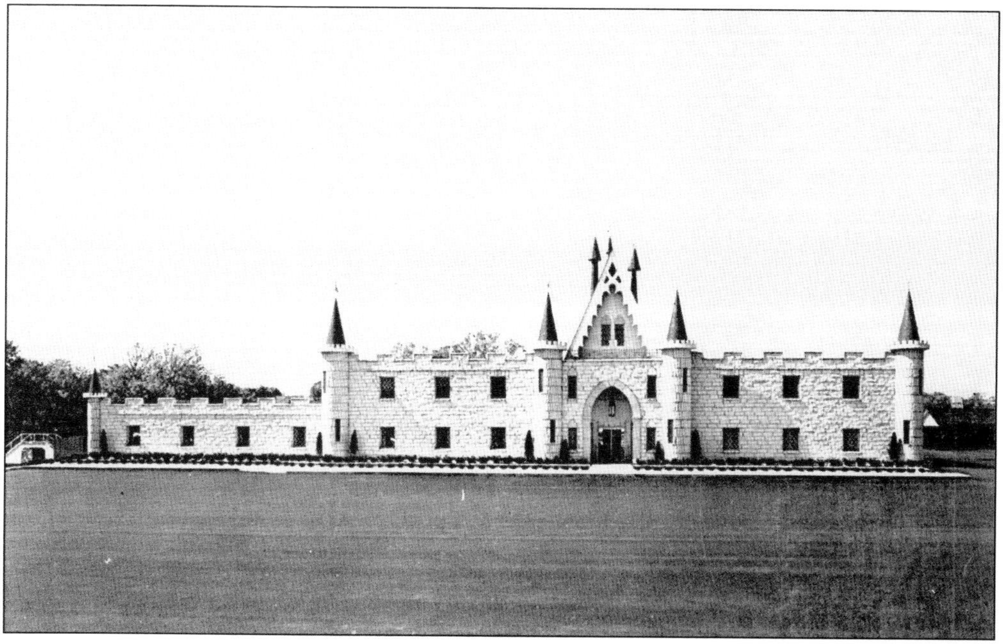

Dutch Wonderland's Castle Gift Shop fronted a 34-acre "wonderland of enchantment and fantasy" just east of Lancaster. The attraction offered "adventure" for the entire family, while the gift shop featured exclusive gifts and gourmet items from all over the world. Earl E. Clark was the owner and manager.

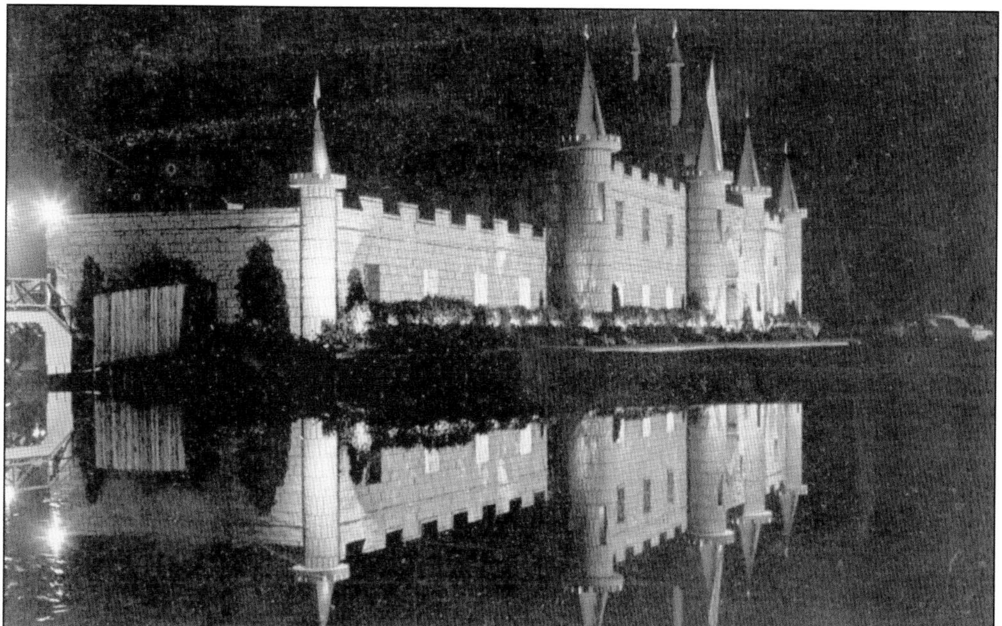

In the early 1960s, when this card was published, Dutch Wonderland was a only a 14-acre site along the highway. The popular park offered animals, puppets, a coffee shop, bake shop, and the famous Castle Gift Shop.

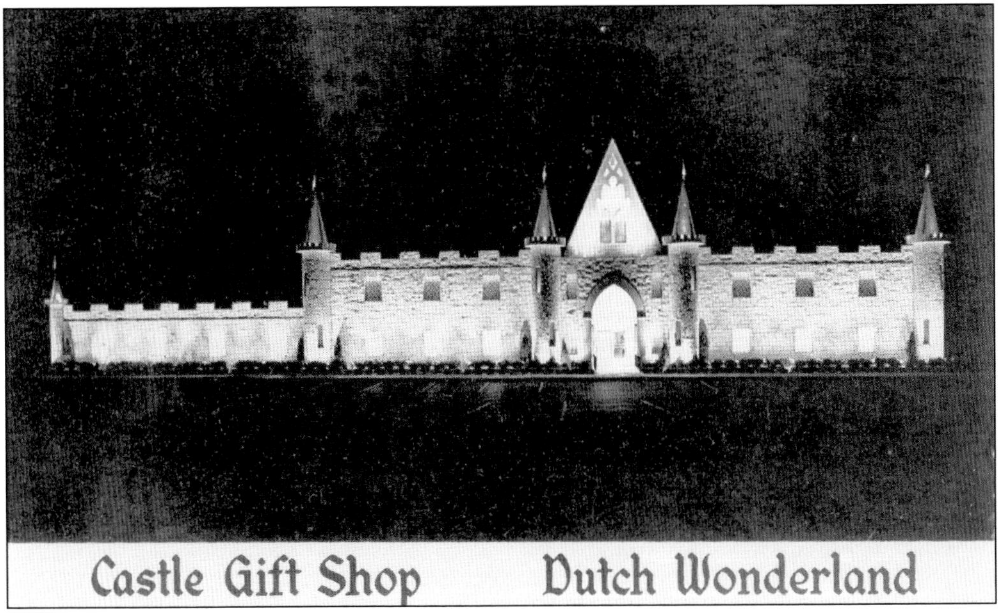

At night, Dutch Wonderland's Castle Gift Shop, a beacon to travelers, served as a roadside advertisement.

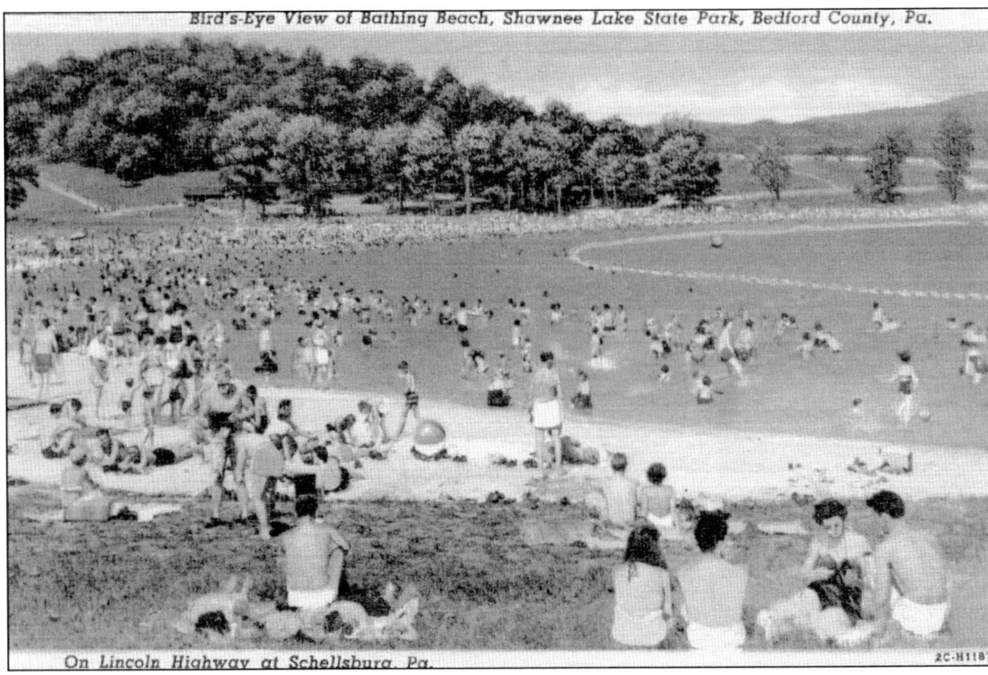

The 451-acre lake at Shawnee State Park was constructed primarily as a flood-control project but is also a popular recreation area. Just off U.S. Route 30 near Schellsburg, the Bedford County park attracts thousands of people for swimming, camping, and fishing.

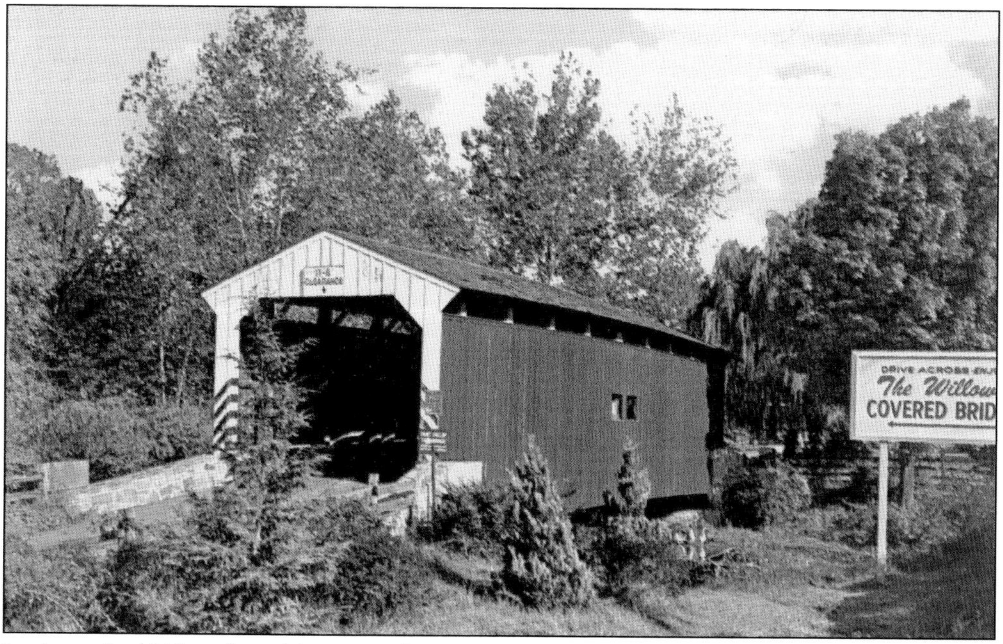

In the early 1960s, when this postcard was published, the Willows Covered Bridge, six miles east of Lancaster, was 180 years old. In 1962 and 1963, this wooden bridge was rebuilt over the stream at the Amish Farm and House, a local tourist attraction.

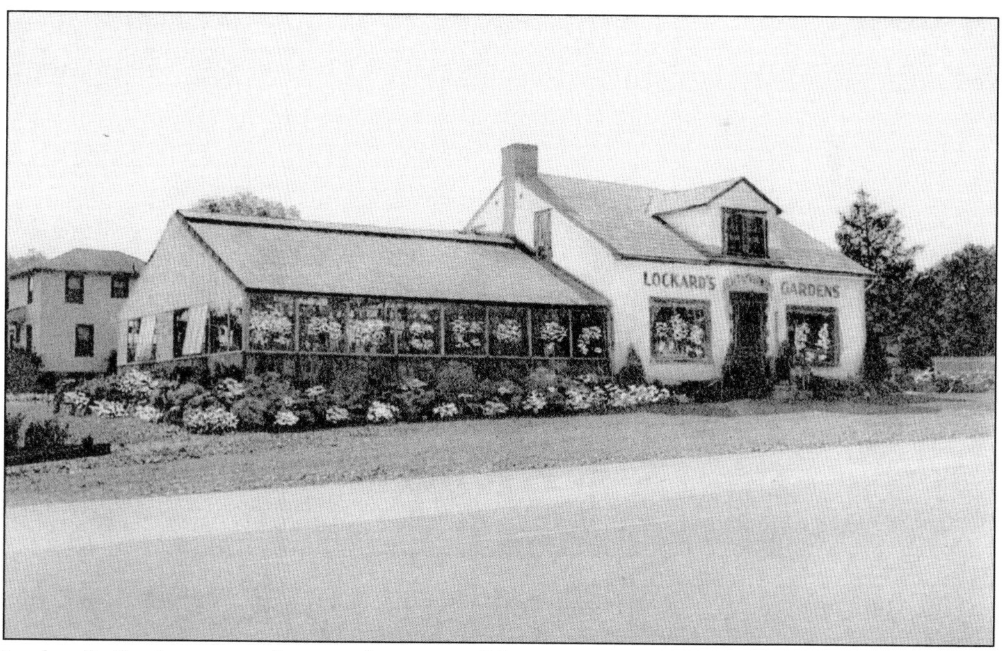

Lockard's Gardens was only one of many small businesses along the Lincoln Highway, likely in the eastern part of the state.

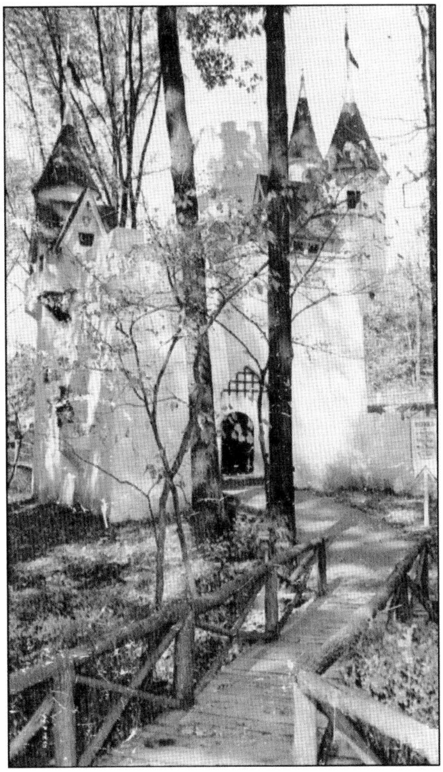

The Enchanted Castle at Story Book Forest is pictured in this *c.* 1961 postcard view. There children could talk with the Golden Knight or see the Genie in the Magic Mirror. At 17 acres, Story Book Forest opened for business in 1956 and continues to attract families to Ligonier.

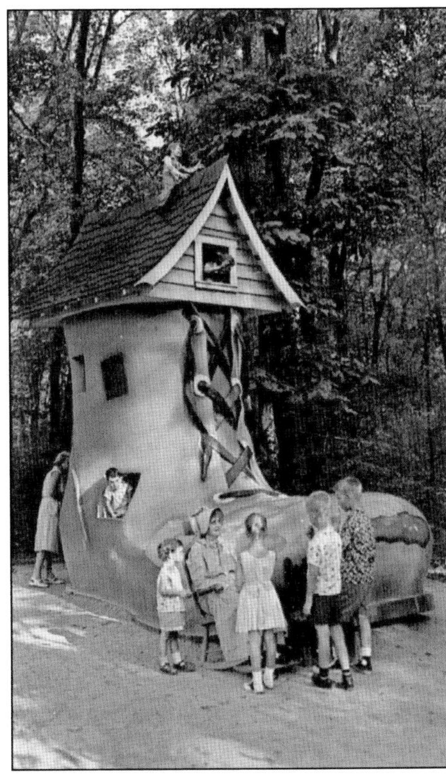

At Story Book Forest, one of the favorites among young children was the Old Lady in the Shoe, who told stories to visitors.

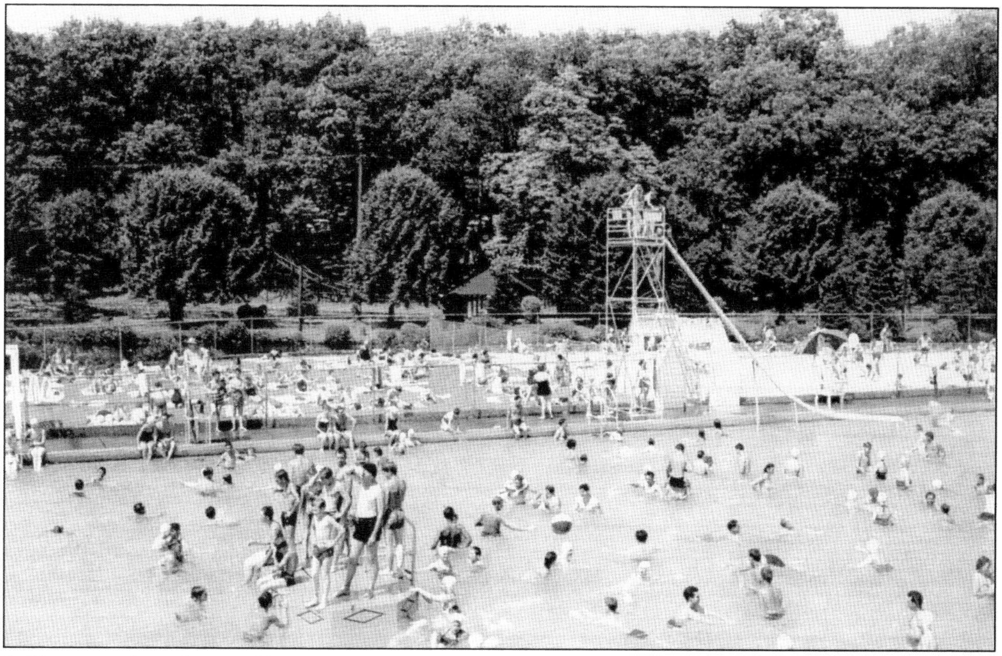

Still a popular place, Idlewild Park started as a picnic ground and eventually grew into an amusement park serviced by the narrow-gauge Ligonier Valley Railroad. The large swimming area was created by an artificial lake and also offered boating and fishing. This pre-1964 view shows the bathing area and "sun beaches."

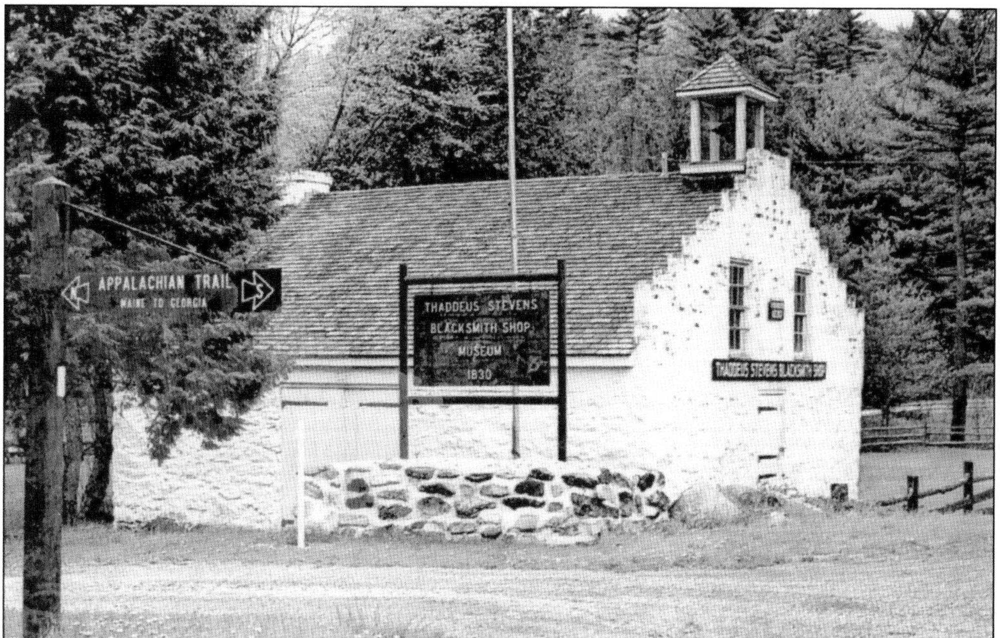

Some eight miles east of Chambersburg, the Thaddeus Stevens Blacksmith Shop is a historical site in Caledonia State Park. The shop was burned by the Confederate army in 1863 and later rebuilt. Stevens was an emancipator and advocate of public education, who also owned and operated the nearby Caledonia Furnace.

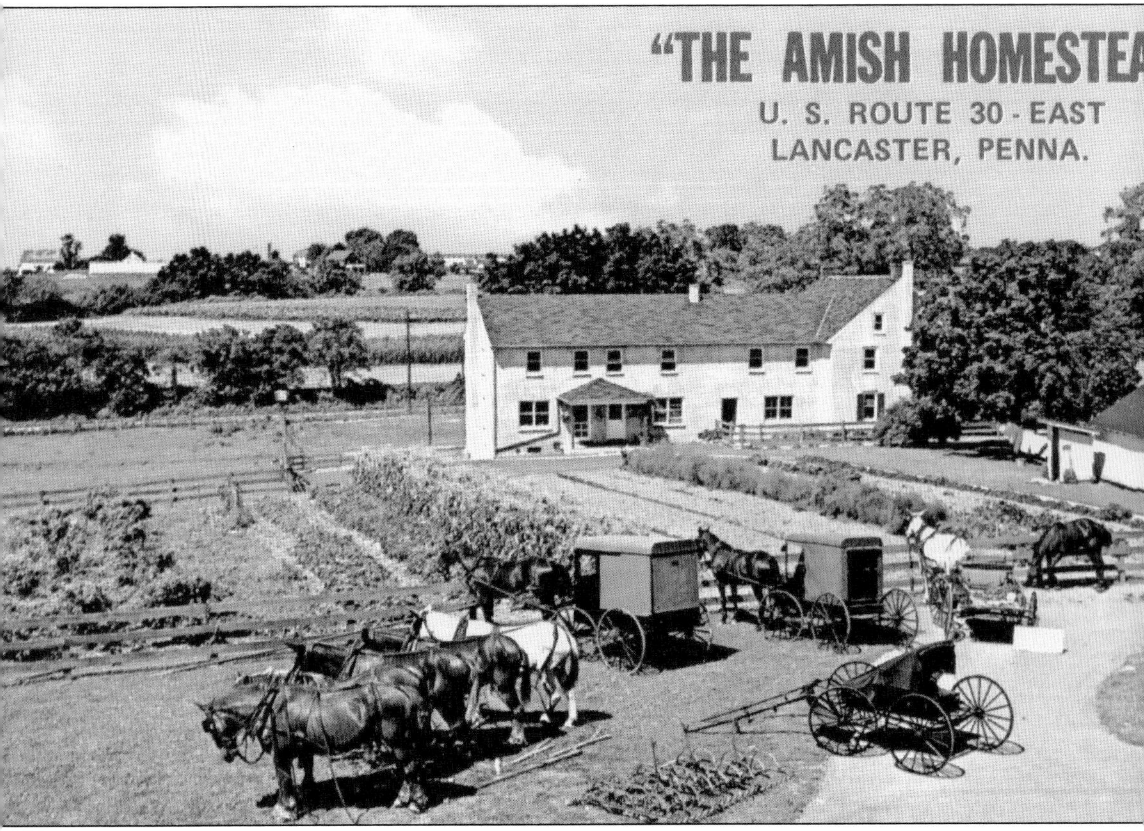

With Lancaster the center of the Old Order Amish community, it was natural that many tourist-oriented businesses would locate nearby. The Amish Homestead stood three miles east of the city and opposite Garden Spot Gifts. Visitors could enjoy a 71-acre farm that dated from 1744 and was occupied by an Amish family. Advertised as being the "experience of a lifetime," the site is now occupied by a Wal-Mart.

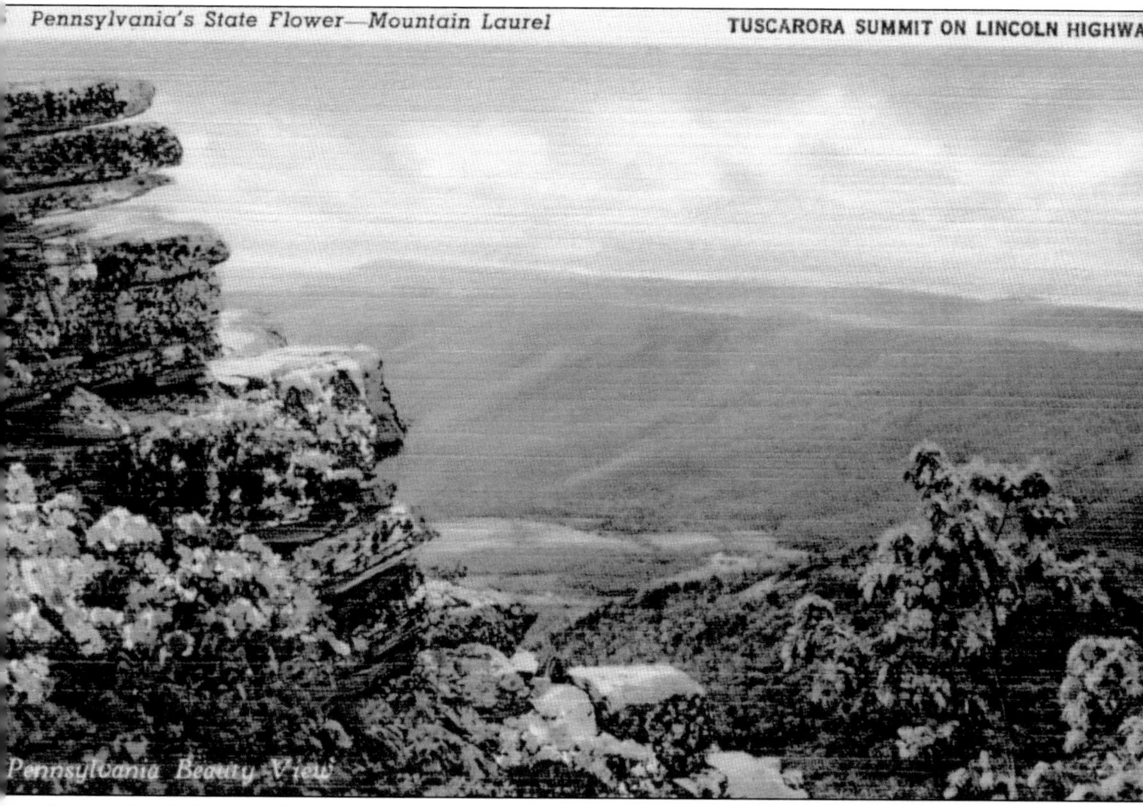

Pennsylvania's state flower, the mountain laurel, scientifically knows as *Kaimia Latifolia*, grows in abundance on the mountains crossed by the Lincoln Highway. This view is from Tuscarora Summit.